Scott,

Hope our book can provide ideas for how to reduce operating costs. Properly implemented, LEAN/Six Sigma is an effective approach.

Enjoy!

Dick Smith

STRATEGIC
SIX
SIGMA

STRATEGIC SIX SIGMA

BEST PRACTICES FROM THE EXECUTIVE SUITE

**Dick Smith and Jerry Blakeslee
with Richard Koonce**

JOHN WILEY & SONS, INC.

Published by John Wiley & Sons, Inc., Hoboken, New Jersey.
Published simultaneously in Canada.

Six Sigma is a registered trademark of Motorola, Inc. Use of the spelling "6 Sigma" for Six Sigma occurs in this book when referencing Caterpillar's use of the methodology.

For general information on our other products and services please contact our Customer Care Department within the U.S. at (800) 762-2974, outside the United States at (317) 572-3993 or fax (317) 572-4002.

Wiley also publishes its books in a variety of electronic formats. Some content that appears in print may not be available in electronic books.

ISBN 0-471-23294-7

Printed in the United States of America.

10 9 8 7 6 5 4 3 2 1

If you think about Six Sigma as another quality program, then it deserves as much intensity as all the other initiatives that can go on in a big company. [But] to the degree that you see Six Sigma as a culture changer—something that will profoundly affect the organization—then by definition, it takes the passion and obsession of the CEO to make it happen. We saw Six Sigma—and by the way we call it Raytheon Six Sigma—as a way to profoundly change our culture, and therefore it started with me and ends with me. I include language on it at almost every meeting that I have, to the extent that people's lips almost move in synch with mine on this subject.

—Dan Burnham, Chairman and CEO
Raytheon Corporation

Contents

Acknowledgments

Writing a book, as you might imagine, is a highly collaborative endeavor. It is an intense, creative, and *interactive* enterprise from initial thoughts to finished text. For that reason, we want to recognize the many friends, clients, and colleagues, without whose constant involvement and steady interest *Strategic Six Sigma: Best Practices from the Executive Suite,* would not have been written.

To our clients and friends who so willingly shared their stories of leadership, change, and transformation with us, we are extremely grateful for your participation in this project. At Dow Chemical, special thanks to Mike Parker, Kathleen Bader, Tom Gurd, Darlene MacKinnon, Jeff Schatzer, Matt Rassette, Shelly Bartosek, and Nancy Weiss. At Caterpillar, our gratitude to Glen Barton, Dave Burritt, Geoff Turk, Julie Hammond, Denny Huber, Diana Shankwitz, Jill Keel, and Phil Thannert. At Bombardier Transportation, our appreciation to Pierre Lortie, Desmond Bell, and Marlene Girard. At Service-Master, Jon Ward, Phil Rooney, Pat Asp, and John Biedry. At Raytheon, Dan Burnham, David Polk, and Ann Psilekas. At Air Products & Chemicals, George Diehl. At Lockheed Martin, our thanks to Mike Joyce and Shirley Pitts. And at J.P. Morgan Chase, our appreciation to Debbie Neuscheler-Fritsch.

At PricewaterhouseCoopers, we gratefully acknowledge the assistance of a number of key colleagues including: Grady

Means, Bill Trahant, Joe DeVittorio, Warner Burke, Steve Yearout, Jim Prendergast, Monica Painter, David Wilkerson, Cathy Neuman, Jim Niemes, Tom McElwee, Charlie Streeter, Peter Amico, George Byrne, Steve Marra, Dan Arnott, Bob Norris, Dawn Edmiston, Mary Trotter, Teddy Regio, Shruti Chandra, Rita Thomas, Bertha Ballard, Robin Masinter, Yolanda Ortiz, Don McCartney, and Allyson Woodruff. This book is incalculably richer for the comments, insights, and ideas each of you suggested as we proceeded with the writing of the manuscript.

To our agent Doris Michaels of the Doris Michaels Literary Agency in New York, and our editor, Matt Holt at John Wiley & Sons. We are grateful for your support of and steadfast interest in this project, and for your continuing advice and counsel as we prepared the manuscript for publication.

To our friends at The American Society for Training & Development and at *T & D* magazine, including Pat Galagan, Haidee Allerton, Valerie Small, Mark Morrow, and Tresa Sullivan; and at the *Journal of Organizational Excellence (JOE)*, Jane Bensahel and Mary Ann C. Fusco. We thank you all for the opportunities you gave us in the past to publish our ideas about Strategic Six Sigma in your publications. Many of those ideas have been further developed, refined, field-tested, and presented in this book, as insights and approaches from which we hope others will learn.

To Roxanne O'Brasky and her colleagues at the International Society of Six Sigma Professionals in Scottsdale, Arizona: Thank you for your interest and involvement in supporting this project.

To Tim Jubach, an independent consultant and president of Lean Enterprise, Inc. Thanks for your help in arranging the Raytheon interview.

To our friends at Video-on-Location in Rockville, Maryland, who gave us invaluable assistance in producing the video interviews on which much of the book's text was based, and which have been subsequently produced, in CD-ROM form, as a leadership training tool (and companion) to *Strategic Six Sigma: Best Practices from the Executive Suite.* In particular, we want to acknowledge the involvement of Dino Veizis, Jim Veizis, Alex Veizis, Jerry Moxley, Chris Houck, and Henry Heuscher. Thanks guys!

To our collaborator and friend, Rick Koonce, who was continually challenged to collect and integrate our thoughts on Strategic Six Sigma based on countless cell phone calls, meetings, hallway discussions, and e-mails. Thanks, Rick, for helping us to produce a smooth-flowing, reader-friendly text from which CEOs and other senior leaders will undoubtedly gain insights and learnings that they can use to implement Strategic Six Sigma in their own organizations!

To our families, especially our wives, Bonnie and Nancy, who have patiently put up with years of us being on the road for business week after week. We are humbly indebted to you both, for all you do.

Finally, we want to thank you, our readers. We hope that you find *Strategic Six Sigma* to be a valuable tool that you can use to introduce Strategic Six Sigma thinking and best practices into your organization. Please feel free to contact us at the e-mail addresses included in the book's introduction. We'd enjoy hearing from you, and learning what you yourselves have learned from introducing Strategic Six Sigma in your company.

Dick Smith and Jerry Blakeslee

Introduction: From Factory Floor to Executive Suite: The Emergence of Strategic Six Sigma as a Business and Leadership Imperative

Six Sigma, the highly statistical quality improvement technique born in the manufacturing bays of Motorola in the mid-1980s, is often used at an *operational* level inside companies today to help them cut costs, improve processes, and reduce business cycle times. Its value in this regard is well understood by business leaders today, and has been the topic of numerous business books and articles in recent years.

Less well known, however, is the potential of Six Sigma to serve as a means to help companies formulate and deploy their business strategies, and bring about broad-gauge transformational change—to serve, in other words, as a high-order leadership approach, philosophy, and change methodology. Strategic Six Sigma principles and practices can, for example, be used to help companies:

➤ Formulate, integrate, and execute new (or existing) business strategies and missions

➤ Deal with constantly changing (and increasingly complex) customer requirements

➤ Accelerate a company's globalization (and global integration) efforts

➤ Facilitate mergers and acquisitions (Dow's merger with Union Carbide, for example)

➤ Ensure effective implementation of e-business ventures with their associated strategies and infrastructure

➤ Drive revenue growth

➤ Accelerate innovation

➤ Improve marketing channels

➤ Enhance and condense the corporate learning cycle—the time it takes to translate market intelligence and competitive data into new business practices

➤ Win the customer care war

➤ Drive systemic and sustainable culture change

➤ Improve financial and corporate reporting

➤ Manage and mitigate business risk

■ A VEHICLE FOR DEPLOYING CORPORATE STRATEGIES

A growing number of companies today are beginning to realize the full, strategic implications of Six Sigma, especially as an engine to accelerate corporate strategy and organizational transformation. Former General Electric (GE) CEO Jack Welch, for example, says that Six Sigma has forever "changed the DNA" of how GE operates. Before his first retirement as Honeywell's larger-than-life CEO, Larry Bossidy used to tell Honeywell employees and shareholders alike that Six Sigma was the key to Honeywell realizing annual 6 percent gains in productivity "forever." At Citibank, meanwhile, Six Sigma was recently implemented to accelerate the bank's customer care approaches around the world. Du Pont and Dow Chemical are both using it to propel sustainable growth, and to position themselves in an industry notorious for both static product prices and thin operating margins. Even hotel chains, like Starwood Hotels and Resorts, are employing it to overhaul their corporate culture, create blissful customer service experiences for travelers, and to radically alter the nature of their hospitality services. (See the sidebar, "What Is Sigma?")

The potential of Strategic Six Sigma to serve such transformational purposes (and others) has profound implications for today's CEOs and their top leadership teams. A recent story in *Fortune* noted that one of the biggest causes of business failures today is the inability of companies to effectively execute their strategies. Because Six Sigma methodology, at its core, relies on the use of factual data, statistical measurement techniques, and robust feedback mechanisms to drive decision making, it's able to unify top leadership teams behind a common language (and a set of data points), making strategic planning and execution more efficient and *successful.* Because it aligns a company's people and processes behind commonly agreed-to goals, it helps companies achieve entirely new levels of profitability and corporate performance

---

WHAT IS SIGMA?

In the world of Six Sigma companies, the term *sigma* has come to signify how well a business process, product, or service is meeting the requirements of the marketplace. *Six Sigma* has come to mean failing to meet a customer requirement only 3.4 times out of a million opportunities.

in less time than traditional strategy implementation does. And because Strategic Six Sigma increases a company's focus, speed, and organizational resilience, it helps organizations respond quickly to changing market conditions, move in new business directions, and improve customer responsiveness, thus enhancing customer relationships, while increasing shareholder value. (See the sidebar, "Six Sigma in Brief: A Catalyst for Change at the Transformational and Operational Levels of an Organization.")

SIX SIGMA IN BRIEF: A CATALYST FOR CHANGE AT THE TRANSFORMATIONAL AND OPERATIONAL LEVELS OF AN ORGANIZATION

Six Sigma is a high-performance, data-driven approach to analyzing the root causes of business problems and solving them. It ties the outputs of a business directly to marketplace requirements. (See Figure I.1) At the strategic, or *transformational,* level, the goal of Six Sigma is to align an organization keenly to its marketplace and deliver real improvements (and dollars) to the bottom line. Strategic Six Sigma approaches provide a framework that potentially can be used to bring about large-scale integration of a company's strategies, processes, culture, and customers to achieve and sustain breakaway business results.

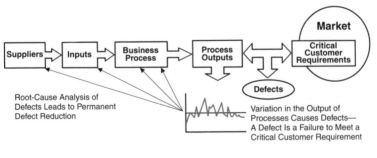

Figure I.1 Six Sigma business improvement.

At the operational or process level, Six Sigma's goal is to move business product or service attributes within the zone of customer specifications and to dramatically shrink process variation—the cause of defects that negatively affect customers. (See Figure I.2) It provides specific tools and approaches (process analysis, statistical analysis, lean techniques, root-cause methods, etc.) that can be used to reduce defects and dramatically improve processes to increase customer satisfaction and drive down costs as a result. (See Figure I.2)

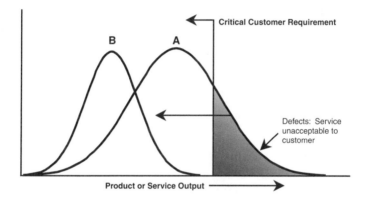

Figure I.2 Six Sigma reduces variation in business processes. An objective of Six Sigma is to reduce variation and move product or service outputs permanently inside customer requirements (curve A to B).

■ STRATEGIC SIX SIGMA GENERATES RESULTS ACROSS MANY INDICATORS

In companies where Strategic Six Sigma has been implemented (Dow, Caterpillar, Raytheon, Bombardier, Lockheed Martin, etc.), it has radically and quickly improved business performance across a wide family of performance indicators—in everything from return on assets (an internal business indicator) to customer satisfaction and timely order fulfillment (external performance metrics.)

Just what's driving the transmutation of Six Sigma from process improvement technique into an accelerator of business strategy and implementation, and a tool of organizational transformation? To answer that question, one needs only to look at the rapidly changing nature of today's business environment and the multiple drivers and pressures that are exerting themselves on the daily operations of companies. Today, for example, companies are under more pressure than ever to:

➤ Develop, implement, and often rapidly revise their business strategy
➤ Attract, service, and retain customers (often by anticipating their needs before they do)
➤ Globalize business operations
➤ Accelerate innovation and research and development (R&D)
➤ Redesign their sales and marketing channels rapidly
➤ Manage business risk
➤ Develop and introduce new products and services faster and more efficiently
➤ Build national and global brands
➤ Develop and implement effective supply chains
➤ Implement transformational change

A recent survey of corporate CEOs commissioned by the Foundation for the Malcolm Baldrige National Quality Award confirms this.[1] The study identified a number of significant trends that are exerting a transformational influence on the nature of global business today. All of them have profound implications for the productivity and profitability of companies worldwide. For example, of the more than 300 CEOs who answered the survey:

➤ Ninety-four percent cited globalization as a major trend impacting the life and livelihood of companies today. Yet, only 18 percent of respondents rated major U.S. companies as excellent in dealing with this trend.

➤ Eighty-eight percent of survey respondents said that improving knowledge management was critical to their business operations. Yet, only 23 percent rated major U.S. companies as excellent in this category.

➤ Seventy nine percent of CEOs polled in the survey rated cost and cycle time reduction as a major need and trend in their companies today. Yet, only 31 percent indicated that U.S. companies, in their view, do an excellent job at these activities.

Still other major trends and issues identified by respondents as critical to business operations today included:[1]

➤ Improving global supply chains (78 percent)
➤ Manufacturing at multiple locations in many countries (76 percent)
➤ Developing new employee relationships based on performance (69 percent)
➤ Improving the execution of strategic plans (68 percent)
➤ Developing more appropriate strategic plans (64 percent)
➤ Ensuring effective measurement and analysis of organizational processes (60 percent)

Any company's performance, of course, is closely related to corporate leadership—and to specific leadership competencies. Thus, another interesting cluster of findings to emerge from the Baldrige survey pointed to the fact that in many cases today, business leaders view themselves as lacking certain key competencies, and in need of upgrading others. Over half of the CEOs in the Baldrige survey, for example, believe that they (and their peers) need to improve their skills in the following areas "a great deal."[1]

- ➤ The ability to think globally—72 percent
- ➤ The ability to execute strategies successfully—66 percent
- ➤ Flexibility in a changing world—63 percent
- ➤ The ability to develop appropriate strategies—60 percent
- ➤ The ability to rapidly redefine their business—54 percent
- ➤ Understanding new technologies—52 percent
- ➤ The ability to work well with different stakeholders—50 percent
- ➤ Creating learning organizations—49 percent[1]

What's the common thread running throughout all these survey findings?

■ IMPROVING PERFORMANCE IS A UNIVERSAL BUSINESS PRIORITY

First, all of them have implications for a company's ability to compete effectively in an increasingly brutal business environment. They suggest that companies (and their leaders) today need to focus on improving business performance both at a process level (the level of actual, everyday work) and at a much higher organizational level as well—the level of strategy development, planning, and deployment.

Second, the findings suggest that companies today are in need of a strong strategic framework and language, not only to help them define their vision and articulate their mission, but also to define, measure, analyze, and improve their performance whether the specific goal is to build market share, enhance customer loyalty, accelerate the R&D process, or improve shareholder value.

Six Sigma principles and approaches—and especially those that are applied in a systematic and strategic way as we describe in this book—can have a tremendous impact both on a company's bottom-line business performance and on its potential for true, top-line business growth. Why? Because the statistically rigorous and robust approaches to business improvement that Six Sigma principles embody provide companies with a common vehicle and language with which to frame business goals, align people and processes, focus organizational energy, and drive results. Six Sigma tools and concepts provide a means to optimally align all of an organization's components—from *leaders, culture,* and *mission and strategy* on the one hand, to *structure, management practices, systems, work climate,* and *employee skill sets and behaviors* on the other—to help a company achieve breakthrough levels of business performance. These variables, as change consultant and author W. Warner Burke puts it, represent the full range of "transformational and transactional" drivers at work in any organization today, and therefore constitute the full productive potential of any business enterprise.

We refer to companies that effectively employ Strategic Six Sigma as *market-smart.* That's because they typically share a number of crucial characteristics: a well-developed (yet constantly revisited) business strategy; a laserlike focus on customers; and a strong internal *climate of alignment* to support strategic business goals.

Because Strategic Six Sigma practices are necessarily built on a foundation of knowledgeable and committed leaders, beginning with the CEO and cascading down throughout all levels of the organization, we have titled this book, *Strategic Six Sigma: Best Practices from the Executive Suite.* Within its pages, we've attempted to capture key insights, anecdotes, wisdom, and stories gathered from interviews conducted with many of today's most successful business executives—people who've both discovered and leveraged the benefits of Strategic Six Sigma thinking and best practices inside their *own* organizations.

In *Strategic Six Sigma: Best Practices from the Executive Suite,* our goal is to outline the key elements of Strategic Six Sigma leadership in companies today, and to provide readers with the guideposts necessary to apply these same practices and approaches in their own companies. To that end, the book is divided into three sections.

Part 1 (Introduction, Chapters 1 and 2) focuses on why every company today needs to become a market-smart company if it is to survive in the marketplace, build customer loyalty, and provide high-quality products and services to customers. We look at the tyranny of environmental forces at work in the business environment today that are compelling companies of all kinds (and in all industries) to develop increasingly robust approaches to ensuring high performance, and how market-smart companies do this through effective implementation of Strategic Six Sigma within their businesses. We also delve in-depth into the compelling strategic mega-applications of Strategic Six Sigma that are emerging as part of leadership practice in market-smart companies today.

Part 2 (Chapters 3 through 9) profiles most market-smart companies (e.g., GE, ___ _____ _____, Raytheon, Caterpillar, Lockheed Martin, Bombardier) that are now using Strategic Six Sigma for the kinds of transformational purposes described earlier. It also provides readers with a roadmap that *any* company can use to effectively implement Strategic Six Sigma methods (and leadership approaches).

How is this done? How *does* a company take the principles of Six Sigma and introduce them into the executive suite? Into a company's strategic planning processes? Basically, it's accomplished when a company's CEO and senior leadership team follow seven critical steps. Simply put, they must:

1. Develop a committed team of leaders to support Six Sigma initiatives.
2. Integrate Strategic Six Sigma thinking and best practices into the company's strategy planning and deployment processes.
3. Ensure that the company is both passionate and consistent about being in touch with customers.
4. Create a business process framework to sustain Strategic Six Sigma for the long term.
5. Develop quantifiable measures—then demand tangible results from people.
6. Develop incentives/create accountability/reward performance.
7. Be committed to having full-time and well-trained Six Sigma Leaders in place to sustain initiatives over time.

As noted, effective implementation of Strategic Six Sigma initiatives requires strong leadership resolve and organizational intent. It also requires that organizations nurture strong groups of leaders at *all* levels to drive Strategic Six Sigma efforts forward. This begs the question, of course, "Just what kinds of skills do the leaders of my company need to possess to be credible and competent catalysts for implementation of Strategic Six Sigma within the organization?"

Part 3 of *Strategic Six Sigma: Best Practices from the Executive Suite* (Chapters 10 and 11) thus delves into the details of how best to develop leaders with strong Strategic Six Sigma expertise, including both technical skills, and critical people and change management skills. As we outline, executives acquire such skills through intensive training and action learning programs; programs that also help them to clarify their goals, quantify business objectives, leverage knowledge of customers and the marketplace, and build the infrastructure of people and systems to drive fundamental and lasting change in their organizations. This section of the book also examines the future of Strategic Six Sigma, and how to sustain initiatives by *building commitment* (not just driving compliance with) Six Sigma thinking and methods. (See the sidebar, "Six Sigma Measurement: At What Sigma Do Your Processes Operate?")

SIX SIGMA MEASUREMENT: AT WHAT SIGMA DO YOUR PROCESSES OPERATE?

Six Sigma Value	DPMO*	Percent Defect-Free
2	308,537	69.20%
3	66,807	93.32%
4	6,210	99.38%
5	233	99.98%
6	3.4	99.99966%

*DPMO: defects per million opportunities.

Strategic Six Sigma: Best Practices from the Executive Suite isn't just about improving business process performance. It's about fundamentally transforming the nature of relationships companies have externally with customers, suppliers, shareholders, analysts, and in some cases, competitors. It's also about transforming the relationships companies have *internally*—with their own employees on whose shoulders the success of Strategic Six Sigma ultimately rests. Our goal in this book is to help you and your company develop the ability to see and structure your business from your customer's perspective; to develop an outside-in perspective to business transactions and to meet customer and marketplace requirements. The days when companies could afford to be lumbering behemoths, inattentive to marketplace requirements, and insensitive to customer needs, have long since passed. So, too, have the days when companies could afford to think of their products or their customers as mere commodities. In the age of "e"—e-transactions, e-marketplaces, e-alliances, and e-business—everything is about speed, communication, customization, and perfection. It's about responding to customer pull, not simply pushing products onto a marketplace you think you own. Companies today have got to get their customer and marketplace stuff right because the customer is in the driver's seat. And meeting customer needs and requirements is what business is all about—today more than ever.

We hope you'll find *Strategic Six Sigma: Best Practices from the Executive Suite* to be a useful book in helping create awareness of and expertise in the use of Strategic Six Sigma principles and practices in your organization. Each chapter is written in a lively, narrative style, interweaving anecdotes and quotations from CEOs, senior executives, change leaders, front-line Six Sigma Black Belts, project managers, process owners, and others. The book is also laced with pull-quotes, strategically placed chapter sidebars that delve into specific points in more detail, and other materials to provide visual variety to the text.

The seven principles of Strategic Six Sigma we write about here have been rigorously field-tested through years of experience with clients, and through robust, documented research. We've used them in companies in a wide array of industries. In each case, they have generated concrete, measurable results and helped boost business performance in myriad ways. We know that you'll find them useful tools in your organization as well—whether your goal is to cut costs, improve productivity, enhance customer loyalty and satisfaction, or spark strong top-line growth.

Remember, implementing Strategic Six Sigma principles isn't easy. Above all else, it requires strong leadership commitment and intense employee commitment (buy-in) to succeed. Having said that, the results from deploying it are nothing short of miraculous for those organizations daring and courageous enough to embark on the Strategic Six Sigma journey to breakaway performance. Good Luck!

Dick Smith
Partner
PwC Consulting
richard.c.smith@us.pwcglobal.com

Jerry Blakeslee
Partner
PwC Consulting
jerry.blakeslee@us
.pwcglobal.com

Strategic Six Sigma

Current and Emerging Applications

We are living, once and for all, in the Age of the Customer. Did you hear what we said? There has never been a better time to be a customer—or a tougher time to be a supplier. Customers have higher expectations and more choices than ever. Which means that you have to listen more closely than ever. Forget building a learning organization. You first have to build a listening *organization—a company whose people have their ears to the ground.*

> —Rekha Balu, Senior Writer
> *Fast Company*
> May 2000

Six Sigma. For years it was viewed simply as a process improvement tool (like total quality management) to help companies improve their manufacturing operations and reduce product defects. So why has it suddenly emerged as a methodology for driving business strategy and transforming organizations? Why are companies as diverse as General Electric (GE), JPMorgan Chase, Caterpillar, Raytheon, Dow Chemical, and Bombardier Transportation all using it, not just to cut costs and reduce product defects, but to drive and shape business strategy and transform how people work?

To understand that, one must understand the nature of business competition today and the nature of the business environment. Companies of all kinds today are facing crush-

1

ing business pressures, not just to continuously streamline their operations and cut costs (perennial issues facing all business enterprises), but also to grow their businesses, nurture innovation, and realize continuous gains in productivity.

In recent years, the pressure on companies to realize continuous productivity and profitability gains has been spurred not only by rising shareholder expectations. It has also intensified as the result of market consolidation, industry convergence, the growth of e-business, the scrutiny of Wall Street analysts (whose daily reassessments of corporate health and vitality can cause the capital valuations of companies to fluctuate by billions of dollars on a daily basis), and by the accelerating pace of business change.

As a result, the ability of companies to bring speed, agility, quality, and leanness to everything they do (e.g., to be fast to market, to shrink cycle times, to make global supply chains more efficient and responsive, and handle just-in-time inventory management and order fulfillment precisely) has become critical, not just to business success, but to business survival. The need for companies to serve these four marketplace masters puts enormous strains on businesses, not just in terms of infrastructure, design, and business practices, but also in terms of how they measure performance, leverage knowledge, serve customers, gauge productivity, and build competitive advantage.

■ DOING BUSINESS IN A WORLD OF GROWING RISK

There's yet another, very sobering reason why Strategic Six Sigma practices are emerging as important to companies today: the escalating prospect of catastrophic business risk. In the wake of the events of September 11, 2001, which took over 3,000 lives and are estimated to have cost global companies in excess of $150 billion, companies are recognizing the need not only to reorder their priorities, but in many cases, to anticipate new risks—from bioterrorism and airliner attacks on skyscrapers, to the potential cascade effect that such catastrophic events can have on all sectors of the economy. After the events of September 11, virtually the entire world economy paused, thousands of people were laid off from their jobs in hundreds of industries, and hundreds of companies had to declare Chapter 11—all of this the result of one unanticipated terrorist event! As one quality expert put it at the time, "The tragic and catastrophic events of September 11 revealed a massive 'quality system failure' in the U.S.'s intelligence system—from security lapses and a lack of on-the-ground human intelligence on the one hand, to the inability of different federal agencies to work together effectively beforehand to avoid such a disaster."

■ QUALITY SYSTEM FAILURES ARE MORE COMMON THAN WE WANT TO BELIEVE

Sadly, however, the failure of such high-profile quality systems is not limited to the events of September 11 or to the public arena. In recent years, there have been numerous quality failures, many of them in the industrial and commercial arenas. The Chernobyl nuclear reactor accident, the worst nuclear industry accident in history, took 125,000 lives, caused 3.5 million people to become ill (according to the Ukrainian Health Ministry), and has cost countless billions to clean up so far. The Challenger space shuttle disaster took seven lives and cost U.S. taxpayers between $5 billion and 10 billion. The Bridgestone/Firestone/Ford tire failures have, to date, taken 203 lives and already cost those two companies in excess of $4 billion—to say nothing of the hidden and intangible costs associated with lost sales, diminished prestige, reduced consumer confidence, damaged brand identity, and so forth.

What could have been done to avoid these disasters? What performance metrics or fail-safe manufacturing systems could have been put in place to avoid them? It begs the question, of course, of how we, as businesspeople (and human beings) define *quality*. Compounding the importance of answering this question is the fact that the events we've just described are only the most public and egregious examples of "quality failures" out there today. Many others, with untold financial, commercial, and even human ramifications, no doubt go unreported or even unknown in business every day.

For example, consider the fact that as we write these words, public scrutiny is focusing on the composite materials that in recent years have been used as a replacement for traditional aluminum in the construction of commercial aircraft, specifically in the tail section of airliners. In the wake of the crash of an American Airlines jet just moments after takeoff from New York's Kennedy Airport, transportation engineers, material specialists, and public safety advocates began raising questions about whether the honeycomb construction of these composite materials is of sufficient strength and durability to make it a worthy replacement for traditional alloys. Is there a potential quality issue here? You bet.

■ HOW DOES YOUR ORGANIZATION DEFINE *QUALITY?*

Renowned quality pioneer Phillip Crosby defined poor quality as ". . . conformance to requirements . . . doing it right the first time." Genichi Taguchi, another quality pioneer who coined the term *loss function* to denote the degree of customer dissatisfaction with a product, has described poor quality as the "loss a product causes to society after being shipped. . . ." Meanwhile, Dr. Joseph Juran, one of the early fathers of the quality movement in the United States referred to quality as "those product features which meet the needs of a customer . . . and provide product satisfaction."

Perhaps quality guru Edwards Deming, however, came closest to describing the modern-day idea of what quality needs to mean for companies today. He observed that "quality must be defined in terms of customer satisfaction. . . . [and requires the total] transformation of . . . American management."

We agree but with a caveat. In our view, quality, as a guiding principle of business, is—and always has been—about customer satisfaction. After all, nobody in business *stays in business* if they don't please customers. But getting to the point of customer satisfaction with one's customers, especially in the world *after* September 11, requires a new dedication, a new emphasis. Today, it's no longer about any of us doing business as usual. Instead, it's about being more strategic, planning for the unexpected, anticipating problems and challenges ahead of time, dealing with marketplace downturns, and being able to ride through patches of marketplace whitewater. It means that all of us must pay more attention to the business environment, get tighter with our customers, analyze our performance data better, and by the way, avoid disasters. The writing was on the wall even before the events of September 11: The economy was sputtering, and the capital valuations of many companies were caving. Today, however, the message is crystal clear: The business world, if we didn't know it already, is an uncertain place. To build world-class performance and to create cultures of breakaway performance in this brave new world, we need a new resolve and a fresh approach.

In today's new business world, quality can no longer be just about processes, products, services, or people. It must be about all four of these things—together. In other words, our notions of quality need to be both systemic and strategic, not piecemeal, inconsistent, or erratic. Indeed, it is only with a systemic and strategic quality framework in place that we will be able to anticipate the future and build sustainable excellence in meeting customer requirements.

■ CONSIDER A FRESH DEFINITION OF *QUALITY SYSTEMS*

For that reason, and from this point onward, we will speak in this book about the importance of companies creating quality systems to ensure their futures and to assure top-line growth, defect elimination, and customer satisfaction.

We define a *quality system* as an enterprise-wide framework of actively managed business processes that assures (over the long term) not only that the needs of one's customers are met (at a price customers are willing to pay), but also that the enterprise itself remains viable, profitable, and ongoing. To be sure, such systems should be able to prevent catastrophic failure and all the consequences that potentially can flow from such events—from loss of life and property to loss of market share, customer satisfaction, or product and service quality. At the same time, they should be constructed to allow for accurate monitoring and measurement of current performance, the taking of steps to ensure continuous improvement, and the constant infusion and application of new information and knowledge to improve efficiency, productivity, and operational excellence.

Assuring the development of such quality systems will be increasingly vital to companies in the future, not just as a result of the tragic events of September 11, but also as a result of the following:

➤ Increasing business competition
➤ Exploding customer demands for better products and better products faster
➤ Shrinking profit margins in many industries
➤ Skyrocketing costs for raw materials
➤ Growing shareholder pressure for sustainable top-line business growth
➤ The need for new products

■ THE USES OF STRATEGIC SIX SIGMA THINKING AND METHODS

Strategic Six Sigma principles and practices have a potentially huge role to play in the planning, building, management, and improvement of quality systems in companies today. Indeed, Strategic Six Sigma principles and practices, if employed effectively, can help a company turn its quality systems into a potent marketplace and competitive weapon. So, what exactly *is* Strategic Six Sigma? In essence, it is a whole-enterprise strategy of business process management and improvement based on the following four steps:

1. Measuring business and product/service conformance to customer requirements
2. Creating specific continuous actions to reduce variation in existing business processes that cause failures to conform to customer requirements
3. Creating new innovative products/services and pro-

cesses to specifically meet customer and market requirements

4. Repeating steps 1 through 3 continuously as necessary for the enterprise to remain viable and sustain shareholder value over the long term

Following are the three critical components to Strategic Six Sigma initiatives (see Figure 1.1):

1. *Designing processes for customer requirements using Design for Six Sigma (DFSS) teams.* DFSS is a robust and systematic improvement methodology that uses specific Six Sigma tools and metrics to design products, services, and processes that meet customer requirements from the outset, and that can be produced and delivered at Six Sigma quality levels.

2. *Improving existing processes using Define, Measure, Analyze, Improve, and Control (DMAIC) improvement teams.* DMAIC is a fact-based, closed-loop, problem-solving methodology that ensures continued process/product/service improvement. It focuses on eliminating unpro-

• DFSS generates new processes, products, services, and/or plants.

• DMAIC improves existing process performance.

• Process management is the system that enables leverage and sustains gains achieved by DFSS and DMAIC.

• Leaders drive and align the efforts strategically.

PROCESS TEAMS – Real-time process monitoring and analysis

Figure 1.1 What are the elements of Strategic Six Sigma?

ductive steps, developing and applying new metrics, and using technology to drive improvement.

3. *Enterprise-wide process management using process teams that work in real time to gauge, monitor, and analyze ongoing business and organizational performance.* The foundation for sustaining Six Sigma improvements over time is the institutionalizing of business improvement through ongoing process management. Process management requires that a company establish a series of dashboards, metrics, and performance indicators for its core processes through which the top leadership team can continuously monitor and assess performance. These dashboards and metrics typically track and monitor a variety of performance indicators, including: leading indicators, results indicators, customer indicators, and internal indicators.

Some companies, including GE, Honeywell, and Raytheon, are already taking a strategic approach to their use of Six Sigma, using it to integrate their business strategies, and to support the achievement of near-term as well as longer-term business objectives. At GE, for example, Six Sigma is today closely tied to the company's other major strategies, including services, globalization, and e-business. And at GE, individuals can't get ahead in management unless they become knowledgeable about and proficient at using Six Sigma practices in their everyday jobs.

Meanwhile, at Caterpillar, the world's largest manufacturer of construction and mining equipment, diesel and natural gas engines, and gas turbines, CEO Glen Barton is using Strategic Six Sigma principles to totally transform the company's business culture and to change how people work. He wants Six Sigma to be the engine that drives the company to sales and revenues of $30 billion by 2006. "A key part of the strategy is institutionalizing a 6 Sigma culture and philosophy," he writes in the company's 2000 annual report. "6 Sigma is a relentless quest for perfection through the disciplined use of fact-based, data-driven, decision-making methodology. It will enable us to make quantum gains in quality and reliability, and will touch everything we do at Caterpillar." It will also, he says, "become our way of life, benefiting customers, dealers, suppliers, employees, and shareholders. We will become the benchmark for institutionalizing 6 Sigma culture deployment excellence."[1]

Other companies are moving toward implementation of Strategic Six Sigma initiatives as well. A well-known automotive parts supplier in the Midwest is using Strategic Six Sigma practices in conjunction with Lean Manufacturing, Shainin statistical engineering techniques, and DFSS/Robust Engineering approaches to fortify and accelerate its product and process improvement efforts. The marketplace pressures to do this are extreme, notes the company's manager for innovation and continuous improvement. "To compete in the marketplace, we must have Lean Manufacturing processes, we must optimize our product and process designs, and we must do effective problem resolution—all at the same time," he says. "We get the maximum benefit from all of these if they work in a strategic way to support one another."

Meanwhile, an aftermarket manufacturer of custom automotive products is using Strategic Six Sigma principles, again in tandem with Lean Manufacturing techniques, to drive improvements in quality, costs, and product delivery. Use of Six Sigma principles and practices, according to one of the company's Six Sigma Black Belts, is helping to create a common language of change within the company and is driving all company employees to take a process thinking approach to getting their work done. The downstream results are that the company is more focused on the customer than it has ever been, is using Six Sigma to eliminate the root causes of product and service defects, and is building brand equity and customer loyalty in the process.

Other companies, such as Lockheed-Martin, recently awarded the largest defense contract in history to build the F-35 fighter (see Chapter 5) are using Six Sigma in various combinations with Lean Manufacturing, Kaizen projects, and other approaches. All this is to drive process, product, and service improvements that support overall strategy execution and ensure the health and vitality of the company's business processes on a sustained basis. "Businesses create earnings on the strength of their operating system," notes Mike Joyce, vice president of Lockheed-Martin's corporate-wide improvement initiative, known as LM-21 (for Lockheed-Martin 21st Century). "Look across our corporation and you'll see hundreds of processes that define what we do—in engineering, marketing, supply chain management, manufacturing, and so forth. Given the pace of change in today's marketplace, operating systems can't stand still."[2]

Joyce says Lockheed-Martin, which launched LM-21 in 1998, expects to capture "$3.7 billion in annual, steady-state cost savings in 2002" by leveraging "lean processes that operate at Six Sigma capability" across all areas of the company. "The integration of Lean thinking and Six Sigma methodologies forces us to change our paradigm of routine day-to-day work practices," he says. The goal is to "achieve waste-free products and defect-free processes that deliver sustained, increased earnings and customer loyalty."[2]

Despite the increasingly strategic orientation of many corporate Six Sigma initiatives today, many other companies continue to limit the use of Six Sigma principles and practices to the local levels of their organizations, where they are used to incrementally improve process performance, reduce process defects, or to enhance performance in other, narrowly defined operational areas.

We submit, however, that the integrated use of Strategic Six Sigma approaches and principles will be increasingly critical to corporate success in the years just ahead. Because companies today face constant change, a proliferating number of risks, and must get to market with ever greater speed, Strategic Six Sigma practices and methods will be used to support not just individual improvement projects, but entire business strategies. For example, let's look at how strategic (transformational) use of Six Sigma principles can help companies with the challenges of:

➤ Globalization and mergers and acquisitions (M&A)
➤ E-business planning and implementation
➤ Supply chain design and planning
➤ Customer relationship management
➤ National and global brand building
➤ New product development
➤ Sustainable growth
➤ Management of innovation/emerging technologies
➤ Business risk management

➤ Globalization and M&A

Globalization and M&A are trends impacting the operations of virtually all businesses today. They are being driven by a variety of forces: tightening profit margins in mature markets, customers who demand increasingly diverse product sets, new enabling technologies that facilitate the merging of corporate cultures, the need to acquire new manufacturing competencies, and expanding companies' global market reach. While the benefits of companies going global have been widely proclaimed, doing it successfully requires that a company's leaders ask themselves some thoughtful and probing questions. For example:

➤ How does a company effectively integrate its global business operations and deal with increasingly sophisticated and complicated customer requirements?
➤ How does a company's CEO unify a worldwide workforce under the banner of a common work language, common management practices, and a common culture?
➤ How does a company effectively build (and then protect) the integrity of its national or global brands?
➤ How does a company achieve optimal *speed and scale* so it can stretch itself to operate both *globally* (in terms of market reach and product sets) and *locally* (in terms of product and/or service customization)?

Grady Means, coauthor (with Bill Dauphinais and Colin Price) of *Wisdom of the CEO* (Wiley, 2000), notes that while there is a good deal of evidence linking globalization to high performance, globalization is a high-risk, high-reward proposition. "When a company globalizes from a strong core strategy, it maximizes reward," he says. But "when a company globalizes from a weak core strategy, it maximizes risk."

The implications of this are truly daunting if one considers the complexity of modern transnational M&A, and the requisite meshing of diverse workforces, business practices, and cultures across continents as part of forming modern, global business enterprises. Today, companies are embarking on "large-scale, high-risk global strategies and consolidations aimed at [helping them become] dominant competitors in particular sectors," write Means, Dauphinais, and Price in *Wisdom of the CEO*. "Such business plans require detailed analysis and planning and a major commitment from corporate leadership and the board of directors to move forward."[3]

In our opinion, such plans also require robust systems, methodologies, and disciplines—such as strategic use of Six Sigma—to help companies integrate and deploy their business operations and strategies, while realizing organizational synergies and top-line business growth.

One company that's using Strategic Six Sigma to strengthen its global business operations, build customer loyalty, and accelerate top-line business growth is Dow Chemical. In recent years, Dow has transformed itself from a "geographically organized and functionally driven company into a global, business-led company with annual sales of over $30 billion," notes Dow President and CEO, Mike Parker.[4] It has also embarked on an aggressive growth campaign, focused both on growing top-line business revenue, and on undertaking strategically significant M&A, one of the most important of which was Dow's recent merger with Union Carbide.

To undergird its growth activities, Parker says Dow built a robust global information technology (IT) backbone, and a global enterprise resource planning system to support its business operations. It also instituted use of Strategic Six Sigma to help deploy its strategic blueprint, put in place in 1994. "That blueprint calls for four things," notes Parker:

First, set the competitive standard, business by business. Six Sigma will play a critical role with this by enabling us to become more competitive in everything we do. Second, productivity: Very clearly Six Sigma can play a key role in that because a lot of what we're doing today involves cost savings projects, finding the "hidden factory" [in our operations], and being able to create more capacity out of what we are thinking is a constrained system. Third, value growth: DFSS [is helping us] design processes so they can perform at high sigma levels at the beginning, not at three sigma. Fourth, culture change: [Six Sigma is helping us] develop a mind-set and intolerance for waste . . . it's going to create breakthrough thought in people as they do their everyday jobs . . ."[4]

The decision to adopt Six Sigma as part of the company's strategic planning and execution process was a natural, says Parker. After the company downsized and restructured in the early 1990s, it needed to find new ways to grow and become more customer responsive. "We realized that to continue our journey to getting better, and to actually help us with the challenge of getting bigger—whether from growing our established businesses, doing successful [M&A], or growing new businesses, we needed some different tools. We also needed a different mind-set and some different capabilities, and that's the reason why we started to think about Six Sigma as the way to go."[4]

Today, Dow is aggressively using Six Sigma methods not only to help it deploy its strategic blueprint, but to leverage specific, concrete benefits from completion of successful Six Sigma projects across all areas of the organization. Currently, the company has some 2,400 Six Sigma projects (both DMAIC and DFSS projects) under way. "More than 350 new projects have been leveraged from the existing pool of active projects across the organization," says Kathleen Bader, Dow's Business Group President of Styrenics and Engineered Products. "We're capitalizing on our global infrastructure—our work processes and IT systems, to leverage the value of Six Sigma and incorporate best practices in our operations around the world." Echoing Parker, she says that Six Sigma is being used to accelerate the company's M&A activities, eliminate costs, deal with supply chain issues, reduce redundancies, and manage raw material supplies. "It is helping us take some of the subjectivity out of these processes," she says.[5]

Using Six Sigma to Accelerate M&A

Like Dow, Bombardier Transportation is also using Six Sigma practices to help support its globalization and M&A strategies. The global leader in the rail equipment, manufacturing, and service industry, Bombardier Transportation recently used Strategic Six Sigma concepts and tools to help accelerate and facilitate its 2001 acquisition of DaimlerChrysler Rail Systems (Adtranz.) "It's real impact has been in helping put the new organizational structure in place and mobilize the management team," says Desmond Bell, the company's vice president of Six Sigma. Bell says Six Sigma concepts and tools were used by the companies' management teams to evaluate key business processes in the two companies, identify key executive roles and responsibilities in the new organization, and to integrate the companies' operations by designing a new business process framework linking them together.[6]

Doing this at the outset of the integration "helped to embed process ownership in the new organizational structure," says Bell, and will help tremendously as the company extends itself more deeply into European and Far East markets.[6]

How Strategic Six Sigma Can Support Globalization and M&A Initiatives

We submit that Strategic Six Sigma practices and methods will increasingly play a role in global strategy development, planning, and deployment. How? By helping companies and their leaders build an empirical foundation for decision making, and drive people, processes, and organizations toward common objectives—whether the goal is to articulate a new global vision, define and assess business opportunities in mature and emerging markets, build and protect global brands, or accelerate integration of global business operations in the wake of M&A.

➤ e-Business Planning and Implementation

Consider now how use of Strategic Six Sigma can help mitigate the risks—and enhance the market opportunities—associated with e-business planning and implementation. Today, the Internet and its associated technologies are spawning entirely new business models. Customer *pull* now defines what a company sells the marketplace; no longer can firms simply *push* generic products and services onto customers. Customers are in the driver's seat, telling companies what they want, and *how* and *when* they want it. Businesses are therefore scrambling to become more responsive to customers' needs on the web. They are creating new products, using customer information to ensure competitive advantage, and making strategic IT decisions to support their e-business ventures. Today, "[c]ompanies are working and spending hard to promote their relatively newfound capabilities on the Net. With 'e or be eaten' rapidly becoming both the common mantra and the bottom-line for many businesses," notes Sheelagh Whittaker, President and CEO of EDS Canada.[7]

But as the dot-com train wreck of the last two years illustrates, building web-based business models is fraught with challenges and difficulties. Not only are there issues of capitalization and the smooth integration of click-and-mortar operations to consider, companies must also grapple with a dizzying array of technical concerns, including scalability, multiplatform integration, bandwidth, convergence, storage, and transactional protocols. "As enterprises embark on journeys into e-business waters, headlines over the next few years will be largely consumed with a series of business 'Mayday' distress signals," notes Don McCartney, a Pricewaterhouse Coopers (PwC) e-business expert. "Lying at the base of each distress signal will be one common theme: the failure to properly consider risk."[8] McCartney says, for example, that companies that fail to understand the IT failures of the past are likely to repeat them with their e-business ventures. "Long before e-business, IT projects commonly went astray as a result of project managers that failed to sufficiently define scope, outline change control procedures, and identify and mitigate potential risks."[8]

As companies plan and deploy increasingly sophisticated and complex e-business operations, there are critical strategic questions they must ask themselves to assure success. For example:

➤ In what ways are the critical customer requirements (CCRs) of e-customers different from those of traditional commercial or business customers, and how can such CCRs be effectively determined?

➤ How do we profile and segment customers appropriately, given that web-based business customer interactions are so different in nature and flow from traditional, face-to-face business transactions?

➤ In what ways can CCRs be used to optimally construct e-channels (web sites, portals, etc.) to meet the needs of web customers in both the business-to-business (B2B) and business-to-consumer (B2C) transaction space?

➤ How can a company align traditional brick-and-mortar and web-based business operations in optimal ways? How does this integration take place?

How Strategic Six Sigma Can Support e-Business Planning

As with globalization and M&A activities, we think using Strategic Six Sigma principles and best practices can be extremely valuable when incorporated into e-business planning, design, and implementation.

First, Strategic Six Sigma methods and approaches will prove very powerful in helping companies to profile and prioritize customers by segment, and then drill down to understand the critical customer requirements of each segment in turn. This will prove critical to the success of business web site operations, because customer behavior is markedly different on the web than in face-to-face business transactions, say e-business experts. (See the sidebar, "Using Six Sigma to Drive Web Design and E-Business Implementations.")

Second, Strategic Six Sigma methods and approaches can go far in mitigating the engineering and operational risks associated with the early-stage planning and launch of e-business initiatives. Companies can use methodologies such as DFSS or DFSS-@-e-speed approaches to accelerate and facilitate the design of e-business operations on the web; to drive new process design, and development of e-sales and marketing channels, logistics/distribution capabilities, customer service operations, and supplier interfaces.

Third, Strategic Six Sigma can be used to determine and allocate the appropriate capital and human resources (HR) requirements to e-business ventures. Because Strategic Six Sigma applies specific metrics, goals, and feedback systems to support business performance, it provides a common

USING SIX SIGMA TO DRIVE WEB DESIGN
AND E-BUSINESS IMPLEMENTATIONS

Just how can Six Sigma methods be used to help companies launch e-business ventures? For starters, they can be very helpful to a firm when it comes to designing a web site, or making an existing web site easier to navigate. That's according to Six Sigma design expert and principal PwC consultant Peter Amico, who says that in the last couple of years, a lot of companies have experienced significant start-up pains with their e-business ventures, because they haven't had an accurate handle on customer requirements.*

A lot of the problem, says Amico, stems from the fact that numerous "demographic and psychographic" considerations have to be factored into understanding the needs of customers for web-based services—how a person's thinking processes work, (e.g., the specific kind of information they're looking for, and even whether they are left- or right-handed). Such behavioral traits, which aren't as critical to consider in other transaction environments, come into play on the web whether a company is operating a web site for retail consumers or trying to migrate heavy-volume commercial and industrial business users to the web. "Somewhere between sixty-seven and seventy-eight percent of buying behavior on the web is driven by behaviorially based buying traits, things that customers themselves can't articulate," says Amico.

For example, customers may like a certain web site because of its visual appeal, graphic design, or because it's intuitively easy to navigate. In other cases, a customer may choose (or not choose) to interact with a web site, based on ergonomic factors such as where a company locates an input or dialogue box, or how it words certain questions or statements to a web visitor.

Traditional voice-of-the-customer surveys or customer interviews are likely to miss what really motivates people to buy products from a certain site, or to use a certain company's online customer services. That's because they don't go deeply enough into analyzing psychographic and demographic data points, says Amico.

So how can Six Sigma help? Amico says a company can use

Strategic Six Sigma approaches to help it separate and prioritize customers by segment, and then drill down to understand the CCRs of each segment in turn. "A chemical company might have a web site where customers go to buy things, where company engineers go to look for technical background information, where procurement people go for pricing information, and where sales people go to get warranty information," he says. "You have to be able to customize a web site to meet the needs of a potentially diverse universe of users."

Though in many ways subtle, the design of a web site can make or break a business, says Amico. "A prospective customer may want to find out what products a company offers, but if the web site has been set up to display products and services by business unit, it may fail to meet that customer's need," he says. "The key thing on the web is that you only have one chance to do things right or people are going to click and go somewhere else. You've got to make your site sticky, so people keep coming back to it."

Design for Six Sigma (DFSS) methods and approaches, says Amico, can be very useful in helping a company delineate and differentiate one customer's needs from others. Of particular help, says Amico, is a Six Sigma methodology he has devised called *DFSS @ e-speed.* The measuring phase of this methodology is designed to probe deeply into customer user and buying preferences, not only through traditional voice-of-the-customer surveys and phone interviews, but also through actual observation of web users to understand their behavioral habits in front of a computer terminal.

By using the tools and techniques of *DFSS @ e-speed,* Amico says it's possible for companies to do an almost limitless amount of web site customization to accommodate the needs of different users. However, he says, as part of the web site design process, a company will typically conduct a cost-benefit analysis, prioritize customer requirements using specific *DFSS-@-e-speed* tools, then roll out periodic new releases of its web site as part of "a multi-generation approach to web design and development."—*The Authors*

*Peter Amico, Telephone interview with Richard Koonce, PricewaterhouseCoopers, Los Angeles, CA, 14 December 2001.

language and framework with which to set business goals and targets for e-ventures, and align employees [e.g., in research and development (R&D), sales and marketing, distribution, customer service, order fulfillment, and account management] to meet those goals.

Fourth, Strategic Six Sigma principles and methods will be employed to help companies form e-partnerships with one another. They will be used to develop clearly understood and mutually agreed-to levels of business performance, customer service, and process measurement and improvement to which all parties to such e-partnerships will agree. In so doing, they will help sustain high levels of product quality and service reliability.

Fifth, introduction of Strategic Six Sigma thinking and methods can help identify and codify e-business best practices, in everything from systems technology to security and strategy. The value of this is undeniable. Notes Cathy Neuman, PwC's deputy global e-business leader, "No one wants to slow down in the online industry, but the truth is that we've seen many companies—from start-up dot-coms to household names—trying to sprint ahead with their business plans when they haven't mastered their walking skills or in some cases, their crawling skills."[9] Neuman adds that given the risks involved with any e-business venture, it's critical that a company have frameworks in place so that a company's "progress can be measured, against its competitors, its markets and its industry, [and also] against the company's own expectations and those with whom it does business."[9]

Finally, the power of Strategic Six Sigma thinking and business practices to create synergy and focus among people in an organization (by defining goals and providing feedback mechanisms to monitor performance) will become increasingly important as companies' e-business models mature and as customer needs become more complex. An example would be as a company moves from the relatively simple process of putting sales and marketing channels on the web to transforming its supply chain and managing strategic e-partnerships among customers, suppliers, financial institutions, and other parties to e-business transactions.

➤ Supply Chain Planning and Design

Still other environmental pressures are putting stress on companies today, forcing firms to continuously redesign their business models to keep costs in check, and to ensure sustained customer satisfaction and responsiveness. For example, in today's business environment where speed is everything, the design of responsive supply chains—those that either anticipate or quickly respond to the needs of customers and that create virtual, web-based networks of companies, customers, and suppliers—is becoming a priority for companies. One company we know, a worldwide provider of B2B Internet services, is pioneering the development of such supply chains. It links companies, their customers, and their suppliers together in a virtual worldwide web of interactive and interdependent relationships, with transaction speed being one of the key criteria of its business performance. It keeps track of this performance using a highly unique performance dashboard that incorporates use of Six Sigma principles to gauge business performance on a daily basis.

Other companies using Strategic Six Sigma practices to design (or redesign) their supply chains include 3M, under its new chairman and chief executive, Jim McNerney. In January 2001, McNerney, a GE veteran, told analysts that he expected Six Sigma to save 3M hundreds of millions of dollars through better and more efficient materials sourcing. He also anticipated that Six Sigma would contribute $300 million to $450 million in pretax income in 2001.[10] Much of that, McNerney predicted, would come not just from slashing costs but also from boosting top-line revenue growth. "I've seen firsthand how Six Sigma can energize an organization, how it can lower costs, increase sales and cash flow, and satisfy customers by truly producing higher-quality products and faster response," he notes.[11]

Using Strategic Six Sigma to Facilitate Supply Chain Redesign

If implemented correctly at the leadership level and cascaded throughout all levels of an organization, Strategic Six Sigma methods and work practices can help streamline the design and operation of supply chains in *any* industry. They can

➤ Help link companies, customers, and suppliers together with a common set of metrics, operating parameters, and performance expectations

➤ Be used to align the organizational designs and priorities of different strategic e-partners to meet the needs of common customers

➤ Be used in other ways to integrate new and existing business processes (e.g., Lean Manufacturing, and sales and marketing), increase customer service levels, enhance inventory management, speed deliveries, reduce cycle times, and lower product and supply chain costs.

➤ Customer Relationship Management

In the words of Sergio Zyman, former Chief Marketing Officer of the Coca-Cola Company and author of *The End of Marketing as We Know It,* the business marketplace today is a "consumer democracy," a place where consumers have a proliferating number of options for everything from toasters and computers to industrial machinery and the latest handheld technology. In such an environment, he says, marketing must be a "science." It must be about "experimentation, measurement, analysis, refinement, and replication."[12]

We argue that every process in business nowadays—from product development and sales to R&D, distribution, and customer care—needs to be viewed as a business science. What's more, every business process needs to be subjected to regular experimentation, measurement, analysis, and refinement. That's because companies can no longer rely on guesswork or intuition to help them design their processes or anticipate customer needs. Instead, businesses must be managed by fact, with a scrupulous and robust approach to ascertaining CCRs (regardless of the product or industry) and fulfilling those CCRs on a consistent basis. This, of course, is the very heart of what Six Sigma is about—reducing defects in processes—including a company's customer relationship management processes. Later in this book, we'll describe what companies like Dow Chemical, Johnson Controls, and Air Products and Chemicals are doing to forge strong bonds with their customers, using Strategic Six Sigma principles and practices as the basis for doing this.

Using Strategic Six Sigma to Support Customer Relationship Management

Suffice it to say here, however, that when they are applied systematically to the arena of customer relationship management, Strategic Six Sigma principles and practices can help companies to

➤ Define their customer strategies and better understand the nature and needs of individual customer or market segments

➤ Conduct market research that can be used for product enhancement or the creation of new products and services

➤ Create effective channel and product strategies (in other words, the means by which a company will deliver products and services cost effectively)

➤ Put the right infrastructure in place to support *all* dimensions of customer care: from new business development, market analysis, and segmentation, to the careful development and nurturing of key accounts and creation of long-term customer loyalty

➤ Create the ultimate in customized products and services

➤ Monitor conformance to customer requirements through real-time customer dashboards (see Chapter 6)

➤ National and Global Brand Building

Building (or revitalizing) a brand name is all about enhancing the goodwill and value that customers place on that name, so it's intimately related to customer satisfaction and loyalty. These factors, in turn, help determine the premium that the market will pay for a brand name that is immediately associated with quality, reliability, service, or integrity.

Driving customer brand name recognition to high levels is a two-edged sword. The Firestone brand is a household name in the United States. But after the American public was deluged with negative press coverage following the Ford Explorer/Firestone tire incidents, its market share suffered terribly. And regardless of the final root cause analysis of those events, the Ford and Firestone names have been greatly tarnished.

Notwithstanding that, the tremendous market success of other companies with household names (e.g., IBM, McDonald's, Intel, and Dell) proves that there is tremendous market leverage to be gained from a well-known name and a reliable brand. Consider the example of ServiceMaster, a home services company built on the acquisition of numerous recognizable names including Terminix, TruGreen ChemLawn, TruGreen LandCare, American Residential Services, Rescue Rooter, American Mechanical Services, ServiceMaster Clean, American Home Shield, AmeriSpec, Merry Maids, Furniture Medic, and The ServiceMaster Home Service Center. Recently, the company embraced Six Sigma as part of a multidimensional strategy to enhance market recognition of the ServiceMaster name as a provider of high-value multiple household services and products. The first waves of Six Sigma projects the company undertook focused on identifying CCRs for each customer base within ServiceMaster's various brands, and on improving customer satisfaction while gaining efficiencies. These projects "are proving to us that Six Sigma principles and practices can be readily applied to our business operations quickly, generating concrete and measurable results," notes Patricia Asp, ServiceMaster's Senior Vice President, and one of the company's executive Six Sigma Sponsors.[13]

Asp says that ServiceMaster is committed to building a high-quality national home services brand that can be leveraged successfully in every regional market. As Six Sigma projects are launched and generate results, "building a common umbrella brand around delivering high customer service levels across our many service offerings will be one of the key outcomes of the company's Six Sigma efforts," she says.[13] Indeed, Asp and other ServiceMaster executives recognize that the measurement and continuous improvement dimensions of Strategic Six Sigma will act to drive customer satisfaction levels continuously higher.

➤ New Product Development

In today's business environment, a company's ability to develop and flight-test new products in less time and for less money has become a critical element in remaining competitive. Dow Chemical, for example, has successfully used Six Sigma principles and methods to significantly reduce the time required to grow transgenic cotton, genetically altered cotton that is resistant to pests and certain herbicides.

Shrinking the product development cycle (and at the same time, the corporate learning cycle) is also a huge issue in the pharmaceuticals industry. There, the average R&D time from invention of a new drug through clinical trials, Food and Drug Administration (FDA) approval, and market introduction can run upward of 10 years or more. It requires enormous capital outlays on the part of pharmaceutical manufacturers, with no assurance that their efforts will not be thwarted by some competitor moving faster, who gets the product to market sooner. Issues of long product development cycles are also significant in the aviation and aerospace industries, and in many other areas of the defense establishment. Consequently, a major pharmaceutical company we work with is using Six Sigma to help it prioritize areas for clinical R&D, and to help it design, develop, and field-test new drugs in less time than in the past. In so doing, it is learning and quantifying the effects from the key decisions it makes as part of the pharmaceutical R&D process. This is extremely valuable information for a company to capture and leverage as it makes key decisions about the allocation of people, capital, and resources.

Strategic Six Sigma practices can be of enormous benefit in supporting R&D and new product introductions in many industries. They can

➤ Accelerate a company's learning cycle
➤ Help product development teams do field research more quickly and with more quantification and consistency
➤ Speed the redesign of initial product designs
➤ Ensure rapid information exchange among manufacturers, customers, and suppliers.

How GE Pioneered the Use of Six Sigma for New Product Development

General Electric started using Six Sigma in 1996, and that same year started using Six Sigma statistical tools to fix and design new products. Nowhere did this prove to be more important than in power systems, notes former GE CEO Jack Welch. "In the mid-1990s, when demand for power plants was modest, we were having forced outages in our newly designed gas turbine power plants. Rotors were cracking due to high vibration. A third of the 37 operating units in the installed base had to be removed in 1995."[14] Using Six Sigma methods, however, vibrations were reduced by 300 percent and the problem was totally fixed in late 1996.[14]

In 1998, GE's Medical Systems group introduced a $1.25 million diagnostic scanner, the first GE product ever produced from concept to finish using Six Sigma principles. The scanner, called the Lightspeed, was the end result of some

200 GE employees spending 3 years of work and almost $50 million to run 250 separate Six Sigma analyses. While one team troubleshot the reliability of measurement devices, another team was trying to figure out how to extend the scanner's product life, while still another was "dissecting image quality into factors that could be massaged to filter out picture-blurring electronic noise."[15]

The development of the Lightspeed could not have been accomplished in the absence of a marriage between high-speed computers and Six Sigma quality design methods. The marriage of the two enabled GE's R&D process to conduct thousands of development tests that in the past would not have been humanly feasible. "In Six Sigma analyses, there are thousands of permutations and combinations—probably too many for the human mind to fathom, although easy enough for even a moderately speedy computer," writes *New York Times* business writer Claudia Deutsch, ". . . [M]odern information technology has made Six Sigma a practical way to identify the optimum configuration of most products or processes."[15]

Between 1998 and 2000, GE Medical launched 22 new Six Sigma–designed products, according to Welch, and in 2001, 51 percent of that division's overall revenues were anticipated to come from Six Sigma designs.[14]

GE's Lightspeed project (and others like it) highlight the ways that the strategic use of Six Sigma practices and thinking doesn't just speed up the product development cycle in a company but can also enhance team cohesiveness and organizational alignment in the process. "Six Sigma gets people from all over the organization to work together on improving the end product, not just their individual piece of it," notes Six Sigma consultant Frank Jones.[15]

Other Applications of Strategic Six Sigma Thinking and Methods

There are still other areas of business focus and priority today, where the use of Strategic Six Sigma thinking and best practices can help companies boost business performance and pursue new business strategies.

➤ Sustainable Growth

One of the most interesting and promising new applications of Strategic Six Sigma thinking and business practices is in the chemical and pharmaceutical industries. In the September 2001 issue of *Harvard Business Review,* Du Pont CEO Chad Holliday outlines the way in which Six Sigma, in tandem with other approaches, is being used today, not only to accelerate Du Pont's globalization efforts, but also to help it be a responsible global citizen. "At Du Pont, we have set various stretch goals for 2010, including a reduction of greenhouse gas emissions by two-thirds while holding our energy use flat (using 1990 as a base year). We also plan to increase our use of renewable resources to 10% of our global energy needs," he writes.[16]

How will Du Pont achieve these goals? In big part it will be through a strategy of productivity improvement that includes Six Sigma. Holliday describes how Six Sigma, as a component of Du Pont's productivity improvement efforts, improved the productivity of a plant in Buffalo, New York, by 10 percent without the need for any capital outlays. At this plant, which manufactures Corian, an acrylic-based material used for solid surfaces such as kitchen and bath countertops, a project team discovered that it could accelerate manufacturing lines by boosting the concentration of a catalyst used to make Corian products. The result was $26 million in added revenue in 2000. This figure might not seem too significant for a company with $30 billion sales, notes Holliday. He adds however, that Du Pont has thousands of such projects underway and is adding 200 new ones each month. "Altogether, our projects using [Six Sigma] methodology are responsible for savings of more than $1 billion a year, and these efforts to improve productivity invariably result in less waste, both in energy and raw material."[16]

Taking a Strategic Approach to Operational Improvement

The Six Sigma projects under way today at Du Pont are all part of a strategic approach to operational improvement that's intended not just to create leaner, more efficient processes but also robust, top-line growth as well. The company's focus on business improvement "elevates productivity from an operational to a more central, strategic level. Many companies consider productivity to be a cost-saving operational issue. We at Du Pont have elevated productivity to the strategic level because we believe that it is central to our efforts in sustainability."[16]

➤ Thinking Big: Using Strategic Six Sigma to Manage Innovation and Assess Emerging Technologies

Traditionally, discussion of disruptive new technologies has been limited to the ways that communications, computer, and information processing technologies either accelerate or otherwise change the nature of business transactions and companies' business models. Certainly, the Internet has played a central role in recent years, not only as a disruptive new technology in its own right, but also as an enabler of other technologies. For that reason, as Grady Means and company point out in *Wisdom of the CEO*, the management of technical change has joined the management of capital to define the context of competition for twenty-first-century firms and markets.

In light of this statement, however, we believe the definition of *disruptive technologies* itself needs to be expanded. It needs to include not just technologies of business transaction (computers, networks, telecom links, etc.), but also new technologies born of continuing scientific discoveries and technological breakthroughs. New scientific breakthroughs and technological advances often create unexpected inflection points in the lives of businesses by spawning the development of new products, disrupting the marketplace balance of power among competitors, and causing the fortunes of some companies to soar, while putting others out of business.

Think of how the introduction of the automobile displaced the need for buggy whip manufacturers, for example, and of how VHS tape products are now being rapidly displaced by CD and DVD technologies. More to our point here, consider the commercial and financial implications that may eventually flow from increased emphasis on stem cell research (new drugs and new drug therapies). Or, the likely impact that advances in the manufacture of microchips is likely to have on competition in the computer industry.

A single newspaper article, culled from the oceans of business newsprint generated in the world every day, provides a snapshot of how scientific and technological breakthroughs can, in many cases, have enormous downstream business and commercial implications. An August 27, 2001, article in the *New York Times* outlined how, in a bid to move beyond silicon-based computers, IBM recently built a computer circuit out of a single thread of carbon. The development signifies a significant breakthrough in molecular electronics, the article noted, and a potential inflection point in the life of the computer industry. It holds the promise of enabling IBM to use nanotubes in computer processors, packing up to 10,000 times more transistors into the same amount of space as today's computers do.[17] This could potentially increase the processing power of computer chips exponentially—far beyond anything we know today. In so doing, it could reposition IBM as the sole provider of this new microtechnology to the marketplace!

Using Six Sigma Principles and Practices to Monitor and Manage the Emergence of New Technologies

Increasingly, disruptive new technologies aren't just changing the dynamics of business competition. They are also overturning old, capital-intensive models of business operations and organization, and changing the nature of customer and supplier relationships. In a Darwinian sort of way, they're even responsible, in many cases, for determining which companies become critical business players in rapidly morphing industries. For all these reasons, companies need to be able to tap a host of environmental scanning, strategic planning, measurement, and evaluative tools and techniques that will allow them *with their customers* to understand the potential market impact of new technologies, identify new market opportunities, and create new value propositions.

Given its emphasis on collecting facts from customers and the marketplace, and using that data to drive decision making, Strategic Six Sigma principles and practices hold the promise of helping companies and their customers nurture innovation, assess the viability of emerging technologies, leverage marketplace disruptions, and build new strategic partnerships as never before. Doing this will create new and exciting business opportunities for companies at the nexus of customer need and technological feasibility. (See also the earlier section, "New Product Development.") Once these opportunities are identified, Strategic Six Sigma principles can be used to bring them to the marketplace faster and more effectively.

➤ Managing Business Risk

As we said at the outset of this chapter, no discussion of Strategic Six Sigma would be complete today without mentioning its myriad uses in mitigating business risk, especially in the wake of the financial collapse of companies like Enron and Global Crossing, and the events of September 11. Business risk today takes many forms, of course: capital exposure, market exposure, exposure of individuals to hazardous situations, potential disruption of Internet and local area network operations, potential disruption of corporate intranet networks, failures of computer security and electronic exchange protocols, cyberespionage, computer hacking, and other forms.

In the wake of the World Trade Center and Pentagon terrorist tragedies of last year, however, discussion of business risk takes on a new meaning—and a new urgency. The events of September 11 brought home the tragic fact that our world is not nearly as secure as we thought. Consequently, we must give more strategic thought to the importance of security and safety issues as part of designing, building, and operating airlines, airports, buildings, and computer systems to eliminate problems that lead to security and safety lapses.

As all businesses today become more global, the business risks associated with operating in a global environment escalate exponentially. "Protecting data and systems worldwide involves far more than technology. Companies are finding it necessary to understand foreign cultures, navigate myriad legal systems, and manage unfamiliar business practices, all the while acknowledging the differences between securing national and international operations," notes technology writer Erik Sherman in the summer 2001 issue of *Catalyst*.[18] Sherman points out that when it comes to managing technology risks, many companies ignore the implications of the weakest-link theory of security. "A company's infrastructure is only as secure as the most vulnerable point of access, including foreign offices and international partners."[18]

Strategic Six Sigma thinking and business practices will no doubt be of great help to companies as they assess the weakest links in their computer, IT, and telecommunications systems; as they brainstorm worst-case business scenarios, develop fail-safe disaster recovery plans, and work to ensure the security of airport and airline customers, tenants of large buildings, and computer and Internet users. All of this has been necessitated as our society comes to grips with operating in a new global environment where customer care strategies, antiterrorism approaches, and high-tech security planning will all need to be considered within the same strategic business context.

■ CONCLUSIONS

As this chapter has shown, Strategic Six Sigma thinking is emerging today as a powerful vehicle that companies can use to operationalize their global strategies, deal with business challenges, and accelerate the achievement of their business goals. Because Strategic Six Sigma emphasizes the use of data (management by fact) and root cause analysis to drive decision-making, it can invigorate the strategic planning and visioning processes of any company. It can help to foster strong organizational alignment and create leadership focus and commitment around critical business goals and objectives.

Most important, of course, Strategic Six Sigma thinking and best practices can be used in powerful ways to help companies become more customer-centric in everything they do—whether their customers are retail or commercial, in heavy industry, transportation, defense, aerospace, pharmaceuticals, petrochemicals, entertainment, home services, or high tech. Becoming customer-centric is the best edge that any company can develop today, not just to ensure its business survival, but also to guarantee its success in a boisterous new business marketplace. That new marketplace is one in which customers are increasingly in the driver's seat, and where market dominance is determined not by pushing products, but by a firm's ingenuity, agility, and responsiveness in meeting critical customer requirements.

Many years ago, legendary management consultant and author Peter Drucker remarked that the purpose of business is to "create a satisfied customer." This book is designed to show how, by adopting Strategic Six Sigma practices and principles within your organization, you can do exactly that—and create robust quality systems in the process.

But implementing Strategic Six Sigma thinking and methods into an organization is no easy task. It takes strong commitment from the top of an organization, and a clear realization by an organization's top leaders of its potential value to the health and vitality of a company. What's more, implementing successful Strategic Six Sigma initiatives requires a keen understanding of the dynamics of organizational change, and especially the intangible soft sides of managing people as part of that process.

In Chapter 2, we examine the reason that some Six Sigma initiatives fail to achieve their goals, or fail at least to live up to their full billing. We also suggest ways that any Six Sigma initiative can be effectively implemented and sustained, if a strategic point of view is taken to its implementation, and if people *at all levels* of the organization are engaged to make such initiatives succeed.

Chapter 2

Rocky Road or Trajectory of Transformation? What Makes Strategic Six Sigma Efforts Successful?

The big myth is that Six Sigma is about quality control and statistics. It is that—but it's a helluva lot more. Ultimately, it drives leadership to be better by providing tools to think through tough issues. At Six Sigma's core is an idea that can turn a company inside out, focusing the organization outward on the customer.

—Jack Welch, Former CEO
General Electric

By now you have glimpsed at the potential of Strategic Six Sigma to help companies operationalize their business strategies and become more customer-centric. The question that arises at this point is what drives Six Sigma implementations to achieve their maximum return on investment (ROI)? What is it that some business leaders do to create and *sustain* the kind of results we benchmark at the best Six Sigma companies [e.g., General Electric (GE), Honeywell, Dow]?

Six Sigma implementations typically follow one of several possible organizational paths over time. Those that achieve the greatest results over time are those that ultimately drive change not just at a *transactional* level inside companies (the level of "processes, management practices, systems, and technology where normal, everyday work gets done," in the words of change management practitioner and author Warner Burke, Ph.D., of Columbia University), but also at a larger-gauge *transformational* level.

At the transformational level (the level of leadership, culture, strategy, mission, and vision), the entire nature of a business enterprise is likely to morph as Six Sigma methods and approaches are deployed throughout the organization. Why? Because the broadly based, enterprise-wide deployment of Six Sigma methods and practices doesn't just generate incremental improvements in discrete work processes or business units of a company. Instead, it totally transforms how people at all levels *throughout* the organization do their work—how their work objectives are determined, how their productivity and job performance are measured, what tasks make up their jobs, how they interrelate with others in the organization and with customers, and so forth. This happens as individuals, groups, and business units all become aligned with corporate goals, and as a direct line-of-sight view is created between a company's processes and people on the one hand, and the needs and requirements of the customers on the other.

Let's look now at the potential trajectories of Strategic Six Sigma deployments in more detail, to understand the characteristics associated with each. (See Figure 2.1.)

There is a very critical period at the beginning of Six Sigma initiatives when a visionary leader reaches the decision to invest in a strategy of systematic improvement using

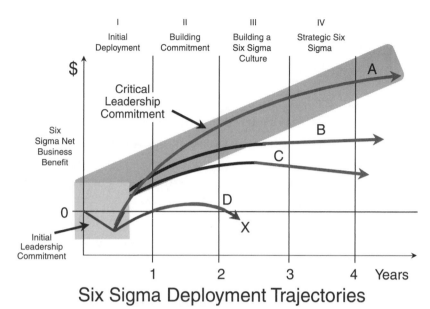

Six Sigma Deployment Trajectories

• The end game is achieving dynamic, customer-coupled process performance.
• It takes a sustained commitment to stay on Trajectory A.
• The zone of critical commitment begins around the end of year 1 and has no ending.

Figure 2.1   Six Sigma deployment trajectories.

Six Sigma methods. This initial commitment and energy generally result in initiatives taking one of several potential flight paths in subsequent years.

Curve D implementations, shown in Figure 2.1, are generally localized (rather than enterprise-wide) efforts. They typically are initiated by a single visionary business unit leader who undertakes a handful of projects to demonstrate that Six Sigma methods work. While these projects may succeed in producing real financial benefits for the organization, quite often there are so few of them that they don't generate the amount of attention necessary to warrant a full-scale implementation. At the same time, they don't result in the building of the necessary infrastructure (e.g., communications channels, training, incentives, a strong coalition of sponsors/champions) to sustain a longer-term effort. As a result, Black Belts often perform their work part-time, which results in far less than optimal results. In addition, because few projects are undertaken, and because there may be only a few (or even just one) committed business leader/Six Sigma champion, a critical mass or community of leaders committed to the effort never develops. Worst case here: leaders outside the process don't support it, and in some cases wait patiently for it to die.

Curve C implementations fare much better in achieving longer-term results. They are characterized by significant implementation efforts across the company, or at least within one major business division. A cadre of full-time Black Belts, approaching 1 percent of the employee population, is typically involved. Curve C implementations focus on solving tough operational issues and on reducing costs or optimizing product quality as viewed by the business. These implementations, while often supported by a larger group of committed executives and a significant infrastructure, realize diminishing returns over time. This occurs because they are often internally focused projects that don't give primacy to customer and marketplace requirements.

Curve B implementations *do* focus on meeting customer or marketplace requirements. They, too, are concerned with cost reduction, the efficiency of the company's current business model, and/or the processes that compose it. Typically, the people who lead these efforts possess an outside-in (customer/marketplace) focus, not an inside-out (company) orientation. Champions of curve B implementations understand that to keep one's business model viable, a company must be in touch with marketplace requirements and trends. Moreover, companies that undertake curve B projects recognize that to succeed in the long term, they need to fundamentally understand the nature of their customers' needs, and the nature of their customers' businesses. They concern themselves with the entire value chain out to the final customer, recognizing that successful customers are of greater long-term value to their own shareowners. Companies in this category also invite their key suppliers into their Six Sigma community to create extended-enterprise Six Sigma deployments. They do Six Sigma projects with and for suppliers and customers, all to retain and enhance the long-term value of the existing customer base. These initiatives enjoy a good deal of top leadership support.

What is it that sustains the curve A (Strategic Six Sigma) implementations in Figure 2.1? What enables curve A implementations to achieve and maintain a Generation IV— Strategic Six Sigma state? Companies on this trajectory have succeeded in both improving the existing business model and creating a new one. They are using Six Sigma business improvement to grow the business—to nurture new ideas, develop new products and services, to undertake new acquisitions, or to acquire new customers. Ultimately, their focus on these areas generates profitable top-line business growth and revenue. Companies that undertake curve A implementations have successfully migrated Six Sigma thinking into their growth and renewal processes by combining Design for Six Sigma (DFSS) concepts into research, new product and service development, sales and marketing, and acquisition processes. Curve A companies use Six Sigma process management as a core strategy to operate the business and to operationalize their business goals. They are characterized by leaders who have a clear vision and commitment to developing a culture of continuous improvement. As part of doing this, leaders actively and consistently promote Six Sigma as "the way we will do our work" on a going-forward basis.

WHY RAYTHEON DEPLOYED SIX SIGMA

We launched Raytheon Six Sigma in January 1999. The driver was that we were a company that had come together by acquisitions in '96 and '97. A number of deals were done very quickly of companies that while in the same market (defense) had been, in many cases, blood competitors previously. So, you can imagine the intensity of feelings that were taken on in this new company, as everybody came together under the same umbrella. It was clear that we needed to do something to bring this organization together. In essence, we needed to create a common language throughout the organization. I also had a view at the time that we were a technology company, an engineering company with over 25,000 engineers. What do you know about engineers? You know they're smart, that they love to solve problems, and that they're *data-driven*. It was clear to me that this confluence of things—the tension that existed in the organization, the need for a common language, and our competencies—all conspired to say there was one clear answer for us: Six Sigma.

Dan Burnham, Chairman and Chief Executive Officer
Raytheon

Achieving maximum returns from Six Sigma requires careful attention to initial deployment of an initiative, and a sustained long-term commitment from the leaders of the organization to making it bear a great amount of fruit. In fact, to deploy Strategic Six Sigma initiatives rapidly and with sufficient speed and scale to ensure optimal success requires that CEOs do seven things:

Step 1: Build a committed leadership team. Effective implementation of Strategic Six Sigma is dependent not just on one person (e.g., a CEO) acting as a Six Sigma advocate, but on a strong community of leaders at *all* levels inside the organization working together to drive initiatives forward. Developing this cadre of Six Sigma supporters is absolutely essential to achieve success with Strategic Six Sigma initiatives. Each member of this team must champion Six Sigma principles at every turn and generate buy-in, commitment, and participation to them within their own spheres of organizational influence. Failure to create this "guiding coalition" for change, as Harvard professor John Kotter puts it, means that even the most thoughtfully conceived Six Sigma plans will fail (due to organizational indifference) or become readily derailed. (For more information on this topic, see Chapter 3.)

Step 2: Integrate Strategic Six Sigma principles into the company's strategy planning and deployment processes. For many companies today, corporate strategy planning efforts are a haphazard affair, made difficult by turf wars and competing political agendas among members of a company's top leadership team. However, by introducing Strategic Six Sigma thinking into a company's planning processes, it can greatly enhance and accelerate the development, direction, and clarity of business goals and targets. Successful implementation requires integrating Strategic Six Sigma initiatives with existing initiatives, business strategies, and strategic improvement goals (SIGs), creating what we call a *line-of-sight* approach to business transformation. This occurs as business leaders become personally involved in generating annual key improvement goals and an active portfolio of projects to achieve these goals.

Often, a significant by-product of this process is the forging of tight team unity in senior executive teams. This occurs because the objective and quantitative elements of Strategic Six Sigma thinking accelerate the storming and norming processes of senior leadership teams and facilitate faster decision making. The use of hard, empirical data, if you will, helps harmonize the chorus of competing individual voices that often keep top leadership teams from operating as effectively as they need to in today's business environment. (For more information on this topic, see Chapter 4.)

Step 3: Ensure that the company is both passionate and consistent about how it stays in touch with customers. Developing a disciplined approach to track and capture existing levels of customer satisfaction and loyalty is critical to the implementation of Strategic Six Sigma initiatives. Such customer intelligence should not be anecdotal, because the critical customer requirements (CCRs) must be quantitatively known and therefore measurable. In addition, the organization must have an up-to-the-minute grasp of what the large-scale marketplace is doing and where it is going. This knowledge serves to drive improvement goals to gain marketshare.

A good example of a company that takes a disciplined approach to customer relationship management is Lockheed-Martin, the Bethesda, Maryland–based defense contractor recently awarded the largest defense contract ever ($200 billion) to produce a new, next-generation jet fighter—the F-35 Joint Strike Fighter for the U.S. military. Building this plane, which calls for developing some 6 million lines of computer code to run its many systems, will require exacting precision and intense focus on meeting CCRs over the plane's incredible eight-year development cycle. *Strategic Six Sigma: Best Practices from the Executive Suite* showcases what Lockheed-Martin and other market-smart companies are doing to create and sustain intense relationships with their customers. (See Chapter 5.)

Step 4: Design, organize, and run the business using a business process framework. To ensure optimal results, Strategic Six Sigma initiatives should be undertaken supported by a framework of process management. This means viewing one's company not as a set of functional silos, but as a *family* of interrelated processes—processes that must be synchronized and aligned to support business goals. Being able to examine the gap between what the business produces and what customers demand (and closing it) is the essence of Six Sigma. The width of the gap can then be used to prioritize Strategic Six Sigma efforts, and thus realize a faster improvement rate. In the long run, it's critical for leaders (a CEO or business unit heads) to manage their businesses by processes with clear, accountable process owners, metrics, and cycles of improvement. Leading Six Sigma companies, such as GE, Dow, and Raytheon, are very intentional about sustaining Six Sigma using a process management approach. They build business process dashboards that display, in real time, their company's performance against CCRs, and how individual business units are managing leading business process variables that impact the customer. (For more about this, see Chapter 6.)

We must institutionalize 6 Sigma to drive continuous improvement throughout the value chain. We will adopt and apply 6 Sigma methodology across the extended enterprise . . . We will apply 6 Sigma to our transactional as well as manufacturing processes . . . to drive growth and cost reduction, and to improve product quality and reliability.

Glen Barton, CEO
Caterpillar
(In a January 2001 message to all 75,000 Caterpillar employees)

Step 5: Develop quantifiable measures—then demand tangible results from people. Quantum performance and Strategic Six Sigma are all about developing appropriate metrics, and then linking individual and team performance by people—

at *all* levels—to these job expectations. From the very beginning, benefits from Strategic Six Sigma initiatives must be
carefully calculated and documented. This requires active
involvement from the controller's office as project results are
directly tied to the profit and loss statement. It also requires
that a company's top leaders develop quantifiable measures
with which to measure the success of Six Sigma projects, and
to which they will hold people accountable over time. (Read
more about this in Chapter 7.)

*Step 6: Establish incentives, create accountability, and
reward performance.* No set of metrics will work effectively,
unless employees are given incentives both to change their
current work behaviors and to embrace new work values and
attitudes, such as team-based, project-driven work. Therefore,
to establish Strategic Six Sigma as a lasting business initiative,
and to drive results, new incentives should be devised to reinforce new work behaviors, drive job redesign, and to ensure
that business leaders are held accountable for project results.
In many cases, this means human resource processes and systems must be reconfigured to reward new things, support new
ways of working, and create a climate of organizational alignment that supports high performance. (See Chapter 8.)

*Step 7: Recognize that success with Strategic Six Sigma
means making a full-time commitment and applying the
manpower to ensure that Six Sigma projects succeed.* Besides lacking strong executive-level support for Six Sigma
efforts, many companies fail with Six Sigma because they
don't staff themselves with the right internal leaders to effectively implement and manage Six Sigma projects over time.
They either take a shotgun approach to implementing it
everywhere in their organization (without having the right

leadership/management framework in place to support it), or they undertake individual quality improvement projects, but without having critical, strategic goals in mind when they do so. We continually tell clients:

The right people + the right processes = desired results

For companies to realize the highly desirable curve A trajectories with their Six Sigma initiatives that we just described, companies must commit themselves to creating full-time Six Sigma leadership teams of Master Black Belts and Black Belts. A firm should dedicate between 2 and 3 percent of its employee population to Six Sigma roles, much as companies such as Caterpillar and Dow do. Competing priorities and part-time team leaders compromise achievement of Strategic Six Sigma project objectives. Agreeing on a team structure, realistic resources, and key skill requirements prior to commencing Strategic Six Sigma projects will ensure that maximum results are derived from these initiatives and that momentum to sustain a Strategic Six Sigma philosophy and way of doing business is established within the organization from the moment of initial deployment. (See Chapter 9.)

◼ HOW STRATEGIC SIX SIGMA CREATES A POWERFUL ENGINE OF CHANGE

When Six Sigma methods and practices are employed enterprise-wide and individual Six Sigma projects are deployed to support achievement of specific business goals or strategies, it creates a powerful engine for change—a common language of performance metrics and expectations to propel an organization forward and bring about true organizational transformation. Typically, it also results in significant productivity and efficiency gains, stimulating in many cases breakaway improvements in business performance. The transforming power of Six Sigma practices and methods is further increased when they are used not just to cut costs or eliminate product defects (e.g., in existing processes and services), but also for higher-order purposes (e.g., to drive innovation, stimulate R&D, or transform a company's culture).

This is the trajectory that Six Sigma deployment took at GE after first being introduced there in 1995–1996. General Electric began by using Six Sigma to cut manufacturing costs and to improve the efficiency of key business processes. As it did, it trained a cadre of Black Belts as Six Sigma leaders in all its businesses, and soon pegged 40 percent of executive compensation to Six Sigma results. Soon, "Black Belt projects sprang up in every business, improving call center response rates, increasing factory capacity, and reducing billing errors and inventories," notes former GE CEO Jack Welch in his autobiography, *JACK: Straight from the Gut*.[1]

In the first full year of Six Sigma implementation, GE trained 30,000 employees, spent roughly $200 million on Six Sigma training, and realized roughly $150 million in savings.[2] Typical of the projects launched was one that GE Capital undertook to improve its response rates to mortgage customers. At the time, GE Capital typically handled some 300,000 calls a year from mortgage customers who had to leave messages or call back roughly 25 percent of the time because GE Capital reps were not available to talk to them. After a Six Sigma team mapped the call handling processes in one highly successful call center, it then applied those same methods to the other 41 call centers. The result was that customers who once found it difficult to reach a live body on the other end of the phone at GE Capital soon "had a 99.9 percent chance of getting a GE person on the first try."[2]

■ FROM PROCESS IMPROVEMENTS TO NEW GE PRODUCTS

After its early successes using Six Sigma to improve manufacturing and customer service processes, GE began employing Six Sigma to fix and create new products. The company undertook efforts in virtually every GE business from power systems and medical systems, to plastics and airline engines. From 1996 onward, Welch's commitment to Six Sigma principles and practices expanded. "We went from 3,000 Six Sigma projects in 1996 to 6,000 in 1997, when we achieved $320 million in productivity gains and profits, more than double our original goal of $150 million," he says. "The benefits were showing up in our financial results. By 1998, we had generated $750 million in Six Sigma savings over and above our investment and would get $1.5 billion in savings the next year. Our operating margins went from 14.8 percent in 1996 to 18.9 percent in 2000."[3]

As important as project benchmarks, careful planning, and business objectives were in effectively launching and sustaining Six Sigma projects within GE, other factors were critical as well, especially Welch's ability to build employee buy-in and support for Six Sigma, to communicate its importance to GE's future, and to create a strong internal climate of alignment to support its use over time.

■ A HIGHLY VISIBLE CHAMPION OF SIX SIGMA

Welch became a highly visible, vocal (even vociferous) champion of Six Sigma at GE. Using a combination of personal intensity, behind-the-scenes arm-twisting, and a muscular leadership approach that demanded results, he made it clear to all GE employees that Six Sigma was a critical business initiative for GE to undertake. At the same time, he linked Six Sigma's successful implementation within the company to people's future job prospects and opportunities for advancement. "I became a fanatic about it, insisting that no one would be considered for a management job without at least Green Belt training by the end of 1998," he notes.[4]

Welch also worked hard to craft a down-to-earth, keep-it-simple message about the importance of Six Sigma to GE's bottom line. This became important one day when Welch realized that while the company was achieving vastly improved levels of performance and cost reductions with Six Sigma, customers weren't necessarily experiencing improved levels of service or product quality. Part of the reason was how people inside GE perceived Six Sigma. Up to this point, most people within GE had viewed Six Sigma as a highly effective—though somewhat complex statistical measurement technique—for improving business processes. Getting a grasp on what Six Sigma was all about, however, especially for customers, involved something else. After huddling with GE colleagues on a trip to Cartagena, Spain, Welch came to the conclusion that more than anything else, Six Sigma was about one thing, variation, and that for Six Sigma to benefit customers, the company had to do more than just improve average performance—it had to reduce the amount of variation, or span, around mean performance. For Welch and others at GE, it was like a lightbulb going on.

"Span reduction was easy for everyone to understand and became a rallying cry at every level of the organization. It was just what we needed to take the complexity out of Six Sigma. Our plastics business reduced their span from 50 days to 5, aircraft engines from 80 days to 5, and mortgage insurance from 54 days to 1."[5]

■ USING SIX SIGMA FOR NUMEROUS END GOALS

Before Jack Welch, Honeywell CEO Larry Bossidy had long believed that to maximize returns from Six Sigma, it must be used not just to improve manufacturing processes or reduce product defects, but also to deploy broad-based organizational goals and priorities. Between 1994 and 1998, Bossidy introduced Six Sigma into a wide array of business operations within AlliedSignal (the predecessor organization to Honeywell.) He used it to shrink cycle times, improve order processing, tighten up shipping and procurement procedures, and to accelerate new product development and innovation.

Bossidy took a systematic and escalated approach to implementing Six Sigma across a range of activities and functions, thus optimizing Six Sigma's power both to improve processes and transform the company at the same time. Building on previous quality programs, "[we took] the difficult but basic Six Sigma skill of reducing defects and applied it to every business process, from inventing and commercializing a new product all the way to billing and collection after the product is delivered," he noted in the company's 1998 Annual Report.[6] In recent years, Honeywell has made particular use of Six Sigma to help drive new product development and innovation. "Innovation is the underpinning of perpetuating an organization," noted Bossidy in the late 1990s as he pushed the company to achieve between $3 billion and $4 billion in new products by the year 2000.[7]

Honeywell has saved an estimated $3.5 billion from Six Sigma–related activities since 1995.[8] It has also differentiated itself with a new version of Six Sigma, known as *Six Sigma Plus*. Developed as a result of the 1999 merger of AlliedSignal and Honeywell, the program's methodology combines Lean Manufacturing with Six Sigma and is based on a series of steps [Define, Measure, Analyze, Improve, and Control (DMAIC)] that are applied to a wide array of projects across all Honeywell businesses including aerospace, specialty materials, automation and control solutions, transportation, and power systems. Honeywell also uses it with all of its administrative functions.[8]

Bossidy has made it clear to Honeywell employees over the years that use of Six Sigma methods and practices is critical to the company's future. To emphasize that point, all Honeywell managers, supervisors, and other professionals are today required to become certified (at a minimum) at the Six Sigma Plus expert level of Green Belt™.[8]

While Welch and Bossidy are among the best-known early adopters and advocates of Six Sigma thinking and methodologies, it should not be inferred from their success that introducing these techniques into their organizations was easy. Far from it.

■ DEALING WITH ORGANIZATIONAL RESISTANCE

Welch, for example, notes that early on, he experienced a lot of pushback from GE managers when it came to integrating Six Sigma thinking into the company's business planning activities and daily operations. It was particularly apparent, says Welch, when he asked senior GE managers to offer their highest potential employees up as candidates for Black Belt training. "We got pushback on the Six Sigma initiative [because] No one wants to give up their best talent on a full-time basis. They've got high targets to reach and need their best managers to make them. At first, only a quarter or perhaps half of the Black Belt candidates were the best and brightest. They faked the rest."[9]

In the early days of Six Sigma at AlliedSignal, Bossidy encountered similar challenges. Miscommunication occurred around how project teams were supposed to go about their work, especially in light of other initiatives (e.g., total quality, customer excellence) and other programs that had periodically been put in place since the early 1990s. What's more, confusion arose as Black Belts, fresh from initial training, began talking to others within the company, trying to build support for Six Sigma projects and initiatives, but confusing people more often than they won converts. These problems only started to be overcome when Bossidy and company realized the importance of cascading the goals, principles, and intended results of Six Sigma to *all* levels of management within AlliedSignal.[10]

■ BRINGING CHANGE LEADERSHIP SKILLS TO SIX SIGMA IMPLEMENTATIONS

What's the lesson in this? While implementing Six Sigma projects in an organization is partly about bringing statistically driven methods to strategic planning, goal setting, and corporate decision making, it's also about conveying change messages to people in compelling yet simple ways. In essence, it means bringing effective change leadership practices to an organization, and using them in clear and consistent ways to drive Six Sigma deployment efforts forward.

The importance of Six Sigma leaders wearing hats as change agents and transformational leaders is a point we can't overemphasize. While effective technical implementation is always essential to successful Six Sigma deployments, so, too, is the ability of leaders to rally an organization to accept such initiatives and, in time, to embrace them as key to the organization's future. "In terms of what makes Six Sigma successful in an organization, it's probably 25 percent technical ability and 75 percent leadership and people," says Desmond Bell, Vice President of Six Sigma for Bombardier Transportation.[11]

The organizational momentum—to say nothing of the personal energy—required of leaders to drive the introduction of Six Sigma thinking and methods in a big company requires uncommon leadership. In essence, it requires leaders who possess what Noel Tichy describes in his book, *The Leadership Engine,* as "edge."

■ SIX SIGMA LEADERS NEED EDGE

Tichy defines *edge* as a top leader's ability to make tough decisions affecting the long-term success of a business. Such leaders challenge conventional thinking and sometimes recommend unpopular or unusual ideas as part of focusing the organization on needed change. Both Welch and Bossidy are leaders who can be described as possessing leadership edge. Each man's commitment to Six Sigma in his organization has been demonstrated through time, energy, resource allocation, and behavior on the job. For example, as we noted earlier, during his tenure at GE, Welch made it clear that Six Sigma was not optional. Forty percent of executive incentives were thus tied to key Six Sigma annual achievements. Meanwhile, Bossidy continues to tell Honeywell employees and shareholders that continued emphasis on Six Sigma is central to the company's drive of realizing "six percent productivity improvement forever."

Leaders with edge are often deft communicators. In ways reminiscent of a John Kennedy or Ronald Reagan, they're able to articulate compelling images of their companies' futures; to evoke, if you will, the organizational equivalent of Reagan's image of America as "a shining city on a hill." The ability to do this—what authors Bruce Pasternack and Albert Viscio describe as the ability to "create coherence" within an organization around new goals and objectives, "is one of the major missions of the CEO," they write in their book, *The Centerless Corporation*. "No one else can do it. It is the heroic leadership challenge."[12]

CEOs like Welch and Bossidy personify the tough, hands-on leadership and edge required at any Six Sigma company today. They recognize that Strategic Six Sigma efforts can't be delegated to others. So, they personally play vigorous roles in driving Six Sigma deployments forward, and in building strong populations of Six Sigma leaders at *all* levels in their organizations to sustain deployments over time. Today, their styles are being emulated by a new generation of Six Sigma leaders, by individuals such as Dow CEO Mike Parker, Caterpillar CEO Glen Barton, and others that we'll talk about in chapters to come.

■ MANAGING THE SOFTER SIDE OF CHANGE

Besides possessing leadership edge, there are still other qualities of transformational leadership that Strategic Six Sigma leaders must bring to their organizations to ensure that Six Sigma initiatives succeed. Paradoxically perhaps, while they must possess leadership edge to make tough decisions and combat organizational resistance to change, they must also possess abilities in managing the soft (people) side of transitions (i.e., by being effective coaches and mentors to others, leading by example, showing vulnerability at times, and by developing leaders *at other levels* in their organizations). Managing this so-called soft side of change is a crucial ingredient in ensuring successful implementation of Strategic Six

Sigma in organizations. Yet, it has received little attention in the business press.

■ STRATEGIC SIX SIGMA LEADERS MUST FRAME THE FUTURE OF THEIR ORGANIZATIONS

We have emphasized that Strategic Six Sigma represents a new leadership approach—both to the day-to-day operations of modern companies and to managing their long-term direction, strategy, and goals. As such, a leader's ability to identify key enablers of change in his (or her) organization would certainly seem helpful in ensuring the success of Six Sigma deployments. For that reason, let's examine those factors that can, in fact, help to accelerate change in organizations, if leaders possess the awareness and skills to leverage these forces to their advantage.

■ PRICEWATERHOUSECOOPERS SURVEY REVEALS BEST PRACTICES THAT CAN ACCELERATE CHANGE

A recent survey of 410 top executives in eight industries conducted by PricewaterhouseCoopers (PwC) determined both key success factors and key organizational obstacles associated with successful corporate transformation efforts. The survey included in-depth interviews with hundreds of executives at the highest level in organizations (including CEOs, CFOs, and senior vice president). It found that senior leadership plays a pivotal role in the success of change efforts of all kinds including Strategic Six Sigma deployments.[13] Leaders of the most successful organizations in this group (44) experience fewer barriers to change efforts than other organizations do. They do a better job of securing employee buy-in for initiatives, provide adequate organizational resources to ensure that projects succeed, and either develop (or possess) a higher level of skills/experience in their employees, which helps sustain initiatives over time. By wide margins, organizations that are most successful with change efforts also display tighter alignment and better communications to support change initiatives.[13] Let's now examine these findings in more detail.

➤ Leadership

With regard to leadership, change efforts at the most successful organizations in the survey receive a higher degree of support from senior management than occurs in other organizations. Key organizational supports (e.g., training and communications) are in place to support change initiatives. Moreover, managers at *all* levels play key roles as change advocates and take specific actions to support change.

Practices	Most Successful	Others	Gap
Senior management behaviors	94%	76%	18%
Effective organizational structure	83%	59%	24%
Respected managers are advocates	87%	71%	16%
Leaders of different units work together	70%	54%	16%

This reinforces the idea, of course, that to be effective at driving Strategic Six Sigma initiatives in an organization, a leader must be good at creating an extensive population of leaders at *all* levels to launch and sustain Six Sigma efforts over time.

➤ Alignment

In the organizations judged most successful with transformation, employees also understand the vision and strategy of the change effort and their roles and contributions to that process. For example, two-thirds of the leaders within the most successful organizations say that employee roles and rewards are aligned with change initiatives, and they also say that employees trust senior management actions.

Practices	Most Successful	Others	Gap
Believe daily activities are relevant	66%	43%	23%
Understand vision and strategy	74%	44%	30%
Trust senior management actions	66%	47%	19%
Have rewards for promoting innovation and change	68%	41%	27%
Employees' roles are aligned with goals and objectives	77%	47%	30%

Not surprisingly, we typically see very strong organizational alignment in companies that are successful with Strategic Six Sigma deployments. General Electric, Caterpillar, and Dow Chemical, for example, all make strong organizational alignment a key support strut of their Six Sigma initiatives. At Caterpillar that alignment was so strong, even in the company's first year of Six Sigma deployment (2001), that the company racked up cost savings and benefits that were more than double the implementation costs—effectively paying for deployment expenses in just nine months!

➤ Communication

With regard to communication, the most successful organizations report (by wide margins) having effective communications strategies in place, and being in frequent contact with employees as change efforts proceed.

Practices	Most Successful	Others	Gap
Frequent progress reports	66%	42%	24%
An effective communications strategy	64%	44%	20%
Encourage open and honest communication	81%	71%	10%

When leaders of the organizations judged most successful with transformation efforts were asked how a company can best leverage communications efforts for successful change, they responded that the most effective messengers of communications about change are senior-level executives (e.g., the CEO, chairman, or president). They also noted that in-person discussions and meetings are the most effective vehicles for communications about change efforts.

Taken together, what the survey findings suggest is that involved, top-level leadership of change efforts (including Strategic Six Sigma initiatives) is absolutely vital to their success. What's more, that leadership must take a variety of forms and be leveraged in critical ways at critical times far down the leadership line to ensure that change efforts succeed. Strategic Six Sigma leaders, in other words, must create a powerful context for change within their organizations and act as the principal catalysts in driving it forward. As you will see, the case studies of Six Sigma leadership outlined later in this book showcase exactly these kinds of leadership best practices—and others as well. At Dow Chemical, for example, CEO Mike Parker is adamant about getting total engagement of all Dow employees in Six Sigma efforts. At Caterpillar, CEO Glen Barton repeatedly tells employees that

Six Sigma will influence everything the company does, and because he believed that it was so important to Six Sigma's initial deployment at Caterpillar in January 2001, he made Six Sigma the number one critical success factor by which business performance and individual job performance would be judged.

■ CHAPTER SUMMARY

As this chapter has shown, the successful introduction of Strategic Six Sigma thinking and business practices into an organization requires more than a focus on statistically driven performance improvement, or even the use of robust metrics to measure as-is business performance against desired future-state or to-be results. It also requires strong change leadership skills—vision setting, leadership development, project management, communications, team building, and goal setting. Finally, Strategic Six Sigma leadership requires the ability to effectively implement Strategic Six Sigma thinking at both the *transformational* and *transactional* levels of an organization simultaneously, so that Six Sigma efforts realize maximum ROI. As we noted earlier, ensuring optimal success with Strategic Six Sigma initiatives requires attention to seven key success factors. (See Figure 2.2.) A company must do the following:

1. Develop a committed coalition of leaders at *all* levels of an organization to launch and sustain Strategic Six Sigma initiatives over time.
2. Integrate Strategic Six Sigma principles into the company's strategy planning and deployment processes.
3. Ensure that the company is both passionate and consistent about how it stays in touch with customers.

Establishing these factors provides the seeds of success.

They need to be integrated uniquely to fit each business.

They are all necessary for the best result.

The most powerful success factor is committed leadership.

Figure 2.2 Strategic Six Sigma success factors.

4. Design, organize, and run the business using a business process framework.
5. Develop quantifiable measures, then demand tangible results from people.
6. Establish incentives, create accountability, and reward performance.
7. Recognize that success with Strategic Six Sigma means making a full-time commitment to it principles and applying the manpower to ensure that Six Sigma projects succeed.

Let's go on to Chapter 3, where we look at the first of these critical successful factors in more detail: the importance of building a committed leadership team to drive Strategic Six Sigma efforts in a company forward.

Chapter 3

Develop a Committed Team of Leaders to Drive Strategic Six Sigma Initiatives

We started planning the implementation of Six Sigma in the summer of 2001. Jon Ward, our Chairman and CEO, worked closely with the executive team that includes our business unit presidents to define our business imperatives, which include quality, customer satisfaction, and becoming the employer of choice. We then chose Six Sigma as the methodology we would use not just to drive performance improvement, but also to transform company operations, that is, how we work, across all our brands. Today, we've only begun to implement Six Sigma but by the end of 2002 we will have over 2000 trained Six Sigma professionals in place, driving projects across all of ServiceMaster.

—Patricia Asp,
Senior Vice President
ServiceMaster

In Chapter 2, we noted that for business leaders to successfully introduce Strategic Six Sigma into their organizations, they must display leadership edge and the ability to personally engage people as part of Six Sigma initiatives. These qualities of change leadership are essential, because implementing Six Sigma principles and practices in a company brings about a fundamental change in how people complete their work, and thus affects everything from the design of work processes and people's jobs to organizational culture and the nature of a company's performance appraisal and reward systems.

Given that, this chapter builds on the themes of transformational leadership introduced in Chapter 2. It showcases how truly successful Strategic Six Sigma leaders today not only clearly articulate the need for Six Sigma thinking and methodologies in their organizations, but also successfully build the organizational infrastructure and leadership coalitions necessary to launch and sustain Six Sigma initiatives.

It is no doubt clear at this point that successful introduction of Strategic Six Sigma into an organization requires more than the exhortations of a charismatic CEO, or even the effective use of communications to frequently and consistently articulate key messages of change to an employee population. Much more is required, including strong top-team unity around Strategic Six Sigma goals, consistent leadership behavior across *all* levels of an organization, and the ability of a company's senior leaders to create a strong climate of organizational alignment to support Six Sigma initiatives. In essence, committed leadership is the single most important ingredient in the successful implementation of Strategic Six Sigma principles and practices within an organization, beginning with the CEO and cascading down through all levels of the organization.

■ CREATING THE CONTEXT FOR LEADERSHIP COMMITMENT TO SIX SIGMA—AT ALL LEVELS

How does one go about creating these conditions? In his book, *Leading Change,* Harvard business professor John Kotter outlines a powerful eight-step process for driving change within any organization. The steps include:[1]

1. Establishing a sense of urgency around change initiatives
2. Creating a guiding coalition to support change initiatives
3. Developing a clear vision and strategy for driving change
4. Communicating the change vision
5. Empowering employees for broad-based action
6. Generating short-term wins
7. Consolidating gains and producing more change
8. Anchoring new approaches to business and work in the organization's culture

Let's apply this framework now to how you and your organization can go about creating a committed population of leaders to drive Strategic Six Sigma initiatives forward in *your* organization.

➤ Step 1: Establish a Sense of Urgency

Clearly, as we've seen from the Six Sigma case studies discussed thus far [General Electric (GE), Dow, Caterpillar, Honeywell, and Raytheon], creating a sense of urgency around the importance of Six Sigma to an organization's success and ability to meet the needs of customers is critical. Both Welch and Bossidy—who between them wrote the early book on effective Six Sigma leadership—instinctively knew that if Six Sigma principles and practices were to take root in their organizations, they needed enormous amounts of top-level leadership support and sponsorship to succeed.

Thus, the importance of Six Sigma was constantly trumpeted to everyone from employees and customers to stakeholders and Wall Street.

Today, a new generation of Strategic Six Sigma leaders is following in the footsteps of Welch and Bossidy, making implementation of Six Sigma methods and practices within their companies a high priority. One of the most prominent of these is Jim McNerney, chief executive of 3M and a GE veteran, who just a month after assuming the leadership reins at 3M in January 2001, held a three-day Six Sigma seminar for about 80 high-level executives. McNerney moved quickly to name Brad Sauer, an executive of 3M Korea to head up 3M's Six Sigma initiative. He also outlined three priorities to be the initial focus of the company's Six Sigma efforts: (1) getting products to market faster, (2) improving cash flow, and (3) enhancing productivity. Thus far, 3M Six Sigma project teams have identified more than 100 projects to undertake in quest of those goals.[2]

Dow is another emerging Strategic Six Sigma champion. Kathleen Bader, Business Group President of Styrenics and Engineered Products and Corporate Vice President for Quality and Business Excellence, says that Dow's Six Sigma vision is to "become recognized and lauded as one of the premier companies of the [twenty-first] century, driven by an insatiable desire to achieve a Six Sigma level of performance and excellence in all that we do."[3]

To do that, however, means that Dow must not only drive down costs, but also eliminate inefficiencies from current business processes. Noting that bottom-line concerns about productivity and profitability are "where everybody's heads are on Six Sigma," Bader says Dow is committed to achieving savings of $250,000 per Six Sigma project, and that Six Sigma's potential to drive out waste, improve quality, boost customer loyalty, and create sales growth will yield enormous financial benefits in the years ahead.[4]

Still other Strategic Six Sigma champions who have placed great urgency on the adoption of Strategic Six Sigma thinking and practices in their organizations today are Caterpillar and Du Pont. Caterpillar is using Six Sigma methods to support a trio of business strategies: (1) increased sales, (2) reductions in manufacturing defects, and (3) higher levels of quality and product reliability. At Du Pont, meanwhile, Six Sigma methods and practices have now been introduced into every business unit and global region, according to corporate Six Sigma champion Don Linsenmann. Like many companies, Du Pont started by using Six Sigma methods and practices in manufacturing. Today, however, there are Six Sigma projects underway in virtually all parts of the company: in distribution, manufacturing, finance, sales and marketing, human resources, and elsewhere.

Clearly, today's Strategic Six Sigma leaders are companies that dedicate not only resources to Six Sigma implementation, but also the time, energy, and attention of their top executives to seeing that Six Sigma methods and approaches get the focus they need to succeed.

➤ Step 2: Create a Guiding Coalition to Support Implementation of Six Sigma Initiatives

We've noted elsewhere that introducing Strategic Six Sigma thinking and methods into an organization isn't easy. Indeed, far from being a silver bullet, it is a process that can take anywhere from three to five years to realize maximum results. The reason?

Many companies begin by using Six Sigma to improve existing processes, and only later begin to replace them with better processes, more attuned to customer needs. In other cases, they introduce Six Sigma practices into a single business unit, get projects going, generate early results, then introduce it elsewhere in the organization.

However, regardless of the specific route an organization takes to implement Six Sigma, building internal support for Strategic Six Sigma practices requires that a company build a strong population of leaders at *all* levels to embrace and advocate Strategic Six Sigma concepts and work approaches.

At Dow, these efforts are being undertaken by creating a culture of accountability, says Bader. It means "changing how we do our work, adopting an intolerance for variation, measuring inputs not just outputs, and demanding measurement and accountability in all we do," she says. It also means building sustainable productivity gains, delivering on customer satisfaction, building loyalty, and leveraging all the organization's resources to competitive advantage.[5]

Besides driving culture change to accelerate Six Sigma acceptance, the company is also committed to building a strong population of Six Sigma leaders throughout the organization. For Dow, this consists of intensive skills training for Six Sigma practitioners, baseline Six Sigma training for all Dow employees, a specialized Six Sigma training exercise for corporate leaders (Green Belts, Black Belts, Master Black Belts, and Champions), and the total engagement of the organization in understanding the importance of Six Sigma to the company's goals of sustainable growth.

Dow's results to date in building a strong cadre of Six Sigma leaders have been impressive. The company is committed to having a constant 3 percent of its employee population working full-time as Black Belt Six Sigma practitioners. Already it has certified more than 90 Master Black Belts who oversee Black Belt training and coaching, and trained over

1,500 full-time Black Belts who are involved in 2,800 active Six Sigma projects company wide. Meanwhile, more than 20 percent of employees (50,000) participate on various Six Sigma project teams, and over 1,500 champions have been through training.[5]

At Du Pont, meanwhile, there is an equally strong focus on developing a strong and robust cadre of Six Sigma champions, project and team leaders. According to Don Linsenmann, one-sixth of Du Pont's employees, some 15,000 people, are now involved in Six Sigma projects, either as trainees or as active project participants. The company currently has 160 Master Black Belts, and it has introduced 2,100 Green Belts to the ranks in the last two years. According to *Chemical Week,* the company is intensifying its training of these individuals, who work part-time on Six Sigma projects while staying in their everyday jobs.[6]

All these companies, like other Strategic Six Sigma leaders, have determined that the best way to jump-start their Six Sigma efforts is to put high leadership priority and visibility on them. The reasons to develop this ardent (and highly competent) population of Strategic Six Sigma leaders is obvious: Because Six Sigma takes enormous leadership energy to plan and implement, a CEO must have at least 30 percent of his or her top leadership team on board at the start, if efforts are to succeed. The results of creating this alignment can be well worth the effort, however, when it results not only in greater efficiency and cost savings, but also in higher levels of quality and customer satisfaction. Notes Bill Stavropoulos, Chairman of Dow Chemical Company, "Six Sigma will be a vehicle to transform this company to premier status—in the eyes of our competitors, in the eyes of Wall Street, and at the very foundation of our company, in the eyes of our employees. We will use it to drive increased customer loyalty, better bottom line results, and to reduce employee frustration over rework, broken processes, and poor quality."[7]

➤ Step 3: Develop a Clear Vision and Strategy for Driving Change

Being able to articulate a clear vision and strategy for change is one of the most crucial things a transformational leader can do when introducing any kind of change initiative into an organization. It's obviously important when making the case for the introduction of Strategic Six Sigma—for several reasons:

First, because Six Sigma is a statistically driven process for driving performance improvement, and because many of its concepts are unfamiliar to front-line workers and middle managers, it is vital that a company's senior leaders create compelling messages, not only about what Six Sigma is all about and what it can do, but how it will benefit an organization down the line. (See the sidebar, "Dow Drives Commitment to Six Sigma Efforts with Communications".)

In our experience, the most effective Strategic Six Sigma leaders are those who are both consistent and relentless in how they talk about Six Sigma to their organizations, customers, Wall Street, and other stakeholders. At Caterpillar, for example, Chairman Glen Barton is crystal clear about the important role that Six Sigma will play at Caterpillar in the years to come, as the company works to both boost sales and increase product reliability and quality. "Caterpillar has begun the journey to make 6 Sigma an integral part of our culture. 6 Sigma will power our corporate strategy by helping us achieve our growth, cost reduction, and quality improvement goals."[8]

Barton is so emphatic about Six Sigma that back when he introduced it to his leadership team in late 2000 and sensed some hesitation from top executives, he likened its introduc-

DOW DRIVES COMMITMENT TO SIX SIGMA EFFORTS WITH COMMUNICATIONS

Building broad-based employee commitment to Six Sigma requires more than a few exhortations from a company's CEO. As effective as a firm's top leader may be as a salesperson of Six Sigma, getting rank-and-file employees to buy into it requires carefully crafted efforts to reach people with the right messages. Sometimes, that means "employing the age-old advertising concepts of reach and frequency along with a double dose of creativity so that messages really sink in and change peoples' behavior."*

So says Jeff Schatzer, Dow Chemical's Communications Leader for Six Sigma, with a bit of tongue in cheek. Six Sigma communications at Dow is a team effort. A number of people, including Tom Gurd, Dow's Vice President for Quality and Business Excellence; Kathleen Bader, Business Group President for Styrenics and Engineered Products and Corporate Vice President for Quality and Business Excellence; Schatzer; Matt Rassette, e-communications specialist; and a culture team, made up of Business Champions, are continuously developing new communications strategies, tools, and techniques to sell the importance of Six Sigma to Dow's 50,000 employees worldwide. It's a big job, largely because top Dow executives have set a goal of having every Dow employee engaged in a successful Six Sigma project by 2005.

Part of the challenge that communicators face is how to create compelling messages and communications deliverables about a topic (Six Sigma) that doesn't lend itself to easy explanations, tidy sound bites, or easy-to-understand copy on a corporate web site. Six Sigma, after all, is about charts, process variation, statistical tools, and highly quantitative methods for driving process improvement. It's complex and mathematical. Another challenge is to package messages so they stand out from everything else in people's Inboxes and e-mail. "Most employees of large organizations are hit with a barrage of 'critical' messages every day," says Schatzer. Somehow, "we've got to cut through all that noise and clutter to get our message to employees."

(Continued)

(Continued)

OVERCOMING RESISTANCE

Finally, communications have to effectively deal with the issue of resistance to change. Even though the company has reaped massive benefits from Six Sigma thus far, "We're only in our second full year of implementation, and we still have a few people holding out," Schatzer says with a chuckle. Tom Gurd, Vice President for Quality and Business Excellence, notes, "There are people who are as excited as they can be about Six Sigma, others who keep their heads down and hope it will pass them by, and still others who are 'sock sorters' who just don't have a clue."[†]

To make its Six Sigma communications efforts succeed, Dow has developed some creative ways to reach employees with key messages about Six Sigma, and to do so with enough frequency that it builds awareness *and* creates commitment to Six Sigma principles and work practices.

For example, the company developed brightly colored, oversize communications posters and handouts about Six Sigma that it uses in training sessions and team meetings, in Portable Document Format (PDF) form on Dow's web site, and elsewhere within the company. One key item is a large, Day-Glo-yellow, triangular-shaped poster. The poster can be unfolded to reveal many panels, and contains a variety of key Six Sigma messages on it—for example, the importance of Dow employees building *customer loyalty* using Six Sigma, and why it's critical to *leverage the benefits* from Six Sigma projects across the entire company.

Schatzer says that there were good reasons to make this particular communications piece large and triangular in shape. "We made this thing big and obtrusive so it would deliberately get people's attention," says the former ad executive knowingly. "You can't easily ignore it, file it in a file drawer, or hide it under a pile of business papers." Today, in fact, the poster is ubiquitously displayed throughout Dow, on walls, web sites, desktops, and elsewhere.

USING A VARIETY OF COMMUNICATIONS TOOLS

Dow is fortunate to have impassioned and visionary leadership delivering powerful messages on Six Sigma both internally and externally. Both Bader and Gurd keynote at leading Six Sigma conferences and internal communications events. Dow schedules global broadcasts on Six Sigma three or four times a year to update employees worldwide on its implementation of Six Sigma, to keep internal momentum high, and to stir employee involvement. In addition, Dow has quarterly satellite broadcasts to employees around the world. During these *Dow World News* broadcasts, Six Sigma plays a prominent role. Performance metrics for Six Sigma are reviewed and video segments covering Six Sigma and Design for Six Sigma (DFSS) projects are regularly incorporated into the broadcasts.

Other tools Dow has developed include videos and Moving Picture Experts Group (MPEG) files. These tools are used in training programs, investor-analyst meetings, and on people's individual computer terminals to get them excited about Six Sigma. One particular animated MPEG shows a computer-generated duck swimming serenely on the surface of a pond. Underneath the water, however, the viewer sees the duck's legs working frantically to avoid underground obstacles, and to navigate difficult terrain. The showing of the duck MPEG always evokes smiles in Dow employees, says Schatzer. That's because everyone who sees it understands that it represents the way things really work—lots of people working in chaos behind the scenes to make things look perfect to customers. The video has been "a big hit," Schatzer says, and has helped break down people's resistance to Six Sigma by casting it as a team effort, dependent on the participation of everybody in the organization to be successful.

COACHING BLACK BELTS ON COMMUNICATING WITH OTHERS ABOUT THEIR PROJECTS

Another thing Dow's communications professionals and Master Black Belts do to support Dow's Six Sigma communications efforts is to coach company Black Belts on how to

(Continued)

(Continued)

communicate effectively with different audiences about Six Sigma projects, both inside the company and out. For example, they often help Black Belts prepare for corporate road shows and Six Sigma gallery walks, where Six Sigma efforts are showcased to large audiences of employees and senior executives. In each case, Black Belts are encouraged to craft their messages to fit the audience. For example, "A person might not understand Six Sigma methodology very well, but he or she can certainly understand the dire effects of a product or service failure," says Schatzer. Thus, Black Belts who are outlining projects to others outside the Six Sigma community are encouraged to start with a story or, to describe the human impact that completion of a particular Six Sigma project will have on somebody's life. "Doing that sometimes gets you further down the road to acceptance and understanding of Six Sigma than if you try to explain the methodology to people."

USE EVERY COMMUNICATIONS TECHNIQUE YOU CAN

Dow believes that to be effective, Six Sigma communications efforts have to use a variety of methods and approaches, including humor and obtrusiveness. What's more, Six Sigma leaders have to be willing to think outside of the box with their communications approaches and take risks even when ideas don't always work.

Sometimes, edgy approaches to Six Sigma communications efforts are critical. "A lot of companies spend time developing mission statements and action plans, put them in plexiglass boxes on the wall, and that's the last anyone ever hears about them," says Schatzer. To get people to buy into Six Sigma, "You have to break old corporate cultural habits. You have to use every tool at your disposal, apply technology in unique ways, and occasionally make people uncomfortable with the message you're sending. That's how you get people to think and work differently."—*The Authors*

---

*Jeff Schatzer, telephone interview with Richard Koonce, PricewaterhouseCoopers, Arlington, VA, 8 November 2001.

†Tom Gurd, interview with Richard Koonce, PricewaterhouseCoopers, Midland, MI, 20 November 2001.

tion into the company as a "train that was leaving the station" in some cases without key people on board. "I can see who's on the train. Some of you are up in the engine, driving it with me. Some of you are sitting in the club car deciding what to do, and some of you are in the caboose," he told the assembled group. Translation: Barton made it clear in that meeting that he expected everybody on his top management team to not only get "aboard the train," but to move forward toward the engine, because the train was definitely "leaving the station."[9]

In introducing Six Sigma into their organizations, Larry Bossidy and Jack Welch showed similar energy and relentlessness as Six Sigma advocates. Welch, for example, talked endlessly about the importance of linking Six Sigma to other key business initiatives such as globalization, services, and e-business. As we noted in the last chapter, Welch was also known for taking a KISS approach, not just when it came to talking about Six Sigma, but when it came to talking about other business goals and priorities at GE. As we noted in Chapter 2, when he was eventually able to boil the essence of Six Sigma down to a simple sound bite, *span reduction,* it crystallized in his own mind the essential value of Six Sigma to GE's customers. In his autobiography, *Jack: Straight from the Gut,* Welch seems to acknowledge, in a rare moment of self-deprecation, that he was perhaps a little bit slow in coming to the realization of how important it was to reduce the concept of Six Sigma to a simple phrase; in essence to create a memorable sound bite about Six Sigma in the eyes (and ears) of employees. "We were three years into Six sigma before we 'got' it," he says.[10]

➤ Step 4: Communicate the Change Vision

Leaders who are effective at introducing Six Sigma practices into their companies readily recognize the key roles that they, as senior executives, need to play in driving home key change messages. Individuals like Welch, Parker, Bossidy, Burnham, McNerney, and Barton display an uncommon ability to communicate a future vision of their organizations, and to galvanize employees behind achieving new business goals. They are also deft at harnessing what consultants Steve Yearout and Gerry Miles, coauthors of *Growing Leaders,* describe as the power of *organizational thermodynamics* to drive change in their organizations.[11] In essence:

> ➤ They *connect* people to their company's vision and mission.
> ➤ They *create* the conditions for new ways of thinking, working, and acting inside their organizations.
> ➤ They *channel* their organization's energy to achieve new goals and objectives.

Why are these qualities so important as part of implementing Strategic Six Sigma in an organization? Executives contemplating the launch of any kind of change initiative face a variety of challenges from organizational inertia and indifference on one hand to competing political agendas and leadership turf wars on the other. For that reason, at the front end of Six Sigma initiatives, leaders must drive compliance with Six Sigma approaches and metrics, even while working to build people's *commitment* to them over time. It can be an arduous process of one step forward, two steps back. We've seen cases, for example, where companies launch a dozen or more Six Sigma projects, 11 of which generate almost instant results, while one does not. Typically, naysayers of Six Sigma jump on these instances of unsuccessful solitary projects as a major reason to thwart Six Sigma's broader-based implementation in an organization.

We submit, therefore, that a leader's ability to *connect, create,* and *channel* energy within his or her organization is absolutely essential, if Strategic Six Sigma principles and practices are to be embraced by an organization. These abilities are key not just to building organizational resolve and top-team support for Six Sigma, but for then cascading key messages about it to other levels of the organization.

➤ Step 5: Empower Employees for Broad-Based Action

One of the strengths of using Six Sigma methods and practices in organizations is that they create a clear causal (line-of-sight) link between the successful completion of specific Six Sigma projects and the successful execution of business goals and strategies. Indeed, the financial results from projects are, in a very disciplined way, rolled up to support achievement of strategic business objectives. As Six Sigma projects are carefully considered and then launched, based on their relevance to strategic goals or business objectives, it helps individuals and project teams to readily link what they do on an everyday basis to specific goals or priorities of the business. It creates an organizational juggernaut for the systematic linkage of strategic business goals or organizational priorities to individual and group work activities and performance metrics. As a result, work processes can be streamlined (or designed) as necessary, to accommodate both customer needs and clearly identified group or project objectives.

The upshot of this is not only to make work performance more efficient: It also motivates employees who, in many cases, acquire a clearer sense of how their everyday jobs impact the business bottom line than they have ever had before. People's energies begin to be released to tackle the clearly identified work at hand, and this helps create commitment to Six Sigma principles and practices, where perhaps none existed before.

To date, for example, GE has trained more than 100,000 employees in the methodology of Six Sigma, and focused thousands of Six Sigma projects on improving efficiency and reducing variance in operations. As a result, GE has realized Six Sigma benefits of over $5 billion.[12]

Meanwhile, at a leading insurance company, where the firm, though profitable, was having problems with service quality, and the company's CEO was constantly being told that his firm's service quality "stinks," 3,000 employees were introduced to Six Sigma over a nine-month period in the late 1990s. The company undertook 40 different Six Sigma projects and realized over $20 million in savings. At the same time, service levels improved dramatically.[12]

At a prominent financial services firm, where the company was losing market value and was increasingly vulnerable to takeover threats, executives embarked on an aggressive Six Sigma initiative in 1998. Two thousand employees got training on Six Sigma methods and principles and were deployed to more than 40 different projects. They built and used service/quality scorecards and voice-of-the-customer (VOC) surveys to ascertain existing performance problems. They then built a new business process framework in transaction operations to bolster performance levels, cut costs, and improve customer responsiveness. To date, this firm has realized over $400 million in productivity improvements, improvements in transactional capacity, and in improved transaction control and security. The company's chairman and CEO says, "Broad application of Six Sigma will allow us to realize margin benefits through greater efficiency and through increases in revenues. Its application to our business will be a major pillar of our strategy going forward."[12]

➤ Step 6: Generate Short-Term Wins

Today's leading Strategic Six Sigma corporate leaders recognize the benefit and value that come from generating short-term gains from Six Sigma projects. Whereas traditional improvement efforts can take 12 to 14 months to generate concrete results, Six Sigma projects often generate savings and process improvements in as little as 4 to 6 months, quickly generating critical momentum. As companies train cadres of Six Sigma practitioners (e.g., Master Black Belts, Black Belts, Green Belts, and others), savings and process improvements can rack up quickly. Seasoned Black Belts can complete three to five projects annually. Early Six Sigma projects in some companies have generated as much as $1 million or $2 million in savings and process improvements. Average savings per Six Sigma project are generally between $200,000 and $250,000. Annual savings delivered per Black Belt can range from $600,000 to $1,000,000.

➤ Step 7: Consolidate Gains and Produce More Change

As is clear by now, the benefits that can accrue from introducing Strategic Six Sigma methods and practices into an organization can add up quickly. Virtually all of the companies we've talked about in this chapter—Du Pont, Dow Chemical, 3M, Caterpillar, Raytheon, GE, and Honeywell, among others—have used their early successes with Six Sigma (especially in the areas of manufacturing) to then migrate use of Six Sigma practices to other parts of their organization. Du Pont Chairman Chad Holliday, for example, reflecting on Du Pont's first two and a half years of using Six Sigma, says, "The savings are just beginning." That sentiment is echoed by other Six Sigma leaders such as Yong Nam, president and CEO of LG TeleCom, "I don't view Six Sigma as just another thing to do. It is a strategy and one that we must implement to compete successfully in our markets. As a result of using Six Sigma, I expect LG Tele-Com to be a world-class Six Sigma company with the world's best Black Belts and Master Black Belts."[13]

➤ Step 8: Anchor New Approaches to Business and Work in the Organization's Culture

For Strategic Six Sigma efforts in any organization to succeed, they need more than an ardent champion in a company's CEO. They also need to be anchored in the organization's culture, management practices, leadership training, and systems. While Kotter's typology of change is a useful way to approach the introduction and sustaining of Strategic Six Sigma initiatives within an organization—especially as it relates to developing a committed leadership population to support those efforts—other things are required as well. One is thorough and systematic training. (See Chapter 10.) Also required is a careful blending of performance metrics and work incentives to drive changes in people's work behaviors. (See Chapters 7 and 8.)

■ BUILDING COMMITMENT TO SIX SIGMA MEANS YOUR COMPANY'S SENIOR LEADERS MUST DEVELOP SIX SIGMA LEADERS AT OTHER LEVELS

Finally, creating a population of leaders committed to Six Sigma principles and practices requires that a company's top leaders be involved—as much as possible—in coaching and mentoring other leaders at *other levels* of their organizations. This, in fact, is one of the key components of contemporary transformational leadership. (See the sidebar, "Do You Have a Transformational Leadership Style?")

Numerous CEOs today have recognized the value of being teachers and coaches of others within their organizations—especially as they've sought to advance business goals or transformation plans. CEOs such as PepsiCo's Roger Enrico, GE's Jack Welch, Intel's Andy Grove, and Honeywell's Larry Bossidy, among others, are all models of CEOs who have put strong emphasis on leadership development, and on top leaders of organizations being personally involved in the coaching and mentoring of others.

Still others are taking this approach today as part of spreading the gospel about Strategic Six Sigma. Besides Welch and Bossidy, 3M's McNerney, Dow's Mike Parker, Raytheon's Dan Burnham, and Du Pont's Chad Holliday (a Six Sigma Green Belt) have been closely identified with the actual training, coaching, and mentoring of their company's Six Sigma leaders. Their personal involvement in developing other lead-

---

DO YOU HAVE A TRANSFORMATIONAL LEADERSHIP STYLE?

How does a CEO energize members of his or her top leadership team to embrace Six Sigma principles and practices? Noel Tichy, one of the leading thinkers in the field of organizational change, says that nowadays winning organizations are built on clear—and sometimes radical or initially unpopular—ideas, communicated by leaders willing to roll up their sleeves, make tough calls, and become engines of real organizational change. Tichy tells audiences of business executives that there are several secrets to being a transformational leader. The good news is that all these things can be learned. Transformational leaders, such as those who are needed to introduce Strategic Six Sigma thinking and practices into an organization, are created, not born.

(Continued)

(Continued)

First, forget about managing people the way you've tradi-tionally done it (for example, by writing memos or asking your direct reports to do the heavy lifting for you.) Top leaders in business today, regardless of the business initiative (Six Sigma or anything else), get out of the executive suite a lot of the time to meet and interact with employees on the plant floor, and with customers on their own turf. They're confi-dent in their ability to interact with people on a human level. And they are team leaders far more than they are delegators, says Tichy, with a personal vision of their organization's future, and an action plan to get there. When you think about implementing Six Sigma principles and practices in your organization, therefore, begin with the end in mind. Know why implementing Six Sigma is critical to your company's future business success, and to narrowing the gap between your company's business performance on the one hand, and customers' expectations and requirements on the other. Then resolve to communicate the urgency of this to company exec-utives, managers, and employees at every opportunity.

Second, develop a teachable point of view *that you can share with other people, and that you can use to cascade the principles of Strategic Six Sigma to all levels of your organiza-tion.* Top transformational leaders—in any walk of life—craft unique and compelling messages to share with others. They do this through coining new language, couching goals in compelling word pictures, and telling stories of where they see their organization going. Former President George Bush (father of "Dubya") might have disdained the "vision thing" when he was president, but having a teachable point of view is essential to getting others to buy into your ideas and goals, says Tichy. Winston Churchill urged on the forces of freedom during World War II by contrasting the "broad sunlit uplands" with the "deep abyss of a dark new age." Ronald Reagan, as we noted in Chapter 2, knew the value of talking about "the shin-ing city on a hill"; Martin Luther King used the mantra, "I have a dream . . . ," as a way to draw people in with his plans. John F. Kennedy, meanwhile, exhorted this country to "land a man on the moon and return him safely to the earth." We all know what happened as a result.

As the CEO of your organization, or as one if its senior leaders, develop a compelling vision of why Six Sigma is important to your organization's future health and vitality—if you want to bring others along with you. Think of this as a variation on the burning platform idea of years past, which senior executives often used as a compelling word picture for explaining why their organizations had to change if they wanted to survive. To help people make the leap to a new way of working, be sure to articulate the key work values that you see as critical to helping people build a Strategic Six Sigma organization.

For example, you might say, "In the months and years ahead, we must increasingly manage by fact and by listening to our customers more than we ever did in the past." Along the way, you'll encounter resistance, but that's par for the course. Push for compliance even before you have full commitment to Strategic Six Sigma thinking (as Jack Welch did), but be sure to listen to employees as you communicate new work expectations to them.

Finally, give Strategic Six Sigma initiatives more of your personal time as a leader than you think should be necessary. Framing an organization's goals in compelling ways is essential to bringing about change, but it isn't sufficient in itself. Top business leaders, as we noted earlier in this chapter, must also be willing to take personal risks and to spend large amounts of personal time injecting themselves into the details of their businesses, talking with employees, eliciting input and feedback, and working to build collaboration and cooperation up and down organizational levels, and across all organizational functions. This is the way you build not just compliance with Strategic Six Sigma principles, but also commitment to and enthusiasm for the benefits that Six Sigma practices and methods can offer down the line.

—The Authors

ers sends a powerful message about the importance these executives attach to the development of Six Sigma skills and expertise in their leadership teams.

The personal involvement of a company's top leaders is especially important when it comes to building a committed population of Six Sigma leaders for the following five reasons:

1. *Strategic Six Sigma represents an entirely new way for companies to organize work and get tasks done.* As such, it requires enormous amounts of organizational resolve, leadership sponsorship, multilevel planning, and effective engagement of employees to succeed. None of these things can be delegated, and a CEO working by him- or herself simply can't do it alone. A large and committed leadership coalition within an organization is clearly critical to giving Strategic Six Sigma projects the backbone they need to succeed.

2. *Because the data-driven nature of Six Sigma thinking and business processes requires tremendous diffusion of knowledge, expertise, and power throughout a business enterprise, it necessitates the cascading of skills—both of a technical and people nature—through all levels of the organization.* To build compliance with (and eventual commitment to) Six Sigma principles and concepts, this cascade must be continuous and intense. A CEO and his or her top leadership team can effectively mirror the importance of Six Sigma principles and ideas by taking a personal hand in the teaching and conveying of critical concepts and knowledge to others—not just technical knowledge, but also the components of effective leadership. This can go far in engaging and empowering leaders at all levels of an organization to step up to the challenges that Six Sigma implementation presents. "Six Sigma requires motivated employees, stringent financial monitor-

ing, a clear linkage to a company's strategic goals, and a 'program' to guide the company in transforming its culture," notes Tom Gurd, Vice President of Quality and Business Excellence at Dow. The training of Black Belts and other employees should not just involve teaching people about how to use statistical tools, he says. "Leadership skills are crucial too."[14] (See Figure 3.1.)

3. Change leadership (such as that associated with implementing Strategic Six Sigma) always involves the investment of more time and energy than executives imagine it will. Because of the highly robust nature of Strategic Six Sigma methods and practices, the only way to ensure that Six Sigma succeeds is to be prepared to give it as much attention and focus as necessary. Commenting on the time factor associated with effective Six Sigma implementation within an organization, Dow's Kathleen Bader says, "A half-hearted implementation of Six Sigma is worse than no implementation at all."[15]

4. The personal involvement of a company's top leaders in training other leaders can help accelerate an organization's learning curve with Six Sigma by facilitating informality, collaboration, and communication among leaders at different levels, and by emphasizing the critical nature of new organizational learning. The success of Six Sigma projects relies heavily on the use of statistical tools, but even more, it requires intensive team decision making and problem solving. Both of these require high levels of trust, cooperation, and collaboration, not only among members of Six Sigma project teams, but also among different functions within an organization. What better way to show employees of an organization the critical role these skills play in the

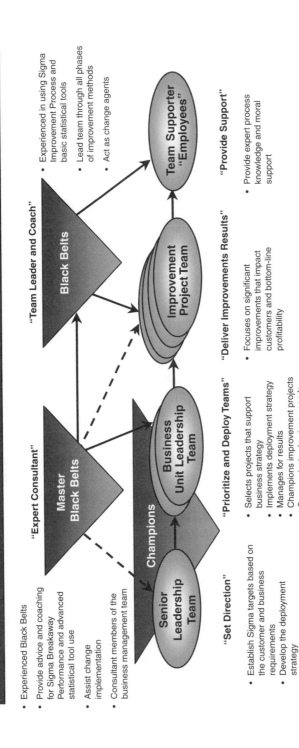

Figure 3.1 Six Sigma leadership roles and responsibilities.

effective implementation of Six Sigma initiatives, than to have a company's top leaders act not just as cheerleaders of Six Sigma initiatives, but as active teachers, coaches, and facilitators of the process?

5. Finally, when an organization promotes the principle of its top leaders developing other leaders with Six Sigma skills, it lays the groundwork for sustaining Six Sigma initiatives over time. How? By fostering strong sponsorship for change and creating leadership alignment across levels. For Six Sigma initiatives to be optimally successful—to be curve A projects as we outlined in Chapter 2—an organization needs to be able to call on an extensive population of leaders within the organization to drive success with Six Sigma over the long term. Leadership leverage with Six Sigma, in other words, derives from having a strong and committed team of Six Sigma leaders throughout one's organization, in every functional area of the enterprise. We submit that when top leaders get involved in teaching other leaders about Six Sigma, it not only provides a vehicle for the deployment of Six Sigma projects. It also provides an important learning ground for a company's future leaders, who ideally should be drawn from the ranks of Master Black Belts, Black Belts, and Green Belts in any case.

The consequences of an organization's top leaders playing roles as coaches and mentors to others has a wealth of significant downstream organization benefits, especially when it comes to successful implementation of Strategic Six Sigma. For example, it can help top leaders articulate their vision for the company to everyone else in the organization. It helps companies establish remarkably consistent leader behaviors across *all* organizational levels. It fosters strong leadership team unity, and it accelerates the transfer of crit-

ical knowledge throughout a company's leadership population. By doing all these things, it also raises morale in organizations and creates strong internal alignment—both of
which are key to successful implementation of Strategic Six
Sigma principles and practices.

■ CHAPTER CONCLUSIONS: LEADERSHIP BEST PRACTICES

As this chapter has stressed, developing a committed leadership team is the single most important success factor in
effectively implementing Strategic Six Sigma principles and
practices inside an organization.

1. **A CEO must effectively articulate compelling reasons for his or her organization to embrace Strategic
Six Sigma.** These are not responsibilities a top business leader can delegate to anyone else.
2. **These messages must be effectively cascaded throughout** *all* **levels of the organization to build a broad base
of leadership and employee support for initiatives.**
Leaders who don't build a strong coalition of support for
Six Sigma are doomed to see Six Sigma initiatives either
fail or derail.
3. **Generating short-term project wins is critical to
building longer-term acceptance of Six Sigma thinking and concepts within the organization.** Because
it represents a radical change in how people do their
work, Six Sigma is initially met with resistance, until
people see how it can provide both structure and clarity to their jobs.
4. **To sustain success as initiatives unfold, a company's
top leaders must effectively manage both the hard**

(performance expectations and metrics) and soft (people and culture) sides of organizational change. Embarking on Strategic Six Sigma requires fundamental culture change, which is partly about performance metrics, partly about processes, and partly about people!

5. **Top leaders must never stop articulating the company's future direction, and why Strategic Six Sigma principles are critical to the company successfully deploying its business strategies!**

Let's go on now to Chapter 4, where we discuss why it's so important for companies to integrate Strategic Six Sigma principles and practices into their strategic planning process.

Chapter
4

Incorporate Strategic Six Sigma Thinking and Best Practices into Your Company's Strategy Planning and Deployment Process

There's a time and place to be directive and when you're launching something powerful like 6 Sigma that's what's required. We have a mantra that says, "We lead with clarity, consistency and commitment in a collaborative way with courage because we have so much to accomplish in such a short period of time."

—Dave Burritt, Corporate 6 Sigma Champion
Caterpillar

By this point, you're undoubtedly beginning to appreciate how the strategic use of Six Sigma principles and practices across your enterprise can (or could) result in dramatic improvements in product, process, and service quality. (See Figure 4.1.) When used in a strategic way, Six Sigma achieves dramatic improvements in business performance because the precise understanding of customers enables an organization to accomplish the following:

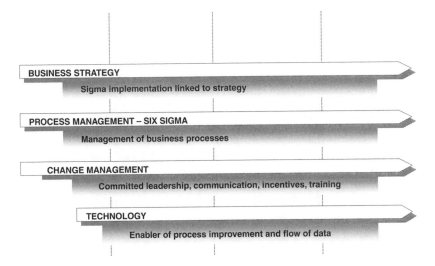

Figure 4.1 Integrating Six Sigma with business strategy. Strategic Six Sigma is based on aligning business strategy with process management/Six Sigma, change management, and information technology to meet critical customer requirements.

➤ Align core business processes with customer and marketplace requirements

➤ Eliminate defects systematically from existing processes, products, services, or plants

➤ Design new processes, products, services, or plants that reliably and consistently meet customer and market requirements

➤ Implement an infrastructure and leadership system to sustain gains and foster continuous improvement

Saying these things is one thing; however, implementing them enterprise-wide inside a company is quite another. How then does one go about it? Think of Six Sigma not simply as a process improvement approach, but also as a deployment vehicle, an enabler, and an integrator of other business-specific strategies or objectives. Taking the vehicle analogy a step further, if Six Sigma is the *vehicle* for deploying a company's strategies, then a company's core processes become its wheels. (Read more about processes in Chapter 6.) The continuous improvement of these core processes (or in other cases their actual design) is what enables the Six Sigma vehicle to move forward and to achieve the results (go in the specific direction) that a company's leaders decide that it should go.

Because Six Sigma is a key vehicle for deploying business strategy, companies must incorporate Six Sigma thinking, methods, and practices into their strategic planning process and use them to execute business objectives.

■ GENERAL ELECTRIC, DOW, DU PONT, AND BOMBARDIER: FOUR COMPANIES THAT LINK STRATEGIC SIX SIGMA WITH STRATEGY DEPLOYMENT

At General Electric (GE), former CEO Jack Welch understands the analogy of Six Sigma as a vehicle very well. That's why he integrated the implementation of Six Sigma with the simultaneous execution of the company's services, globalization, and e-business strategies. In effect, it became a key component of the company's operating system to guide the deployment of these other objectives. Some 100,000 people were trained in the principles and methodology of Six Sigma in the early years, beginning in 1995. "Now Six Sigma is the way we work," notes the GE web site. "We all speak a common language of CTQs [critical-to-quality specifications], DPMOs (defects per million opportunities), FMEAs (failure mode effect analysis), and [needs assessment maps]."[1]

The language of CTQs and DPMOs is very much in evidence in all of GE's operating businesses today—from medical systems and aircraft engines, to GE Plastics and GE Appliances. A senior executive in one GE business unit says that Six

Sigma principles and practices are at the heart of every inter-action and transaction with customers. "You look at your cus-tomer and say, 'What are the four or five things that we have to do absolutely right to ensure he or she is a customer for life?' " he says. "Once you define what those critical-to-quality char-acteristics are, you begin to shape your processes around those customer critical-to-quality characteristics."

At Dow, the company has taken a similarly strategic approach to the implementation of Six Sigma principles and practices across the organization. As noted in Chapter 1, Dow President and CEO Mike Parker views Six Sigma as a key vehi-cle for implementing Dow's strategic blueprint. (See the side-bar, "Using Six Sigma to Drive Business Strategy: The Dow Way.") That theme is echoed by Kathleen Bader, President of Dow's Styrenics and Engineered Products unit, who says that Dow implemented Six Sigma to support three key business goals: (1) customer loyalty and revenue growth, (2) produc-tivity enhancement, and (3) culture and people alignment.[2]

Like Dow and GE, Du Pont has taken decisive steps to employ Six Sigma as a vehicle for deploying its business strategies. As we noted in Chapter 1, it is using Six Sigma to drive sustainable growth, specifically to support three strate-gic initiatives: (1) integrated science, (2) knowledge intensity, and (3) productivity, all of which Du Pont CEO Chad Holliday says are vital to achieving sustainable growth and enhancing the company's understanding of customer needs and markets. "Science is the cornerstone of our ability to build and sustain a richer mix of businesses," he says. "We are focusing on mar-ket needs for electronics and high-performance materials, while we invest in new technology platforms such as plant sci-ence and biomaterials." To help it pursue a knowledge inten-sity business model that "leverages the value of our market knowledge, our brands, our technology, and know-how," Du

USING SIX SIGMA TO DRIVE BUSINESS STRATEGY: THE DOW WAY

Six Sigma is sometimes referred to humorously as "a total quality management (TQM) or business process reengineering (BPR) program on steroids." That's because it's a powerhouse way to drive defect and cost reduction and to support deployment of a company's business strategies. GE is probably the best-known example of a company that has used Six Sigma to drive deployment of its strategic priorities, among them globalization, services, and e-business. But today, another company is quickly ramping up to challenge GE for that distinction: Dow.

At Dow, Michael Parker, the company's president and CEO, is working rapidly to transform Dow into the world's largest and most diverse chemical company.* It is a Herculean challenge that involves a creative blend of cost reduction, mergers and acquisitions (Dow recently bought rival Union Carbide for $7.4 billion), and aggressive top-line business growth. To make all these initiatives work (and to do it within Dow's vertically integrated framework of global business units), Parker is relying on a twofold approach: a newly formed corporate operating board structure that brings members of his top executive team together from all over the world for regular consultations, and on Six Sigma. Strategic Six Sigma work practices are being applied today in virtually every area of Dow, says Parker, to help drive organizational alignment, to build customer loyalty, and to help the company make its strategic blueprint a reality.

That blueprint (in place since 1994) calls for Dow to set the competitive standard in the chemical industry, improve productivity, achieve aggressive value growth, and transform its business culture from one that traditionally has been inside-out in its approach to products and customer relationships, into one that is fiercely customer-centric.

In early 2001, Parker reaffirmed to chemical industry analysts that he expects Six Sigma to contribute $1.5 billion (cumulatively) to corporate earnings before interest and taxes by the end of 2003. To achieve that, Dow has launched

(Continued)

(Continued)

more than 2,400 DMAIC and 50 DFSS projects internally in the last two years, with more being launched or replicated almost weekly. They include projects such as "The Perfect Order" (designed to streamline the ordering process for Dow customers and improve customer loyalty). Dow has also spearheaded improvement projects in manufacturing, administration, and in product R&D—in one unique case to accelerate the growth of transgenic cottonseeds. Still other projects are under way to streamline development of uniform service agreements between Dow and its thousands of suppliers and contractors.

Parker is a passionate believer in the power of Six Sigma to create a performance culture at Dow, and to imbue employees with the mind-sets and toolsets to accomplish the company's aggressive strategic goals. In the past, "we thought in a 3 or 3.5 Sigma [mind-set]," he told us in an interview. "We've had to recognize that our old ways of doing business— of simply being a great manufacturing and technology company—are no longer enough." Indeed, that old way of doing business kept Dow "far back from the ultimate consumer in most of the things it does," Parker says. Consequently, "We had a tendency not to look to the outside [marketplace] as much as we might have, to understand that there is a consumer-driven reality to who we are."

Today, Dow's web site proudly proclaims that it is in business not just to make great products, but also to be a solutions-oriented company that helps its customers solve their business problems. "Becoming solutions-oriented demands that we combine our formidable 'old economy' strengths with the very best traits of the new economy, including speed, flexibility, an outside-in focus, constant innovation, and sustainability," says Parker. Six Sigma's robust data-driven approach to decision making, and its strong focus on metrics and accountability will enable Dow not just "to run its established businesses or do successful [M&A], but [also] to come up with new opportunities for growth."

While most of Dow's Six Sigma projects to date have been DMAIC projects, Parker sees tools such as DFSS as strategically critical to building the foundation for Dow's future business performance, once the company wrings as many productivity gains as possible out of its current efforts. "If you can design your processes so that they can perform at Six Sigma at the beginning, not at 3 Sigma, you will achieve a huge breakthrough in performance," he says. And although he admits that Dow is only now in the "early stages of customer loyalty-driven Six Sigma" projects, he emphasizes that Six Sigma projects such as "The Perfect Order" are making extensive use of voice-of-the-customer (VOC) and voice-of-the-marketplace (VOM) data to drive new design efforts.

STRONG TOP-DOWN LEADERSHIP COMMITMENT TO SIX SIGMA

Parker's goal to have Six Sigma support the deployment of Dow's business strategies is clear and unequivocal. "Within six years, we want every one of our employees to have experienced Six Sigma," he says. Thus, Dow is on an aggressive campaign to develop Black Belts in tsunami waves of training involving up to 200 Black Belt candidates at a time. The idea is to create sufficient speed and scale to support broad-based deployment of Six Sigma inside the company, and to ensure that Six Sigma thinking and practices quickly permeate and hopefully saturate the way people at *all* levels and in *all* parts of the organization think about their jobs.

Parker himself is deeply committed to fostering a strong cadre of Six Sigma leaders within Dow. He participates actively and visibly in all the waves of Black Belt training the company has done thus far at its Six Sigma training center in Atlanta, Georgia. "I spend hours with each of the waves as they come through." He is particularly energized by participating in gallery walks (reviewing significant Six Sigma Black Belt projects to understand the numerous ways—both monetary and nonmonetary—that they support Dow's business strategies).

So what's Parker's advice to other CEOs who might be contemplating Six Sigma in their organizations? The benefits from Six Sigma can be impressive but require huge amounts of senior leadership support to succeed, he says.

(Continued)

(Continued)

"To move a company from a 3 or 3.5 Sigma performance level to even a 4 Sigma performance level requires extensive training of people and a deep-seated organizational commitment to Six Sigma principles and best practices"—things like data-driven decision making. As for becoming customer-centric, a company must really commit itself to the processes and procedures to make this happen. "You have to really want to hear from customers to understand their needs and what they want from you," Parker says.

Does Parker have any doubts about the Six Sigma journey on which Dow has embarked? Not for a moment. Six Sigma will "go on forever at Dow," he proclaims. That's because its potential for new value creation is almost limitless. "We've made a lot of progress with Six Sigma and we're going to make much more in the next couple of years, as all our folks and businesses become more intimate with the marketplace," he says, adding, "our Six Sigma methodology, married to a [mind-set] of being focused on the customer and defining the dimensions of customer loyalty, is absolutely critical to us at this point in our history." — *The Authors*

*Michael Parker, interview with Richard Koonce, PricewaterhouseCoopers, Midland, MI, 19 November 2001.

Pont is "using Six Sigma to enhance productivity, build marketplace competitiveness, and grow revenues."[3]

Bombardier Transportation, the world leader in the manufacture and supply of railway vehicles and services, is still another company that's taking a strongly strategic approach to deploying Six Sigma in its organization. "Our overarching goal with Six Sigma is to use it to sharpen our appreciation of customer needs and then to design and deliver the appropriate product or service profitably," says Pierre Lortie, Bombardier Transportation's president and chief operating officer. To that end, Lortie says the company is using Six Sigma for four key strategic purposes: (1) to reduce costs and improve operating efficiencies; (2) to surpass customer expectations by margins Bombardier's competitors can't match; (3) to improve the company's performance at a faster rate than its competitors can; and (4) to build a future generation of leaders who will be able to manage in an increasingly complex environment, meeting the needs of customers and giving Bombardier Transportation a sustained competitive advantage.[4]

What steps did each of these companies take to effectively integrate Strategic Six Sigma into the strategy planning and deployment process? In each case, corporate leaders

➤ Articulated their business strategies
➤ Identified strategic improvement goals (SIGs)
➤ Identified and prioritized specific improvement projects to impact those SIGs
➤ Created active Six Sigma projects led by Black Belts

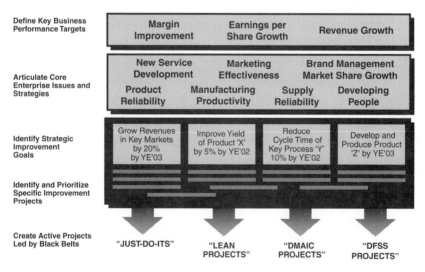

Figure 4.2   Critical steps in Strategic Six Sigma implementation.

■ DRIVING THE STRATEGIC SIX SIGMA IMPROVEMENT ENGINE

Look now at Figure 4.2. For maximum impact, a company must deploy Strategic Six Sigma from the executive suite—the very top of the house—and cascade it down through the leadership chain. As Figure 4.2 shows, the process requires the rigorous alignment of strategies, SIGs, and specific improvement efforts [both Define, Measure, Analyze, Improve, and Control (DMAIC) and Design for Six Sigma (DFSS)] projects to achieve specific improvement results. There are four key steps involved in this process, a discussion of each which follows.

> ➤ **Step 1: Define Key Performance Metrics and Articulate Core Enterprise Issues and Strategies**

In step 1, the company's top leadership team (with assistance from Master Black Belts and Black Belts) needs to huddle for an intense, shirtsleeve discussion of the company's core enterprise issues and strategies. As Figure 4.2 reveals, the issues can include anything from profitability targets and brand strategies, to process performance gaps, product reliability issues, growth issues, or challenges associated with new service development or developing people.

A key focus of discussion at this stage is the company's current performance, key performance indicators (otherwise known as KPIs), and how the company is doing in terms of profitability, productivity, market responsiveness, and customer satisfaction. Is the company meeting its sales targets? Is it meeting customer satisfaction requirements? Are business strategies being executed effectively? Company leaders must answer a number of critical questions as part of their discussions. They include (but are not limited to) the following:

➤ What are our company's core issues and strategies? (Prioritize.) Are they being well executed? How do we know?

➤ Do we quantify our effectiveness in executing strategy, or do we make unwarranted assumptions about how well we're doing?

➤ What are the financial implications of those strategies that are not being well executed? (Quantify costs/revenue impact.)

➤ What issues are adversely affecting customer satisfaction and loyalty?

➤ What are the financial implications of each? (Quantify costs/sigma level.)

➤ Do we have current knowledge of customer needs/ requirements?

➤ What critical customer requirements (CCRs) do we currently meet and which do we not? (Quantify performance gaps.)

➤ What are the means we use (feedback loops, formal channels, and so forth) to stay in touch with customers?

One of the key goals of this first-stage discussion is to get all of the top leaders of the organization onto the same sheet of music when it comes to identifying and ranking priorities and strategies for the company going forward. This discussion, which ideally should be assisted by an outside team of facilitators, is likely to create sparks and heated discussion. (See the sidebar, "Why Is It So Tough to Form Top Leadership Teams?") However, it can be the basis for an organization's top leadership team effectively coalescing around common issues the company must address. It also helps to *connect* the organization's top leaders around a common set of goals, and begins to *create* and *channel* the energy that will be required to drive Strategic Six Sigma implementation efforts forward.

WHY IS IT SO TOUGH TO FORM
TOP LEADERSHIP TEAMS?

Teaming at the top of an organization is often tough to accomplish. There are many reasons for this. For one thing, top executives often have strong control needs. By instinct, they rely more on their own wisdom and experience than on team approaches to solve problems. In their book, *The Wisdom of Teams,* for example, Katzenbach and Smith note that by the time most executives arrive at the top of a company, they are loath to permit their job performance (and ratings) to be dependent on other people.* This can easily keep a top team from coalescing around shared goals, and it can also prevent team energy from ever being optimized.

Second, many senior executives are not temperamentally suited to take on the shirtsleeve work that is required if they are going to be part of a true team, note Steve Yearout and Gerry Miles in their 2001 book, *Growing Leaders.*† The reason, notes Yearout, is that "in their roles as senior executives they have usually managed staffs, been accustomed to delegating work to other people, and relied on key subordinates for background materials, research, idea development, speeches, talking points—and even their 'point of view' about many business and organizational topics."

Third, strong egos can easily get in the way of top executives taking the time—or exerting the energy to bond with their fellow senior executives in true team settings. Because many top executives in organizations view their peers as potential rivals for the CEO job, forming a productive, top-level executive team becomes difficult, and creating strong and synergistic group dynamics can be problematic.

*J. Katzenbach and D. Smith, *The Wisdom of Teams: Creating the High-Performance Organization,* HarperBusiness, New York, 1994, p. 220.

†Adapted from Steve Yearout and Gerry Miles (with Richard Koonce), *Growing Leaders,* American Society for Training and Development, Alexandria, VA, 2001, p. 145.

Finally, top executives have limited free time and may view top-team meetings and assignments (such as Six Sigma implementation) as activities to which they want to devote only the minimal amount of time required. Therefore, they may fail to personally involve themselves in top-team activities, will send subordinates to key meetings, and may in many cases fail to inject themselves personally into the top-team unity building process. This low-key commitment can cause the group identity and dynamics of a top executive team to suffer from the very start.

➤ Step 2: Identify SIGs

At this stage, a broader cross section of the company's leadership (extending down to upper middle management) is brought into leadership discussions. This group meets to further clarify and confirm core business issues and strategic concerns. This group (essentially the business unit leadership of the company) also begins to identify specific SIGs. It discusses the overall outline of performance scorecards and dashboards that will be adopted by the company to measure, gauge, and assess performance as Six Sigma projects are launched. In addition, this team of executives begins drawing up a deployment strategy to meet strategic improvement targets. Among other things, business unit/division leaders must do the following:

➤ Identify SIGs in specific areas and processes
➤ Develop the outlines of performance scorecards and dashboards (the things to be measured and how they will be measured against CCRs)
➤ Prioritize SIGs based on how well they drive the performance metrics in the right direction

➤ Develop a Six Sigma deployment strategy (including a list of those who should play major roles in the deployment process as Master Black Belts, Black Belts, project sponsors, and so forth)

➤ Create strong leadership and employee ownership of Six Sigma methods and approaches

A major goal of step 2 is to engage a group of senior business leaders who will act as hands-on Six Sigma deployment champions (DCs) within the organization. Discussions in step 2 are thus an important ingredient in helping to form the critical infrastructure inside the company that will be needed to launch and *sustain* Strategic Six Sigma initiatives over time. Six Sigma champions actively work to sponsor and drive the use of Six Sigma methods and procedures throughout all parts and levels of the organization. Their early and passionate embrace of Strategic Six Sigma is critical to its then being cascaded as a leadership priority to other leadership levels.

A critical factor in getting business unit leaders on board as Six Sigma champions is to see their organization's top leader taking an active role as the company's number one Six Sigma evangelist, sponsor, and advocate. Dave Burritt, Caterpillar's Corporate Six Sigma Champion, enjoys recalling a time early in 2001 when he and his organization were doing project sponsor workshops and needed help in conveying the urgency of Six Sigma to workshop attendees. He arranged for Caterpillar's Chairman, Glen Barton, to attend three different workshops in the Peoria, Illinois, area on a Saturday, so that attendees would begin to understand how much top company leadership was committed to Six Sigma.

Glen was out of town and had to fly in. He wasn't feeling well—he had a cold. But he came into these project sponsor workshops on a Saturday with no entourage and just started sitting at tables. That created a lot of buzz here in the Peoria area. There are three separate locations here in the Peoria area, and he made a point to hit every one of those sites. And the comments I got were things like, 'Glen was just here. He knows this stuff. He believes in this stuff. We'd better start getting on board with this. . . .' "[5]

➤ Step 3: Identify and Prioritize Specific Improvement Projects

At this stage, with the basic outline of performance metrics now determined and the detail of customer scorecards and process dashboards beginning to take shape, an even wider circle of business leaders (with assistance from Master Black Belts, Black Belts, and Green Belts) meets to identify and prioritize specific improvement projects. How exactly is this accomplished?

"This Six Sigma thing has to pay its own way!" is the cry of most business leaders when they first hear about Six Sigma. The reaction is appropriate. Over the years, other improvement initiatives [total quality management (TQM) and business process reengineering (BPR), to name but two] often have promised a lot but delivered little. For that reason, any Six Sigma program that a company implements should be designed to pay its way, at least from the second year of implementation onward. This means each project must pay its own way.

Some projects that a company selects—the proverbial low-hanging fruit that involves minor tweaking of existing business processes—can quickly result in immediate benefits and payoffs. We identify them in Figure 4.2 as *just-do-its*. Other projects that can be undertaken using lean enterprise techniques are identified in Figure 4.2 as *lean* projects.

Projects that require more extensive process or product improvement or redesign are assigned to cross-functional DMAIC teams. (See Chapter 5.) The DMAIC teams concern themselves with defining business improvement opportunities, measuring performance of current business processes, analyzing the root causes of existing performance gaps, improving performance, and controlling performance of existing or redesigned processes. The goal is to do all of this for the lowest possible cost.

Projects that require *new* process or product development are assigned to cross-functional DFSS teams. (See Chapter 5.) These teams design *new* processes or products using a unique set of methods that accurately determine customer needs; define product/service requirements; and enable teams to explore design alternatives to meet those needs, develop detailed designs, and implement those designs. (Projects handled through DFSS often prove very powerful in accelerating research and development (R&D) efforts and shrinking new product development cycle times.)

In step 3, a company's leadership team should brainstorm numerous potential projects across a wide variety of operations. Each should be assessed for its potential impact on SIGs. When putting together a portfolio of improvement projects to work on, design some projects to have short-term paybacks. This way, an organization is forced to put Six Sigma principles to work immediately, thus quickly generating improved levels of service and quality, which, in turn, improves customer satisfaction and generates increased sales in the long term. Short-term payoffs from Six Sigma projects, which also have the psychological effect of building momentum for change, can include anything from improved process efficiency and increased capacity to lower operating costs and reduced costs from rework.

Other projects should be designed to have longer-term paybacks. For example, working to improve customer satisfaction over time creates a more robust revenue stream, and developing a more motivated workforce creates a stable foundation for sustaining long-term Six Sigma success. Marketing and sales processes are often places to discover opportunities for revenue growth.

Step 3 typically ends once a prioritized slate of Six Sigma projects has been agreed upon by a consensus of the company's leaders, and a business leader sponsor or champion has been assigned to each.

➤ Step 4: Create Active Projects Led by Black Belts and Sponsored by Business Leaders or Champions

In step 4, Six Sigma projects proceed under the guidance of Six Sigma Black Belt team leaders and are based on the deployment strategy and plans developed in step 2. Each project is also assigned a business leader sponsor or champion, who is held accountable to ensure that the project stays aligned with business goals and has the resources needed to be successful.

As the detailed shirtsleeve work of DMAIC and DFSS teams gets under way, the first critical task of assigned Black Belts and project champions is to build a business case for their projects, and to develop detailed project charters. Also, in this stage, the detailed work of developing customer scorecards and process dashboards proceeds. *Customer scorecards,* developed in close cooperation with the customers, focus on helping a business to monitor and gauge its performance from the point of view of the customers' end requirements (on-time deliveries, fulfillment of critical functions or activities, transactions satisfactorily completed, etc.). At the same time, *process dashboards* are created to help the company keep track of how it is doing—to monitor, track, and gauge the nature of process inputs and outputs generated in fulfilling customers' end requirements. (For more about scorecards and dashboards, see Chapters 6 and 7.)

As already noted, some Six Sigma projects (the so-called just-do-its and the lean projects) are designed to score quick wins and provide early financial and productivity paybacks. Other projects (specifically DMAIC and DFSS projects) need to be analyzed more carefully and will provide payback over a longer period of time: from three months to one year.

■ CREATING A CLIMATE OF ALIGNMENT TO SUPPORT STRATEGIC SIX SIGMA DEPLOYMENT

As Strategic Six Sigma is operationalized, it aligns a company's metrics (its family of measures) not only with articulated business strategies, but also with prioritized SIGs that are critical to supporting the strategy. The specific Six Sigma projects that are chosen and launched are intended to directly impact identified SIGs, and, in turn, affect execution of the company's strategy or strategies.

■ BE CONSISTENT AND NEVER LOSE SIGHT OF CUSTOMER REQUIREMENTS

To fully impact a company's customers, implementation of Strategic Six Sigma initiatives needs to be consistently applied across the entire business value stream, encompassing all functions and operations. (This is one reason Six Sigma project teams need to draw members from all organizational functions.) As projects are undertaken and completed, the process of assessing, monitoring, and improving business performance, and addressing customer requirements must become continuous. As it does, the organization creates an engine of continuous improvement with hundreds or even thousands of high-impact projects focused on customer and business priorities. Sustaining this improvement engine requires clear accountability, effective communication, close collaboration, and trust among all parts of an organization. It also requires the elimination of organizational silos and the clear and unequivocal support of a company's top management.

One leading e-business executive that Pricewaterhouse-Coopers (PwC) works with says that continuous improvement ought to be the preeminent ambition and goal of every company today. That's because "getting this activity right" is the key both to continuous customer satisfaction and continued marketplace success. But the key to doing this is to view one's company as a set of highly complex and interrelated processes:

The fundamental principle of Six Sigma is that businesses are all about processes. *Every business has almost an infinite set of processes that make it work, and there's a set of processes that describe commercial transactions between customers and suppliers as well. Six Sigma is about imposing an intellectual discipline on process reengineering. The philosophy of Six Sigma is that to reengineer a process within an enterprise or between enterprises you first have to **define** the process you're trying to reengineer. You must [then] **measure** the outputs of the process using statistically valid techniques. You must **analyze** the outputs of the measure-*

ment process. You then put improvement plans in place to the process. And then the key thing is to take the reengineered process and put it under control.[6]

The ability to put process management under control is in fact one of the key success traits of today's Strategic Six Sigma companies. As this executive points out, it's also one made infinitely more manageable today if a company's IT, e-business, and enterprise resource planning capabilities are applied to the task:

We believe that to successfully place most business processes under control, you have to impose e-commerce technologies onto those processes—or otherwise stated automate those processes. So, when I travel around the world and talk to customers, or to reporters and analysts, the point I always try to make is that . . . to realize quantum improvements in productivity you must constantly be reengineering your processes—both inside your business and with your suppliers and customers . . . The way you put that process of control in place for the long-term is to automate it so the process is repetitive, it's easily measurable, and it's easily improved upon when you start getting results that are out of spec.[7]

We will have much more to say about process management in subsequent chapters.

■ KEY CHALLENGES WITH STRATEGY INTEGRATION

As a company proceeds to integrate Strategic Six Sigma methods and practices with other business strategies and priorities, there are five implementation challenges.

1. It's critical to assign specific financial goals to each Six Sigma project that an organization undertakes. This helps to rank-order projects in terms of their importance in impacting SIGs. It also serves to create tight organizational alignment and focus around achieving concrete and measurable targets as they relate to specific SIGs, such as faster innovation or enhanced customer satisfaction.

2. Be sure to deploy plans from the top down, so that employees understand that top leadership vigorously (and enthusiastically) supports Six Sigma objectives. "If you're the CEO in your organization or one of its senior leaders, embrace the Jack Welch philosophy—'Here's what I want,' "— recommends one corporate quality manager. "It's critical to driving compliance and commitment to Six Sigma—especially on an enterprise-wide basis," he says.

3. Put effective communications channels in place so that deployment plans and objectives are communicated to all parts of the organization in clear, consistent, and frequent ways. Six Sigma deployment veterans say effective communications are key to successful Six Sigma deployments. Why? Because the people who provide the highest (and most visible) level of support to implementation efforts (i.e., a firm's senior leaders) aren't the same people who will be responsible for performing everyday Six Sigma tasks at the *project* level. Clear, consistent, and frequent communications with the troops is thus critical to ensure that rank-and-file employees understand the Six Sigma tasks and goals they must accomplish.

4. Be certain that you put adequate leadership ground forces in place to help Six Sigma project teams punch through organizational roadblocks and deal with other impediments to successful project launch and completion. A veteran Six

Sigma Black Belt in a leading automotive parts manufacturing company says that in his experience, this is key to making sure that Six Sigma project teams don't get mired in organizational quicksand as they begin their work. "Put deployment champions in place at the divisional and regional levels, who will have an on-the-ground feel for what individual project teams need in completing their work, and who can help bust through organizational silos or other barriers to completing [Six Sigma] projects," he suggests.

5. *Put training in place.* We'll have much more to say about Six Sigma leadership training in Chapter 10, but suffice it to say here that providing appropriate amounts of training to *all* levels of leadership and management is critical to the success of Strategic Six Sigma initiatives and to cascading Six Sigma sponsorship, knowledge, and expertise down through all levels of the leadership chain.

■ ONE COMPANY'S RECIPE FOR RAPID STRATEGIC SIX SIGMA DEPLOYMENT

What's the best way to effectively deploy Strategic Six Sigma inside an organization and to be certain Six Sigma projects are optimally aligned to support business strategies? One of the best recent examples of successful Strategic Six Sigma deployment took place in 2001 at Caterpillar.

When it comes to sheer, short-term financial success from deploying Six Sigma, no company can match Caterpillar. In 2001, in its first year of Six Sigma deployment, this Peoria, Illinois–based company, well known for manufacturing heavy-duty earth-moving, construction, and mining equipment, and diesel and natural gas engines, realized accrued benefits of twice the cost of Six Sigma deployment, notes Dave Burritt, Caterpillar's Corporate 6 Sigma Champion. How did Caterpillar do it?

"One of the keys to breakthrough success with 6 Sigma is extremely rapid deployment of 6 Sigma professionals inside the organization, the building of an infrastructure to support success, the training and certification of Black Belts, and the development of a strong team of 6 Sigma Deployment Champions," says Burritt. He adds that Caterpillar introduced 6 Sigma using a *tsunami,* or *big-wave,* approach (a term he borrowed from his friends at Dow) across the entire organization:

> *We rolled 6 Sigma out on January 15, 2001, at 13 locations around the globe—in North America, South America, Europe, and Asia. Everybody was adopting 6 Sigma. What we focused on initially were three critical success factors— growth, cost reduction, and quality/reliability. We made sure that when projects were selected for 6 Sigma they directly connected in with one of these three priorities. In 6 Sigma sessions that followed, where the project sponsor was present and we had 6 Sigma training, we also developed selection filters that started at the top of the organization with strategic goals and then cascaded down to strategic areas of improvement and to critical success factors at the business unit level. At the business unit level, the business units themselves exercised self-determination in picking projects that linked back to the corporate strategies of growth, cost reduction, and quality/reliability.[5]*

As this story shows, Caterpillar was able to bring tremendous organizational focus to its Strategic Six Sigma efforts. It created an organizational line of sight between strategies and critical success factors on the one hand, and SIGs and specific Six Sigma projects at the business unit level on the other. The company thus created a powerful climate of organizational alignment to support pursuit of its business strategies. Breakaway business performance thus became possible almost immediately. Indeed, the company proved so effective at generating cost savings and performance improvements that it more than paid back the costs of deployment in just nine months! This is the first case we know of where a company has more than paid for the cost of Six Sigma deployment in less than a year!

■ CHAPTER SUMMARY

This chapter has outlined how a company's leaders can effectively incorporate Strategic Six Sigma principles and practices into the strategy deployment process. It consists of a four-step process of aligning performance metrics, SIGs, and Six Sigma projects to effectively execute a company's business strategy or strategies. The key to breakaway success with this activity is for a company's CEO to effectively engage progressively larger groups of leaders in increasingly detailed discussions of SIGs, and to prioritize Six Sigma DMAIC and DFSS projects for launch based on their ability to impact SIGs. Leaders must then develop appropriate customer dashboards and performance scorecards with which to manage and monitor Six Sigma projects on a continuous basis.

➤ Best Practices Associated with Incorporating Strategic Six Sigma into a Company's Strategy Planning Process

When applied strategically to business goals, Six Sigma principles provide a common framework of tools, metrics, and methods for organizing, defining, mapping, and measuring work inputs and outputs, as well as for guiding the design or creation of business processes. Because they create strong line-of-sight alignment, linking strategies with SIGs and specific Six Sigma projects, they constitute a powerful engine for driving process improvement and long-term organizational transformation. Nonetheless, to fully harness the power of Six Sigma principles for strategic purposes, a company's top leadership team must first do the following five things:

1. **Come to a clear agreement about the company's business strategy or strategies.** This requires intense teamwork and group focus, the sublimating of individual executive egos in many cases, and close cooperation and collaboration of leaders across *all* of a company's business units, divisions, or functions.

2. **Take painstaking care to identify financial targets, determine how business performance will be assessed, and be certain that all employees of the company understand these performance metrics.** Doing this right requires that all of a company's leaders adhere to the same set of metrics for assessing and evaluating performance, and that they hold their subordinates accountable to these same metrics. At first, it may be difficult to get group consensus about how business performance will be measured, so a company's CEO may need to force the issue with the top leadership team, and get them to agree on a specific family of measures by which their performance (and that of their business units) will be judged.

3. **Be clear about the criteria that will be used for prioritizing Six Sigma projects for launch.** We will have more to say about this in subsequent chapters, but it is critical that leaders develop specific financial targets for individual projects, and that they assess the

appropriateness of individual projects based on the use of specific project filters. (See Chapter 7.) This will ensure that the projects selected have the maximum impact possible on SIGs.

4. **Put adequate leadership ground forces in place throughout the organization to help Six Sigma project teams do their work.** The essence of Six Sigma is the generation of results. For Six Sigma initiatives to succeed, project teams must therefore be empowered with strong sponsors, champions, and leaders. Moreover, senior Six Sigma leaders must play hands-on roles in removing organizational roadblocks to teams effectively completing their work. This will involve helping teams break through organizational silos and getting them the resources (e.g., people, systems) they need to succeed.

5. **Think of Six Sigma not as a process improvement approach, but as a powerful deployment vehicle, enabler, and integrator of business strategies or objectives.** When a company's executives do this, the true power of Six Sigma can be harnessed and channeled to meet any business priorities or goals a company may have. Six Sigma will cease being simply a process improvement methodology, and become an engine for driving tight organizational alignment, leadership focus, and breakaway business performance.

While Strategic Six Sigma can be a valuable and powerful vehicle to drive a company toward attainment of its business goals, it is predicated, of course, on a company first understanding the needs and requirements of its customers. For that reason, we turn now to Chapter 5, where we talk about why it is critical that, as part of deploying Strategic Six Sigma inside an organization, a company develop a disciplined process to stay in touch with its customers and the marketplace.

Chapter

5

Be in Touch with Customers and the Marketplace

Understanding value from the customer's perspective *is the first principle for us because if you get that wrong, then, by definition, the rest of what you do is waste.*

> —Mike Joyce, Vice President
> *LM-21 Operating Excellence/*
> *Lockheed Martin*

When it comes to implementing Strategic Six Sigma practices in a company today, it's essential that a firm develop disciplined processes for assessing customer satisfaction and loyalty, and that it be able to make changes to its core processes when and if it becomes necessary. At the same time, a company must have robust mechanisms in place to capture an up-to-the-minute grasp of what the larger business environment is doing and where it's going. That's because we live today in a dynamic new marketplace, characterized by market turbulence, emerging technologies, shifting competitive dynamics, rapidly changing consumer habits, and of course, increasingly complex demands that commercial and industrial customers make of their suppliers. A company can't afford to be out of touch or out of sync with this marketplace for very long. If it is, it risks being left in the dust by other, more agile and aggressive competitors that are able to leverage customer and market knowledge to competitive advantage. Even if a company is consistently meeting the needs of current customers, it may still fall behind the levels at which its competitors are pleasing *their* customers. Therefore, to grow its share of market it must make customer and marketplace intelligence gathering a continuous priority.

This chapter therefore talks about the importance of a company having robust methods in place to capture both customer and marketplace information, and how these data are then used to define the work of Define, Measure, Analyze, Improve, and Control (DMAIC) and Design for Six Sigma (DFSS) project teams.

■ WHY MANY COMPANIES DO A POOR JOB OF COLLECTING AND USING CUSTOMER AND MARKETPLACE INTELLIGENCE

Many companies do a less-than-adequate job of staying abreast of customer needs and buying requirements, and an even poorer job of tracking marketplace trends and other developments. The marketplace is replete with the wreckage of companies that either misjudged their customers and markets, suffered from poor timing, or took their marketplace dominance for granted—to their regret. Following are some examples.

Some companies believe that they know exactly what their customers require and, consequently, almost never talk to them, at least not in a systematic and consistent way. "We've served that client for years," they'll say. "We know exactly what they need." Such companies often are blind to what "they don't know they don't know" about their customers. Thus, they fail to take stock of changing customer buying habits, shifting purchase patterns and requirements, changing consumer trends and tastes, or competitive and demographic changes in the marketplace. Such companies are often preeminent in their marketplaces for a time, able to rest on the laurels of past business successes for many years. Eventually, however, they're awakened from their complacency when a pesky competitor comes to the marketplace and eats their lunch, offering better and cheaper products, for example, or by otherwise altering the marketplace balance of power among competitors. One example would be when a fledgling upstart displaces a long-time market leader. Or when a savvy newcomer (e.g., Dell Computer) assumes the role of disintermediator, shaking up the marketplace, and totally rewriting the rules of business engagement for everybody else.

Look at what happened to the Swiss watchmaking industry in the 1970s and 1980s, for example, as Japanese and U.S. watchmakers flooded the global consumer market with quartz watches and literally cleaned the clocks of Swiss watchmakers. They offered cheaper, in many cases disposable, watches that proved very popular with young consumers. Swiss watchmakers, who traditionally had relied on consumers putting high value on Swiss craftsmanship, and the willingness of consumers to automatically pay for it in stores, did not foresee the appearance of such watches.

Meanwhile, everybody is familiar with the story of Dell Computer, which roared into the computer marketplace 15 years ago, leapfrogging over traditional competitors like Compaq, Hewlett-Packard (HP), and IBM to sell computers directly to retail customers—and in a fraction of the time typically associated with computer purchases up to that time.

Dell's continuing innovation in the areas of customer sales, service, and care—its offering of online system configurators to retail computer purchasers, for example—continues to help it stay ahead of its competitors in the retail computer space, because Dell realizes that retail computer buyers want computer buying to be simple, easy, fast, and hassle-free.

Other companies recognize no distinction between momentary customer satisfaction and long-term customer loyalty. Thus, they may squander the opportunity to translate existing customer satisfaction into longer-term customer loyalty and retention. Until they wise up, of course!

Years ago, the Customer Loyalty Institute of Ann Arbor, Michigan, helped Dunkin' Donuts discover that it was the retail chain's coffee, not its doughnuts, that brought customers back to Dunkin' Donuts shops time and time again. After discovering this, the doughnut maker aimed its promotional efforts at getting new customers to come in and try the coffee. Doughnuts didn't even figure in the ad campaign. The moral of this story? Don't always assume you know what keeps your customers coming back to you. Instead, ask questions and do research. Be driven in your approach to customers not by intuition or gut, but by data points. And go after *new* data on a regular basis. Learning about one's customers is often an eye-opening process of peeling back layers of onion skin, getting past personal intuition and marketplace perceptions to arrive at real, documentable business fact about customers!

Still other companies have lots of good data about their customers and their marketplace lying around inside the organization, but these data either are hoarded, siloed, or held hostage to organizational politics. In any case, data are not easily leveraged in a cross-functional or cross-process way across the organization.

Collecting information from customers and the marketplace and ensuring the continuous *exchange* of information between companies and their customers are both key to helping companies assure high levels of customer care, service, and responsiveness today. Accurate customer and marketplace data collection is the fruitful end product of careful customer listening. It's key to effective competitive positioning, and it's the essential lubricant that facilitates modern customer-supplier communications. Perhaps most important, getting good, hard reliable data about customers and the marketplace is critical to effectively executing business strategies today, and to creating a business culture based on a strategic approach to customer care.

■ HARDWIRING PROCESS IMPROVEMENT TO CUSTOMER AND MARKETPLACE REQUIREMENTS

One of the big advantages of implementing Strategic Six Sigma inside an organization is that it hardwires process improvements (via Six Sigma projects) not only to business strategy, but also to customer requirements and broad marketplace analysis. (See Figure 5.1.) As this figure shows, the systematic and consistent collection of customer and marketplace data (e.g., market trends, competitor data, customer requirements) provides a rich mix of information that, when synthesized and looped back to the organization, feeds both the strategy development process and core process improvement. Taking an even longer view, it provides the basis for continuous organizational transformation and sustained process management. Process management is the desired end game of Strategic Six Sigma deployment in an organization. It institutionalizes the end-to-end design and

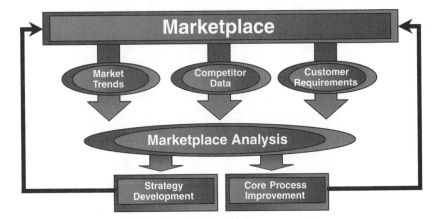

Figure 5.1 Defining customer and market requirements. Strategic Six Sigma analyzes market trends, competitive data, and customer requirements, and it uses these data to drive strategy development and core process improvement enterprise-wide.

operation of business processes to function in a synchronized, organic way to meet customer requirements on a continuous basis.

Nowadays it is critical that companies understand the needs of customers more intimately than ever before. In an era of rapid change and intense competition, the companies that establish and maintain the clearest, most consistent understanding of their customers' requirements, and that can organizationally meet those requirements on an ongoing basis, are going to become and remain market leaders. That's why Strategic Six Sigma is fundamentally concerned with understanding the needs of customers and the marketplace, and then using those data to drive both strategy and core process improvements. (See Figure 5.1 and the sidebar, "At Caterpillar, Getting to the Voice of the Customer Is Still a Work in Progress.")

AT CATERPILLAR, GETTING TO THE VOICE OF THE CUSTOMER IS STILL A WORK IN PROGRESS

Caterpillar had remarkable success with 6 Sigma worldwide in 2001—realizing benefits of more than double its implementation costs. Nonetheless, Caterpillar's Corporate 6 Sigma Champion Dave Burritt acknowledges that the company still has a lot of work to do when it comes to listening to and understanding the needs of customers. "In the first year, we focused on driving [short-term] benefits through very quickly, and proving we could be accretive with our goals," he says.*

For example, in the initial nine months of its 6 Sigma deployment, Caterpillar cleaned up many customer problems relating to timely delivery of product orders to dealers, and tackled a lot of quality and capacity issues relating to production and product design. "We cleaned up some problems, but we're not, in all cases, getting to the Voice of the Customer," says Burritt.

One example: Caterpillar still has work to do to fully apply 6 Sigma to product innovation, new product introductions, and top-line business growth, says Burritt. To do those things, "we need a more robust system." Geoff Turk, Caterpillar's Six Sigma Methodology and Training Development manager, agrees:

At Caterpillar, 6 Sigma is about turning strategy into action and reality. Our strategy is to grow profitably, reduce non-value-added cost, and dramatically improve our product and services quality and reliability. We can't achieve any of these without firmly embedding 6 Sigma into new product and service development, production processes and product problem resolution. We have to do it across the board with DMAIC, DMEDI, and process management or, our strategy will not become reality.†

*David Burritt, Interview with Richard Koonce, Peoria, IL: PricewaterhouseCoopers, 4 December 2001.

†Caterpillar's own version of Design for Six Sigma, *DMEDI* stands for *Define, Measure, Explore, Develop, and Implement.*

(Continued)

(Continued)

Burritt says corporate executives will focus year-two 6 Sigma efforts "on looking through Caterpillar's entire value chain into our dealer organization." To do that, the company has breathed new life into its in-house business intelligence group. What's more, it's using various *industry councils* (created to research industry sectors like quarry, aggregates, and mining) to reach further into various subsegments of the Caterpillar marketplace to better understand customers' needs. That research will help Caterpillar's Black Belts determine where to focus 6 Sigma project efforts on a going-forward basis, says Burritt. "We have a dealer organization that we rely on heavily to tell us what the voice of the customer is, [but] now we [also] have 715 Black Belts—soon to be double that number—with a lot of questions about who the real end customer is," he says. "That's the next dimension of our 6 Sigma efforts."—*The Authors*

The intended end result of implementing Strategic Six Sigma in an organization is to create a finely honed organizational machine, a machine whose core business processes are so finely attuned and aligned to customer requirements that they constantly meet or exceed expectations, creating not only satisfied customers, but also highly loyal customers who stay with a company because they know it delivers what it promises.

Figure 5.2 reveals how this ideal state of sustained process management is supposed to be created within a company. As this graphic reveals, *inputs* (in this case, both customer specifications and raw materials from suppliers) enter into a company's production processes yielding *outputs* (finished products), which, according to the figure, meet all the needs of the customer as noted on the *customer scorecards* shown.

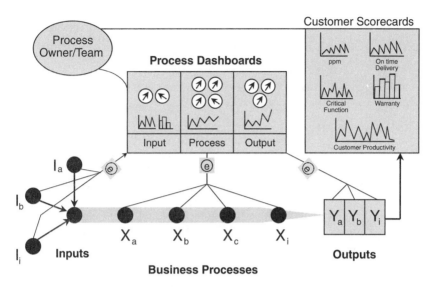

Figure 5.2 The elements of process management.

At the same time, in this ideal state of affairs, *process dashboards* (the tools by which the company ensures that inputs, processes, and outputs are all meeting the specifications of customers) are all glowing green, showing that all requirements of inputs, processes, and outputs are being met. Meanwhile, the whole process is being watched over by process owners and process teams that monitor the mechanism to make sure this company remains a well-oiled commercial machine, meeting the needs of customers in efficient, cost-effective ways. (Read more about this in Chapter 6.)

That's the way Six Sigma works. It effectively aligns all of the organizational components necessary (i.e., suppliers, process inputs, business processes, process outputs) to meet the needs of customers on a consistent, continuing basis. But how does an organization get to the point of sustained process management? Or move toward it?

The first challenge a company faces is to gather high-quality information about customers and the marketplace, and to leverage this internally to drive process development or redesign. Only with good information in hand can a company configure or design its processes to meet the requirements of customers. But as Figure 5.3 reveals, it can be a challenge to understand what customers really want and need. For example:

➤ Do your customers make purchase decisions based on quality, cost, delivery, service/safety, the degree to which a company demonstrates corporate responsibility? Or on some mix of all of these?
➤ Do you actually know your customers' critical customer requirements (CCRs), their rates of repurchase, and the degree to which sales of one product lead to others?

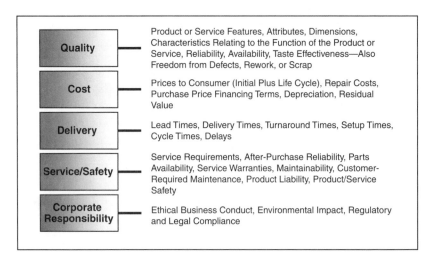

Figure 5.3 What do customers want? The challenge is to understand how your customers define and prioritize the various needs and expectations they have of your products and services.

➤ Can you distinguish between those variables that influence customer satisfaction and those that contribute to long-term customer loyalty and retention?

➤ How can you effectively collect these facts not just once but on a continual basis—as part of process development and design, and as part of strategy development and execution?

■ DON'T ASSUME YOU UNDERSTAND WHAT YOUR CUSTOMERS NEED (WANT)

As we said earlier, a company shouldn't take it for granted that it can read the minds of its customers, or that it intuitively understands their needs, which may be more complex or changeable than a company wants to believe. For that reason, a key tenet of Strategic Six Sigma philosophy is to take an *outside-in* approach to building a business. In other words, a company must build and configure itself to meet the needs of the external marketplace, not the other way around. Organizational consultant and change author Dr. Warner Burke of Teacher's College, Columbia University, describes this as the modern-day business imperative companies face to "let service to customers drive their organizational structure." Consequently, a key component of Strategic Six Sigma requires listening to the voice of the customer (VOC) in all the venues where customers interact with a company, so that it can develop a comprehensive understanding of customers' requirements.

■ TAKE AN OUTSIDE-IN PERSPECTIVE TO UNDERSTANDING YOUR CUSTOMERS

More than that, however, the goal of Strategic Six Sigma is to develop a comprehensive profile of customers—to understand a customer's industry, its operating constraints, competitive pressures, trends in its own marketplace, its relationships with its own customers, and other forces that impact the customer's buying attitudes, its profit margins, and how that customer interacts with *you*, their supplier.

It is for this reason that *market-smart* Strategic Six Sigma companies like Dow and Caterpillar make the leveraging of customer loyalty a key business goal. They see it as the foundation for enduring marketplace predominance, sustained financial strength, and continuing revenue growth. Dow is involved in a number of Six Sigma projects designed to better understand customer loyalty issues and to leverage this understanding into all Dow businesses. Caterpillar, meanwhile, is employing the use of a newly revitalized internal business intelligence unit, numerous Six Sigma tools and teams, and various industry councils to better understand the needs of Caterpillar customers worldwide, and to leverage this understanding across the company's entire value chain—from research and development (R&D) and product testing through manufacturing, sales, marketing, distribution, servicing, and account management.

There are many potential ways for companies to tap the VOCs. In the past, anecdotal information gathered from salespeople, customer service representatives, and others on a business's front lines often played a major role in the development of corporate marketing strategies, sales approaches, and product and service sets. While still helpful, such data do not provide the statistical validity or reliability required for the expenditure of large amounts of capital for product development or business strategy execution today. Moreover, such anecdotal information can be like Swiss cheese—full of holes and gaps, the knowledge of which is essential to effective strategy planning and business execution—especially today.

Similarly, while the firsthand street wisdom about markets and customers often shared by members of top leadership teams in discussions of business strategy has always factored in the formulation of business plans and strategic goals, this kind of information can be flawed as well, and should never be used as the sole data source in planning and executing business strategy. It is often subjective, sometimes dated, and seldom substantive enough to provide a real-time basis for the rapid development of business strategies and marketplace goals in a quickly changing business environment.

ROBUST APPROACHES FOR GATHERING VOC INFORMATION

What's needed today are more rigorous and systematic tools for gathering customer data and market intelligence. Tools such as focus groups; VOC surveys; telephone interviews; transaction surveys (which probe individual customers' experiences of specific customer transactions); customer panels; intense, on-site customer visits by executives and Six Sigma process teams; and client education events are just a few of the mechanisms a company can use to gather customer requirements and market intelligence data.

It's also important to have disciplined and consistent mechanisms in place to capture and resolve customer complaints, deal with customer queries, and leverage the knowledge gathered in these interactions back into the design or redesign of business processes, marketing strategies, and changes in work habits or business activities. Companies such as American Express, L.L. Bean, Mercedes-Benz, USAA Insurance, and Sun MicroSystems are especially well known for leveraging customer intelligence back into the modification of existing processes, and into the development of new systems and approaches to service customers and manage customer relationships.

"Voice-of-the-Customer Surveys and other, rigorously developed customer engagement tools can help companies acquire a wealth of customer data and marketplace intelligence," notes Jim Niemes, a senior PricewaterhouseCoopers (PwC) consultant who has worked with several PwC clients in implementing Six Sigma programs. "If carefully analyzed and sorted, that information can then be fed back into the organization, affecting how key processes are designed, and how the organization relates to customers on a going-forward basis."[1]

Unfortunately, many companies experience roadblocks in reaching out to customers, gathering critical data, and leveraging that knowledge to tweak work processes, change workflows, or change how customers are serviced. Turf wars among competing parts of an organization can be one problem, when people hoard information and don't collaborate with others to solve company-wide customer problems.

A bigger problem, according to Niemes, is that many companies simply don't know what questions to ask their customers in order to develop a better and more detailed understanding of customer needs. "A couple of years ago my bank called me—of course it was at dinnertime—and wanted to ask me a series of questions about customer service," he says. "A guy asked me five minutes worth of questions and when he finished I said to him, 'You realize that you forgot to ask me one critical question: "What's the most important thing we as a bank do to keep you happy as a customer?"'" Niemes says something as simple as a company committing itself to asking its customers, "What's most important to you about the services we provide?" on a regular basis can make all the difference between business success and failure. "Some companies never ask that question of their customers," he says.[1]

■ KEY STEPS TO MAKE A COMPANY MORE CUSTOMER-CENTRIC

What steps can a company take to ensure that it has the systems in place to capture customer and marketplace data in consistent ways, and on a regular basis? Early on in the Strategic Six Sigma deployment process, (ideally in step 1, discussed in Chapter 4) a CEO and top leadership team must ask themselves some key questions, even before the work of Strategic Six Sigma DMAIC and DFSS teams gets underway. For example:

➤ What are the short- and long-term metrics (with targets) that define success for our business? (In other words, what makes up the company's family of measures?)

➤ How do these metrics roll up into measuring both business unit/division performance and overall customer satisfaction?

➤ What other systems and techniques should we use to capture, analyze, and incorporate customer and marketplace data into the design of business processes, marketing strategies, products, and services?

➤ To what extent does this organization's culture and values currently support enterprise-wide information sharing and the consistent use of customer and marketplace knowledge to drive competitive advantage?

Open-ended questions such as these provide the basis for a CEO and top leadership team to evaluate not only existing performance gaps, but also culture, systems, and organizational design issues that need to be addressed as part of deploying Strategic Six Sigma inside the organization.

For example, if a company's culture doesn't foster collaborative teamwork, enterprise-wide information sharing, or effective coordination and collaboration among operating units or business divisions, these issues need to be addressed, before consistent approaches to customer and marketplace data gathering can be put in place and sustained. If the company's current information technology (IT) systems are outmoded and ill-suited to supporting Six Sigma work approaches and consistent customer and marketplace data collection, these systems must be updated to support these goals.

Finally, if top management is not deeply committed to leveraging customer and marketplace data as a competitive weapon, work is required to instill these imperatives at the top of the organization, and cascade these values down to leaders at *all* levels.

■ LEVERAGING VOC DATA INTO A REFINED SET OF CUSTOMER REQUIREMENTS

Strategic Six Sigma is concerned with translating the raw data collected as part of both anecdotal (and more formal) data-gathering efforts, into precisely defined and well-understood customer requirements, against which current levels of process performance by a company can be measured. Critical customer requirements, in other words, must be known and measured, if a company is to effectively deploy Strategic Six Sigma inside its organization.

■ DEFINING CCRS

To accomplish this, a company must have closed-loop processes in place to gather customer and market intelligence data. Next, it needs the capacity to translate that data into hard measurements that can be analyzed regularly and compared with business process outputs. If CCRs are not defined to the point that a clear target with specifications is established, they are not useful in determining a company's current defect levels. Managing by fact means calibrating and readjusting one's business processes to the point that they exactly meet the needs of customers on a consistent basis—with as little variation from this performance as possible. This is where DMAIC and DFSS Six Sigma project teams begin their important work.

■ COLLECTING CUSTOMER AND MARKET-PLACE DATA AS PART OF LAUNCHING IMPROVEMENT EFFORTS

The collection of raw data from which CCRs are developed is accomplished in two ways: (1) from regular VOC efforts a company undertakes (telephone surveys, periodic focus groups, etc.) and (2) from data gathering that DMAIC and DFSS Six Sigma project teams do, once they've been chartered to tackle specific business problems. While teams may initially be chartered based on the analysis of existing in-house data, they must quickly embark on their own data-gathering efforts to clarify the real customer issues that will become the focus of their improvement efforts. The work of DMAIC and DFSS teams proceeds, therefore, using a rigorous approach to determine CCRs.

■ THE DIFFERENCE BETWEEN DMAIC AND DFSS TEAMS

The DMAIC projects focus on improving existing processes, products, or services by analyzing current problems, identifying defects, and undertaking specific improvement efforts. The DFSS projects, on the other hand, focus on designing *new* processes, products, or services. In either case, customer input (in the form of CCRs) forms the basis of the work that the teams undertake. Upon successfully completing projects and generating concrete and measurable results from them, a company will then take the learning and improvements realized as part of a project and replicate it elsewhere using process management techniques.

➤ What DMAIC Teams Focus On

In DMAIC projects, identifying customers' process, product, or service requirements (CCRs) is a critical part of initially defining the opportunities for process, product, or service improvement. (See Figure 5.4.) In the *Define Opportunities* phase of DMAIC projects, for example, a project team will ask itself questions such as these:

- ➤ Who is our customer?
- ➤ What are we trying to fix or avoid?
- ➤ Where's the variation in meeting CCRs?
- ➤ What is the impact on the business?
- ➤ How will this project benefit the customer?
- ➤ What are the measurable CCRs or CTQs?

Subsequent steps in the DMAIC process involve verifying customers' requirements for product, service, or process changes; analyzing opportunities for improvement; putting

- Focuses on real problems directly related to the bottom line

- Realizes results in 4-6 months

- Utilizes multiple tools and techniques, including rigorous statistical methods when needed

- Sustains improvement over the long term

- Disseminates improvement throughout the organization

- Acts as an agent of change

Figure 5.4   Elements of Strategic Six Sigma: the DMAIC process. The DMAIC methodology focuses on driving process, product, or service improvements by omitting unproductive steps, developing/applying new metrics, and using technology to drive improvement.

improvements in place; and piloting and assessing the success of improved processes.

➤ What DFSS Teams Focus On

Design for Six Sigma projects proceed in a similarly robust way. They undertake data gathering to determine customer and marketplace requirements for new products, services, or processes. They develop customer research plans; identify and segment customers to be researched; determine CCRs through careful data collection, segmentation, and quality function deployment; identify and benchmark levels of performance in other organizations; and develop and implement product, service, or process designs based on their research. Extensive periods of testing, measuring performance, and evaluating and tweaking of designs then follows, leading to finalizing of design efforts and the development of a new process within an organization. (See Figure 5.5.)

Both DMAIC and DFSS project teams undertake their efforts, using what's known as an *action learning approach* to problem solving. Because they deal with product, service, or process issues that may never have been dealt with by their companies before, DMAIC and DFSS projects require enormous amounts of teamwork, trust, creativity, risk taking, and collaborative decision making to succeed— whether the end goal is to pilot concepts for redesigned processes or to field-test new designs of products, services, and processes. Figure 5.6 reveals that the ultimate analysis of CCRs will indicate whether a specific process needs to be improved (a DMAIC initiative) or designed from scratch (a DFSS initiative).

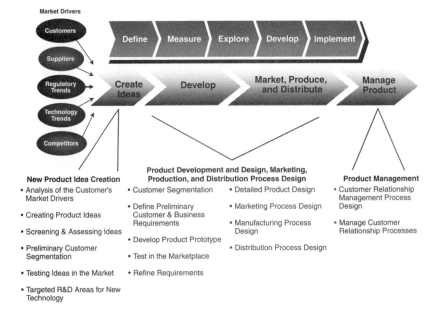

Figure 5.5 The DFSS relationship to product life cycle.

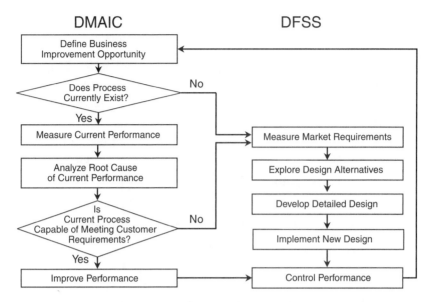

Figure 5.6 Strategic Six Sigma principles. Strategic Six Sigma principles help a company to decide whether to improve (DMAIC) or design (DFSS).

■ DEVELOPING STRONG QUESTION SETS: A CRITICAL PART OF BOTH DMAIC AND DFSS PROJECT TEAM EFFORTS

Because Strategic Six Sigma relies on the careful collection, correlation, analysis, and application of facts to drive both process improvement (DMAIC) and process design (DFSS) efforts, care must be taken in data gathering to accurately determine customers' requirements and to discern market trends that ultimately can affect long-term customer profitability and viability. For these reasons, it's vital that companies develop good question sets for use as part of both DMAIC and DFSS Six Sigma projects. Six Sigma project teams must develop these question sets in such a way that they answer not only basic questions about customer requirements (e.g., what contributes to overall customer satisfaction), but also generate an understanding of what fosters long-term customer loyalty and business retention. In other words, project teams must be certain question sets are rigorous and thorough enough to create a fully developed picture of a customer's requirements not just today but also in the future. This requires that DMAIC and DFSS question sets be able to get at multiple levels of information about specific subjects. For example, as part of determining a customer's key business requirements, it is important to ask detailed questions of the customer regarding

➤ Its own customers and competitors
➤ Its internal business processes
➤ Operating constraints
➤ Supply chain issues and difficulties
➤ Competitive and marketplace pressures
➤ Issues with other suppliers or strategic partners

When we work with companies, we focus a good deal of time on helping them develop the question sets that must be at the heart of determining CCRs and launching both DMAIC and DFSS projects to address them. We can't overstate the importance of data collection as part of determining CCRs. The fact-based nature of Six Sigma requires the rigorous and highly organized collection and leveraging of customer and marketplace data on a continuous basis, not just to cut costs and improve processes, but to help generate growth and drive business strategies forward. (See the sidebar, "How Lockheed Martin Is Using Six Sigma Principles to Develop and Manufacture the F-35 Joint Strike Fighter.")

HOW LOCKHEED MARTIN IS USING SIX SIGMA PRINCIPLES TO DEVELOP AND MANUFACTURE THE F-35 JOINT STRIKE FIGHTER

When it comes to meeting CCRs, few companies face more daunting challenges (or more demanding customers) than Lockheed Martin Corporation. In 2001, the Bethesda, Maryland–based defense contractor, which had 2,000 sales surpassing $25 billion, was chosen by the Pentagon to build the Joint Strike Fighter (JSF), a stealthy, multipurpose, next-generation jet fighter that will be used by the U.S. Air Force, Navy, and Marine Corps, as well as the U.K. Royal Air Force and Royal Navy.

The nearly $200 billion contract, the largest in Department of Defense history, calls for the building of more than 3,000 aircraft over an expected 40-year life of the program. It will involve Lockheed Martin in a joint venture not only with the Pentagon, but also with two strategic business partners: Northrop Grumman and BAE Systems of Great Britain.

To effectively coordinate the building of the JSF will require "enormous focus on critical customer requirements." That's according to Mike Joyce, Vice President of LM-21, Lockheed Martin's enterprise-wide continuous improvement initiative that blends the use of Six Sigma, Lean, and Kaizen improvement approaches to drive process improvements throughout all of Lockheed Martin's business operations.[*] For example, the Pentagon needs an "Air Force version of the JSF that has quick up-and-away range and payload capability," a Navy version "for aircraft carrier operation," and a Marine Corps version that's able to do "vertical launch and setdown like a Harrier Jet," says Joyce. Six Sigma methods and techniques will be critical to meeting all these customer requirements, because they enable "structured problem solving," he says.

[*]Mike Joyce, interview with Richard Koonce, PricewaterhouseCoopers, Bethesda, MD, 11 October 2001.

(Continued)

(Continued)

But while versatile aircraft design is a key priority for the JSF project, so, too, is affordability. "In our product designs, we frequently work at the edge of new technologies. In addition, we must factor in affordability as well," notes Joyce. Already, the value of Six Sigma principles and work practices to JSF design has borne fruit. Before Lockheed Martin was even awarded the JSF contract, Joyce says application of Six Sigma tools and approaches played a big role in helping the company shrink the anticipated production cycle for a single JSF from 12 months (typical today for the F-16) to just 5 months (with a defined path that could get that to 2.1 months.)

As JSF production proceeds, Joyce says Six Sigma will play a vital role in helping to align Lockheed Martin's program management with the Pentagon's own mirror organization that will be overseeing the project. This will ensure that Lockheed Martin engineers, aircraft designers, and technicians engage in a continuously fact-based dialogue with Pentagon officials and military brass about design requirements, and are constantly incorporating those discussions into ongoing efforts. "The program [Six Sigma project] managers we assign to specific projects spend lots of time with the customer," says Joyce. "Moreover, we have a very strong programmatic culture that has ways of cascading customer requirements throughout the organization once they have been identified. This is our structured way of keeping the [critical-to-customer] attributes of the product in front of our design team."

Joyce says Six Sigma work approaches will optimize workflow by streamlining production steps and eliminating waste, variation, and nonproductive activities. That's critical when a firm is building thousands of aircraft over many years, and must coordinate highly complex work efforts on the part of both individuals and teams. "Optimization of [workflow] is very challenging," says Joyce. "In our business, we flow molecules to make products and data bits that lead to decision or action. Typically however, the businesses we've been in have not been optimized for flow. Instead, they've been organized to optimize tasks or functional activity."

Finally, Joyce sees Six Sigma principles (in conjunction with Lean Enterprise and Kaizen techniques) as being crucial to creating a robust value chain to support JSF development and production. For example, Six Sigma work approaches will be vital to developing a reliable, error-free aircraft system design that eliminates as much variability from the weapon system and (eventual performance) as possible. "Where Six Sigma comes in as a tool set, is right upfront in [aircraft] design. It demands that you account for variation in the design process" at the beginning of the R&D cycle, he says. This is important to affordability because shrinking Pentagon budgets and increasingly complex performance requirements no longer allow aircraft manufacturers to take years of test flights and multiple prototypes to develop designs and build systems. Instead, defense contractors face enormous pressures to condense their R&D cycles and embed new technologies in military hardware and equipment as rapidly as possible. When you make "the elimination of variability a design task" in the early stages of aircraft manufacturing, "you can approach 100 percent quality levels [with subsequent production] quickly." — *The Authors*

■ WHY FACTS PROVIDE SUCH A POWERFUL BASIS FOR DECISION MAKING

Today, more than ever, companies need to be managed by *fact,* and use of Six Sigma practices and principles provides a company with a powerful empirical foundation for business decision making. The use of empirical data to drive business decision making has an important effect at catalyzing leadership and organizational energy around critical business goals. When all the members of a corporate leadership team are working with the same fact set, it eliminates the unsupported assertions and unsubstantiated opinions that often factor in corporate decision making in boardrooms today. It can also accelerate development of strong top-team unity, shared perspectives, and collective commitment to specific business goals and how best to achieve them.

Being able to gather customer and marketplace intelligence, analyze it, and act on it on a regular basis is part of ensuring that a company's feedback loop stays closed, and that a company consistently measures its performance against current customer and market requirements. While significant adjustments are often required when incorporating Strategic Six Sigma approaches into the ways a company gathers and analyzes customer/marketplace information, the financial results can be powerful and quickly apparent. Indeed, if a company commits itself to management by fact, it often improves efficiency and cuts the costs of doing business almost immediately. In so doing, it is likely to enhance levels of customer service, increase responsiveness, and create positive marketplace and customer perceptions.

■ CHAPTER SUMMARY

This chapter has focused on the importance of companies developing sophisticated and accurate mechanisms with which to capture and analyze customer and marketplace information. It has also discussed how such data ultimately find their way into the pursuit of specific DMAIC and DFSS Six Sigma projects. Finally, this chapter has emphasized why the consistent and accurate collection of VOC and voice of the marketplace (VOM) data are critical both to ensuring continually high levels of customer satisfaction (as part of Strategic Six Sigma initiatives), and as part of creating a customer-centric culture that emphasizes a strategic approach to customer care.

As this chapter outlines, creating a customer-centric culture is not easy. It requires that a company's leaders pay close attention to creating a business culture that supports team-based work, strong organizational alignment, metrics, and a total focus on serving customer needs. For many companies, this requires that they banish bureaucracy, punch holes in organizational stovepipes, and combat the inertia that often thwarts companies from readily transforming themselves into more efficient and productive enterprises. It also means embracing the idea of *strategic customer care* as a core business value and embedding it in the very DNA of the organization.

➤ Best Practices Associated with Collection of Customer and Marketplace Data

With those things in mind, here are a few best practices that business leaders need to apply as part of planning and launching Strategic Six Sigma initiatives.

1. **Establish customer care as a core organizational and business focus.** Because Strategic Six Sigma is all about understanding the needs of customers and the marketplace, strategic care and servicing of customers needs to be the central tenet of a company's business activities. This is a message that must be continuously articulated by the CEO and top leadership team, and continually cascaded down through *all* levels and parts of the organization on a consistent and frequent basis. It needs to be the driving idea behind how the company functions, how processes are developed and designed, and how the product and service development process within the organization proceeds.

2. **Adopt an outside-in approach to customer and marketplace data collection.** Don't ever assume you

know what your customers need (want) or that you thoroughly understand the dynamics and currents of your industry and marketplace. Instead, assume the opposite, and make the disciplined, consistent, and frequent collection of customer and marketplace data not just an organizational goal but a leadership obsession, as well.

3. **Be ruthless about assessing your company's current VOC and VOM capabilities.** Are robust mechanisms, systems, and channels for collecting customer and marketplace information in place or not? If so, how good and reliable are they? Do they capture VOC and VOM data in frequent, consistent, and accurate ways? If so, is this information regularly fed back into the organization to change how products are produced, services are delivered, or processes are operated and designed? Can you point to an executive who owns the VOC and VOM processes for each market in your company? If VOC and VOM capabilities are weak, you need to bulk up your company's abilities in these areas. You need to align IT and other systems to support consistent and disciplined collection of customer and marketplace data, and create an internal climate of alignment to support enterprise-wide information sharing. The importance of this will be further emphasized in Chapter 6, where we talk about the importance of putting a business process framework in place to guide and sustain Strategic Six Sigma initiatives over the long term.

4. **Determine if you have adequately segmented and profiled your customers.** As a precursor to providing high levels of customer care, you will need to profile and segment your customer base. By grouping

customers according to current revenue stream and enhanced revenue potential (e.g., for sales of other products/services), you can isolate customers that represent the greatest potential for future business and continued customer loyalty.

5. **Be honest in determining whether your company is currently positioned to deploy a strong customer care strategy.** From a change management standpoint, your organization may need to examine what potentially hinders it from embracing change and deploying Strategic Six Sigma principles and practices.

6. **Focus on continuously realigning the top leadership team to support customer care goals and objectives.** As part of deploying Strategic Six Sigma in an organization, it is critical that companies appoint executive process owners to oversee key customer care processes. This creates strong ownership for Six Sigma ways of working, and it broadcasts the message to the organization that the top leadership is serious about deploying Six Sigma throughout the organization and holding both executives and employees accountable to customer care goals.

7. **Continually monitor how the company listens to customers, and be intentional about continuously refining these processes.** As part of fostering a culture of more consistent and strategic customer care, it will be critical to open channels both to customers and the marketplace using surveys, one-on-one telephone interviews, focus groups, and other means, such as benchmarking. Anecdotal information is useful, but only when reinforced with more formal data collection techniques. Many companies look upon customer service/research, account management, customer care

strategies, and complaint handling as cost centers. We submit, however, that in today's business environment, taking a comprehensive approach to customer relationship management is a market-smart strategy. It can help convert currently satisfied customers into long-term loyal customers.

If done well, embracing a strategic approach to customer care creates strong organizational focus, accelerates organizational change, enhances business responsiveness, and spurs customer loyalty. "When strategic customer care is working well, it's a win-win situation for you and your customers," writes Stanley Brown, author of *Strategic Customer Care: An Evolutionary Approach to Increasing Customer Value and Profitability.*[2] "The long-term relationships that result will, in turn, continue the cycle of profitability that will ensure your success."

Now that we've focused on the importance of developing a strong, customer-centric approach to data gathering as part of Strategic Six Sigma deployment, let's move on to Chapter 6. There we focus on the importance of business leaders developing a business process orientation to better organize and configure their companies to meet changing business requirements—based on the data they collect from both customers and the marketplace.

Chapter

Build a Business Process Framework to Sustain Strategic Six Sigma Efforts

[P]rocess management is more than a way of improving the performance of individual processes; it is also a way of operating and managing a business.

> —Dr. Michael Hammer
> "Process Management and
> the Future of Six Sigma"
> *Sloan Management Review,*
> Winter 2001

In Chapter 5, we discussed how critical it is that as part of deploying Strategic Six Sigma initiatives in an organization, a company first put disciplined processes in place to tap the voice of the customer (VOC) and the voice of the market-place (VOM). This enables companies to develop a fact-based knowledge and understanding of customer needs and marketplace trends.

In this chapter, we delve into the mechanics of creating a business process framework that leaders of a company can use to actually implement Strategic Six Sigma initiatives inside their organizations. We discuss process *baselining* and how to create process owners and metrics that will allow leaders to see how a company's key processes are performing against market requirements. We also focus on why leaders must develop a business process mind-set in order to configure their companies to meet changing customer needs, and why maintaining this perspective is imperative to long-term success with Six Sigma.

Because it is such a robust approach to business improvement, Six Sigma can, as noted, help a company realize quantum leaps in business performance improvement and competitiveness. But getting there requires a highly focused approach. For example, because it is based on quantitative analysis of a business and comparing a company's performance with customer requirements, Strategic Six Sigma cannot be implemented effectively in an organization without rigorous mapping of existing business processes. Moreover, there must be broad-based agreement by a company's leaders as to what those processes are, and what kind of output customers expect from them.

A company's core processes [marketing, sales, research and development (R&D), customer service, etc.] define its current business model or theory of how the business creates value for customers and thus shareowners. *Core processes* are characterized as:

> ➤ Delivering products and services that directly meet customer needs (and that customers are willing to pay for!)
> ➤ Being closely tied to the company's competencies
> ➤ Being part of the organization's identity with its customers and the marketplace

➤ Having the means to achieve the organization's expected return on investment (ROI)
➤ Differentiating the business from its competitors

It is the intersection of a company's core process outputs with critical customer requirements (CCRs) that ultimately defines process sigma as well as long-term business success for a company. Being able to examine (and close) the gap between what a business produces and what customers demand is the essence of Six Sigma. The width of the gap (or the process sigma value) can be used to prioritize Six Sigma improvement efforts.

Organizations that identify improvement projects, not as isolated endeavors, but as strategic improvement activities within a company's business process framework will achieve a faster ROI. They're more focused and impactful because they work at the nexus of product or service output and market demand, instead of relying solely on intuition. (See Figure 6.1.)

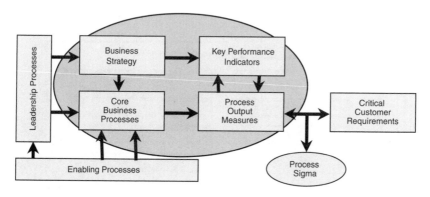

Figure 6.1 Align improvements to core processes and key performance indicators.

■ DRIVING A BUSINESS PROCESS MIND-SET IN YOUR ORGANIZATION

Building a business process framework requires that a CEO and his or her top leadership team first possess a business process orientation to the business. In other words, they must stop seeing their organization as a collection of independent business activities and siloed business functions, and instead view the business as a family of interrelated and interdependent business processes, all of which must be carefully aligned and integrated to meet CCRs. (See Figure 6.2.)

Developing a business process framework is about recognizing the importance of this alignment and constantly adjusting core business processes to stay in sync with customer needs and large-scale marketplace requirements. To achieve this alignment, the business must measure each process comprehensively. (See Figure 6.3.) This mapping and measuring of business processes is referred to as *process baselining* in the GE Six Sigma lexicon, and it provides a perspective on the health of the business that can give its

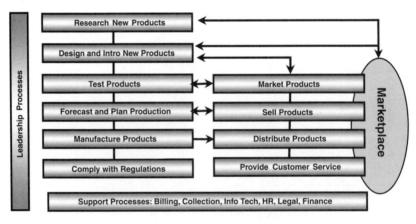

Figure 6.2 Strategic Six Sigma applies Six Sigma practices and principles enterprise-wide.

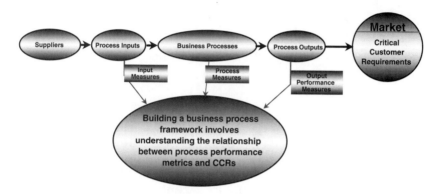

Figure 6.3   Building a business process framework.

leaders key insights into where Six Sigma improvement teams should focus to identify high-yield projects.

The CEO and senior leadership team can begin to build a process mind-set by first understanding their own activities as an integrated portfolio of executive-level governance processes that are required to set corporate direction and strategy: develop and allocate resources, manage risk, and align the organization to assure achievement of its long-term goals. (See Figure 6.4. Also, see the sidebar, "Six Sigma

Figure 6.4   Leadership processes. Leadership processes are owned by the senior leadership team.

Provides a Powerful Approach and Toolkit for Operating a
Business.") Second, the senior leadership team must ask
itself some hard questions. For example:

**SIX SIGMA PROVIDES A POWERFUL APPROACH
AND TOOLKIT FOR OPERATING A BUSINESS**

"Six Sigma provides a powerful approach, toolkit, and mind-
set with which to get all the leaders of a business onto the
same song sheet," says Pierre Lortie, president and chief
operating officer of Bombardier Transportation.* "Going forward, it is going to help us deal with the challenges of history,
geography, and language that now face Bombardier Transportation as it operates on an increasingly global scale."

Lortie made these comments to us as he reflected on
Bombardier's long history of mergers and acquisitions,
including its 2001 acquisition of Adtranz (formerly Daimler-
Chrysler Rail Systems), a move that added thousands of new
employees to Bombardier's payroll in Europe and Asia.

"If you look at Bombardier today, we are an amalgama-
tion of some 40 national companies, each with its own culture and traditions," says Lortie. Bombardier employees in
these formerly independent companies work in some 43
countries and speak languages ranging from Czech and Ger-
man, to Polish and English, he says. And while Lortie
acknowledges that getting them all to operate as part of a single company currently represents a big challenge, he says
that the recent deployment of Six Sigma has already begun to
provide the company's employees worldwide with a "common language of metrics and processes for organizing how
we do our work." This "language of metrics transcends
national and cultural differences." Consequently, "I'm confi-
dent that Six Sigma will make us strong and successful in
meeting our customers needs, wherever our customers are."

—The Authors

*Pierre Lortie, interview with Richard Koonce, PricewaterhouseCoop-
ers, Montreal, PQ, Canada, 7 March 2002.

➤ Do we consistently fulfill customers' requirements or are there gaps in our performance?

➤ How do we measure precisely our customers' view of value?

➤ Where does our business performance stand in relation to our competitors? Do we exceed customer expectations, or do we have significant problems with customer satisfaction levels, customer loyalty, and customer retention?

➤ Do existing improvement initiatives and activities bring continuous, sustainable improvement to business processes (reduction in defects and costs or improvements in productivity and profitability)? Or, has the organization's business performance plateaued?

➤ Have we identified key risks in our business model that could jeopardize our business plan, and are we taking specific actions to assure these risks are minimized? Or, are we constantly in a reactionary, fire-fighting mode responding to regulators and changing market conditions?

➤ Are we (the CEO and senior leadership team) satisfied with how quickly we're able to adjust our business model to accommodate market changes? Or, are technological advances and competitors forcing changes and improvements on our company faster than it is able to accommodate?

➤ Is our organization convinced that it is monitoring the right leading performance indicators within our business processes to assure we will meet our stated business goals? Or, are we just adding up the numbers at the end of each week, month, and quarter and hoping for success?

The senior leadership team must own, measure, and improve the leadership processes in any company. Its responsibilities include keeping the business model continuously viable and profitable, and being certain that employees understand the company's direction and goals and their roles in helping it achieve its objectives. The senior leadership team must also develop the company's high-level strategic plans, and continuously assess performance against the quarterly and annual targets of the business plan. It must develop an expanded leadership team to cascade Six Sigma goals and requirements throughout the organization. Finally, it is responsible for driving continuous improvement in all business processes, which requires routine (at least annual) redefinition of the strategic improvement goals (SIGs) from which all Six Sigma projects are ultimately derived.

■ THE FIVE STEPS TO BUILDING A BUSINESS PROCESS FRAMEWORK

Implementing a business process framework within one's organization consists of five key steps, which a company's top leader must carry out.

➤ Step 1: Identify the Organization's High-Level (Level 1) Process Framework and the Subprocesses (Levels 2 and 3) That Comprise It

The first step in building a process framework is to fully lay out all of an organization's high-level (core) processes and all of the subprocesses that support those core processes. (See Figure 6.5.) Doing so provides an explicit and integrated organizational snapshot that is useful in understanding how

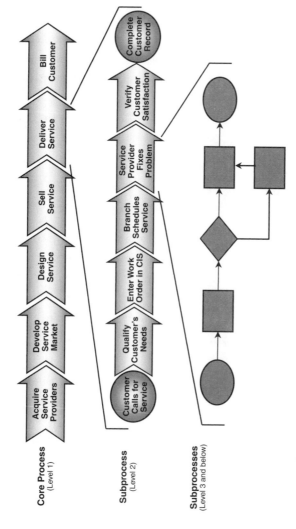

Figure 6.5 Process owners are assigned to core and subprocesses.

157

various processes and subprocesses work and relate to one another. Many companies undertake this endeavor as part of major reengineering or process innovation initiatives. Others build their process networks slowly and deliberately from the bottom up through their Six Sigma project work. In either case, it is important for leaders to create an integrated business process framework because the process-customer intersection that appears defines a business's value proposition to its customers. This intersection then becomes the focus of a company's improvement or design priorities.

➤ Step 2: Identify Key Senior Leaders as Process Owners with Accountability for Assigned Process Performance

In step 2, a company must identify key senior leaders to serve as level 1 process owners, who will be responsible for overseeing process improvement activities in key areas identified in step 1. To ensure that these individuals fulfill their roles effectively, key process improvement targets need to be built into executives' personal performance plans. Process owners also need to be selected to oversee improvements in level 2 and level 3 processes. By assigning clear accountability to key individuals for the improved output of its core processes, a company lays the groundwork to drive necessary changes in business activities at an operational level that will improve operating effectiveness and positively impact customer satisfaction levels. Executives who are chosen to be process owners do not give up their line or functional responsibilities. In most companies, they continue in their traditional functional roles while assuming the added responsibilities of process owners of core processes. In most companies, assigning the most logical person to be a process owner of a core process is a challenging task. That's because most core processes are cross-functional or cross-departmental, which means that finding a person with a sufficiently broad organizational perspective on how the process works can be difficult, especially if the company has historically been organized by functional silos. No one individual may have the breadth of experience needed for the task. This is why companies sometimes find it opportune to assign a process owner team of two or more executives to manage a process. If your company does this, be sure that all members of the process team are held accountable to the same metrics in their personal performance plans.

➤ Step 3: Establish a VOC Process for Internal and External Customers, and Identify CCRs for Each Process

Determining and staying in touch with changing customer and market requirements is a primary responsibility of process owners. Therefore, process owners should also own the VOC and the VOM processes that determine requirements for the product or service produced by their process. This requires that a company use all the information at its disposal to define customer and market trends and requirements. There are many ways to get this information as noted in Chapter 5. (See also Figure 6.6.) In any case, process owners must create continuous processes to convert customer and marketplace intelligence into useful data that can be used in process design or redesign efforts. Process owners must continuously redefine CCRs for each customer segment based on that segment's value equation (i.e., what it is that each customer segment is buying).

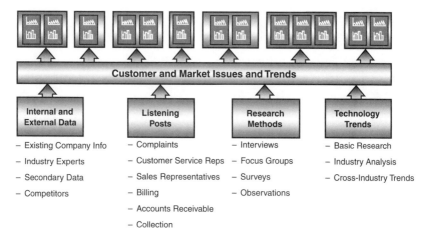

Figure 6.6 Developing CCRs. Customer segmentation and CCRs definition.

The segmentation process itself can be subtle and time-consuming. It may require careful delineation of CCRs within specific customer segments, or linking of CCRs to individual external or internal customers in some cases, if the customer is particularly important, and/or if the CCRs for that customer are unique.

➤ Step 4: Baseline Assigned Processes

Baselining is the practice of documenting the current performance of a process against both customer and business requirements. Defining process performance requires that process owners build an equation that can be described as $Y = f(X_{1,\ldots,n}, I_{1,\ldots,n})$, where Y is a process output measure, X represents the critical controllable metrics in the process that have the greatest impact on output performance, and I represents the critical input metrics that most significantly impact variation in the process outputs. (See Figure 6.7.)

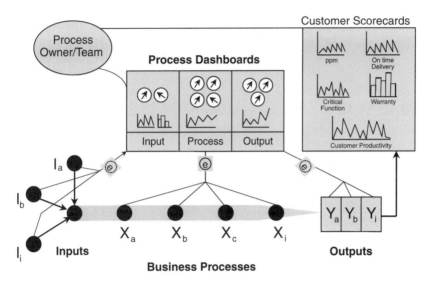

Figure 6.7 Process owners create dashboards and scorecards.

Over time, process owners need to build process dashboards as well as customer scorecards that provide real-time information on process performance. Identifying and wiring up these metrics takes excellent process knowledge, lots of time, and requires the best information technology a company can get its hands on. Often, they must be built manually and wired up as the information technology (IT) becomes capable of supporting the data needs of the process team.

➤ Step 5: Establish SIGs Based on Process Performance Gaps

Another primary responsibility for process owners and their teams is to regularly analyze process performance to identify, prioritize, and commission DMAIC and DFSS Six Sigma projects that continuously improve process metrics and customer satisfaction. Selecting improvement projects from this process performance perspective is one of the significant advantages of Strategic Six Sigma thinking.

■ IS YOUR ORGANIZATION MEASURING THE RIGHT THINGS?

We typically find, as we work with CEOs and senior leadership teams in the early stage of a Strategic Six Sigma deployment effort, that they often are measuring a lot of things, but not necessarily the most important things, or to a sufficient level of granularity. For example, many companies focus almost exclusively on result indicators. A CEO and senior leadership team may be measuring a certain result indicator when, instead, they should be looking at certain predictive or leading indicators. [In our preceding discussion of the process performance equation $Y = F(X, I)$, the leading or predictive indicators are the Xs and Is, while the output or result is the Y.] Predictive or leading indicators help organizations tell ahead of time if a certain level of productivity or efficiency is going to be attained, whether stated sales/revenue targets are going to be reached, or if a certain level of defect reduction will be realized. An example of a predictive measure would be the total number of sales calls and proposals a sales organization generates each month, the number of which helps forecast the likely number of closed sales to be generated within a specified period of time. Six Sigma projects and analysis uncover and help companies to refine and document their knowledge of these vital few predictive indicators. Controlling these critical predictive metrics prevents the creation of rework loops—the hidden factory—and allows the business to prevent defects from reaching the customer.

■ DOES YOUR COMPANY NEED TO DEVELOP A MORE COMPREHENSIVE SET OF INDICATORS?

In other cases, we find that an organization may have to develop a more comprehensive and sophisticated family of performance measures—to track conformance of supplier inputs to standardized requirements, to gauge business performance across a spectrum of internal process indicators (efficiency, productivity, reduced cycle times, etc.), and finally, to fully assess all the dimensions of customer satisfaction. With regard to this last point, for example, it's not enough in business today for a company to simply track overall levels of customer satisfaction. It must track customer satisfaction, loyalty, retention, and repurchase. It must be able to track particulars such as the level of customer satisfaction against key buying attributes, and other key criteria. A CEO and top leadership team need to discuss what will constitute the appropriate family of measures early in the Strategic Six Sigma implementation process, because it lays the critical groundwork for what comes next.

■ DEVELOPING A FAMILY OF MEASURES

In many cases, it will be important for the CEO and senior leadership team to track a family of metrics (e.g., result indicators, customer indicators, and predictive indicators) so that an organization provides itself a wide-angled snapshot of business processes, and the extent to which a given process is exactly meeting the requirements of customers. A study of leading improvement-driven organizations, conducted by a consulting firm, found that such improvement-driven companies typically pay close attention to a family of metrics as part of ensuring continuous process redesign and customer satisfaction; the conviction being that measuring performance based on a single (or small number of) metrics does not provide a comprehensive enough view of business operations and may, in fact, obscure problems or quality issues that need to be addressed. Figure 6.8 provides a snapshot of a typical executive dashboard. Beneath each item is a hot link to specific metrics about that particular metric.

Another thing we find in working with CEOs and their top leadership teams is that, in many cases, a company may be measuring the right things but doesn't have the closed-loop infrastructure, systems, and technology, as well as people in place to actually implement identified improvement initiatives. Still another challenge companies often face in implementing truly enterprise-wide business process frameworks is largely cultural. Many companies are made up

INVENTORY EFFECTIVENESS	DELIVERY RELIABILITY	RETURN MANAGEMENT	ACCTS. RECEIVABLE EFFECTIVENESS	SHIPPING EFFICIENCY	DATA COLLECTION
Inventory Reliability	On Time Delivery Reliability (ICON)	Return Rate	Invoice Aging	Total Shipping Costs and Air/Ground Breakout	Inventory Data
Unfilled Units and Segmentation	Delivery Defects and Segmentation	New Release Return	Key Ratios - As a % of Total Invoiced	Unit Shipping Costs	Delivery Reliability
Zero Ships and Segmentation		Return Processing Efficiency	Segmentation of Key Ratios by Customer	Interbranch Costs	Return Processing
Inventory Level			Credits and Writeoffs by Reason	Carrier Performance Metrics	Shipping Reliability
Forecast and Returns-New Releases			Pricing Discrepancies		Accounts Receivable
Product A/B Ratio					

Figure 6.8 An executive dashboard map. Dashboards enable a company's executives and managers to track the performance of core processes and their alignment with customer expectations.

of individual business divisions that historically have operated independently. To become elements of a business process framework they must learn to become much more *interdependent* in how they work with one another. This is one of the organizational challenges Caterpillar faced at the beginning:

"We're learning a lot about process ownership, and what an organization needs to do to support it," says Dave Burritt, Corporate 6 Sigma Champion at Caterpillar.[1]

One of the things our Chairman did was to put in place a new position, a systems and processes division Vice President, Sid Banwart. He's the CIO of our organization. He has responsibility for IT and Process Improvement and I report to that position. So what we're doing is integrating Processes and IT to make sure there's a unifying framework for pursuing 6 Sigma projects. We're using DMAIC and DMEDI (a.k.a. DFSS). We're using DMAIC for process improvement and DMEDI for process creation. And we're firm with that. We have to refine our processes, identify process owners, we have to give our process owners teeth. We're in the infant stages with this, but there's good work going on.[1]

The process focus that supports 6 Sigma also has to be clearly lined up with a company's strategy, says Burritt. "Your Black Belts have to see how a certain project lines up to support the strategic goals of the organization. And you have to help them focus on the customer, see through the whole value chain, not stop at an internal process partner, but be sure to get to the end of the process, to the end customer."[1]

Like Caterpillar, Bombardier Transportation is also learning a lot about process management today and its importance to sustaining high levels of business performance. The company's recent acquisition of DaimlerChrysler Rail Systems (Adtranz) greatly expanded Bombardier's potential market for rail passenger equipment and transportation systems and its geographical presence. To be effective in these markets, company executives realized that they needed a new business process framework through which to run their increasingly globalized business operations. Building that framework is now a work in progress, says Desmond Bell, Bombardier Transportation's vice president of Six Sigma, and is focused on a number of key areas of the business, including the bidding process, new product development, and project management:

> *Our bidding process is obviously a key process for us because it's the way we win work. We identified it last year as a key process that we had to significantly improve. For one thing we had to take costs out, whilst improving risk management. We also had to reduce cycle times for putting bids together, because there's a growing number of projects on which we're being asked to bid today, especially in Europe. So, we have to have a very nimble process. Another process we're working on is a new product development process. We have full-time Master Agents (MBBs) working with a cross-functional team to develop that process right the first time. Still another process we're working on is our project management process. In the transportation business how you make money is based on how you manage your projects, your contracts, so we're using Six Sigma to help us design and implement a new project management system.[2]*

■ CHAPTER SUMMARY

This chapter has discussed why it is so important for a company's top executives to establish a business process framework (and to adopt a process management mind-set) as part of successfully coordinating and rolling up the financial benefits of individual Six Sigma projects to improve overall business performance. Organizing and managing Strategic Six Sigma initiatives using a process management umbrella affords companies the opportunity to integrate all their Six Sigma initiatives and to leverage project benefits across the organization. (See the sidebar, "Seven Ways Air Products and Chemicals Delivers Customer Value and Business Results.") Furthermore, it enables a company to focus only on those projects that hold the most promise of reaping significant financial results and operational improvements. It does this by creating strong line-of-sight alignment linking individual Six Sigma projects, SIGs, and the ultimate achievement of

---

**SEVEN WAYS AIR PRODUCTS AND CHEMICALS
DELIVERS CUSTOMER VALUE AND BUSINESS RESULTS**

Developing quantitative measures to track and improve business performance is a powerful way for companies to get in touch not just with customer needs, but also with their own business strengths. At Air Products and Chemicals, for example, an international supplier of industrial gases and equipment, and specialty chemicals, the Gases Division determined that it had seven basic processes that added value to customer transactions and impacted financial results. So, the Customer Engagement Team (CET) identified what these seven processes were and developed metrics to go with each. The team also identified the financial impacts associated with delivering customer satisfaction in each process, developed plans to improve

(Continued)

(Continued)

its performance, and identified the key cross-functional players within Air Products' Gases Division that would be critical to making this happen. Developed and known as the *7 Ups,* these seven measures today continue to provide Air Products with critical business indicators for delivering service to customers.

The seven key processes, as shown in Figure 6.9, are:

1. Developing and introducing competitive offerings
2. Pursuing and committing to new customer needs
3. Initiating new customer service
4. Producing and making product available
5. Processing and fulfilling customer orders
6. Delivering payable invoices for cash receipt
7. Resolving customer complaints

Today, Air Products has extended these areas of focus to its global businesses. Notes George F. Diehl, Director of Global Process Management for the Gases Division of Air Products, "Using these metrics to manage the customer-facing processes resulted in higher rates of customer retention while meeting our productivity targets. We found that measurement, in a business process context, was our most important lever of change."

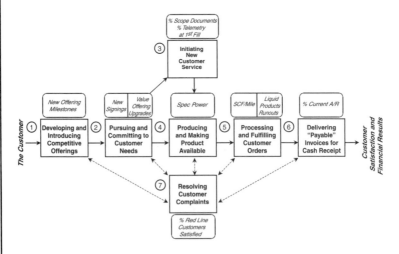

Figure 6.9 Air Products and Chemicals, Inc., Customer Engagement Process (CEP). *(Used by permission of Air Products and Chemicals.)*

168

specific large-gauge business objectives and strategies. In so doing, it avoids organizational confusion and the dissipation of organizational resources on unproductive projects and activities and aligns people, processes, and metrics around customer-focused goals.

➤ Best Practices Associated with Effective Process Management and the Establishment of a Business Process Framework

Establishing a business process framework in which to frame a company's Six Sigma initiatives (DMAIC and DFSS projects) requires a high degree of leadership focus and organizational discipline. Indeed, as the members of a senior leadership team come together to decide how best to move forward with Strategic Six Sigma, it is critical that they do the following:

1. **Think in enterprise-wide ways about the business.** They should avoid making decisions about Six Sigma projects based on strictly functional perspectives or, on where each individual has typically worked in the company's organizational structure. To facilitate executives thinking in boundaryless, enterprise-wide ways about the business, the CEO and top leadership team should develop an enterprise map of the business. Enterprise maps provide a global snapshot of a company's key business processes and subprocesses. They provide a compelling end-to-end visual or blueprint of the company's business model and value proposition.

2. **Come to a firm agreement about the company's overarching business goals, strategies, core processes, and key operational issues.** The CEO and top leadership team should expect discussions on these topics to be intense and even heated at first, especially if the heads

of different business units or divisions have been accustomed to operating independently of one another. Still, such discussions will prove healthy in the end. Such storming and forming in fact are an essential part of the team coming to a newfound consensus about enterprise-wide business issues and priorities, and how Strategic Six Sigma can be used to address them.

3. **Agree on specific performance metrics that will be used to assess business performance on an enterprise-wide basis.** To do this effectively, the CEO will need to challenge his or her direct reports to quantify their business goals and performance metrics. He or she must challenge top executives with questions such as, "What are we measuring now and why?" "How do we actually measure performance?" "Where are the gaps in our performance?" and "Do we truly understand what our customers need, or do we just think we do?"

4. **Cascade responsibility for Six Sigma projects to others in the organization, as appropriate.** As this chapter has shown, driving acceptance of a business process framework inside the organization requires cascading the priorities of Six Sigma initiatives to other levels of leaders inside the organization (Black Belts, process owners, champions, etc.) and driving the alignment of projects with articulated SIGs and business strategies. Leaders must do this both by empowering leaders at other levels, and by holding them accountable to specific and measurable performance targets.

5. **Develop appropriate real-time scorecards and dashboards in order to closely manage business performance (at least with the company's biggest and most significant customers.)** It takes time for a

company to develop finely tuned performance score-cards and process dashboards with which to monitor customer satisfaction and business performance on a real-time basis. Indeed, at the very beginning of a Strategic Six Sigma deployment, putting the systems, mechanisms, and structures in place to gather CCRs in a consistent and disciplined way takes a tremendous amount of legwork and leadership focus. Even then, dashboards and scorecards must periodically be redesigned to reflect changing customer parameters or business requirements. In any case, the payoffs from developing dashboards and scorecards are enormous, once the systems are in place, and leaders are able to monitor real-time company performance. It eliminates guesswork from decision making, and provides companies with a powerful empirical basis of information with which to assess customer satisfaction as well as business performance.

6. **Sustain an all-out commitment to work as an integrated process management executive team, even when difficulties are encountered.** For many companies, developing a business process framework emerges organically out of the task of identifying core processes and prioritizing business goals, priorities, and issues. *Retaining* an enterprise-wide focus to managing the business, and sustaining Strategic Six Sigma improvements through process management requires continued discipline by a CEO and the top leadership team. This can be difficult at times, because individual executives will need to retain a business process perspective on how the business operates, while also handling their day-to-day functional responsibilities within the organization.

7. Finally, as part of establishing process management in the organization, the CEO and top leadership team need to pay attention both to the explicit and implicit messages they send to the organization about its importance. There must be strong top-team unity around the priorities of Strategic Six Sigma deployment and the role that a business process framework plays in sustaining it. Moreover, rank-and-file employees need to see this commitment reflected in both the words and actions of leaders. The display of consistent leader behaviors around Strategic Six Sigma deployment, and the use of process management to sustain it, becomes very critical in building not just employee compliance to Six Sigma, but also long-term commitment to a Strategic Six Sigma way of working.

Let's go on now to Chapter 7, where we discuss the importance of developing quantifiable measures, and achieving concrete results from Strategic Six Sigma projects. Among other things, Chapter 7 will discuss the various filters an organization can use to select and prioritize strategic improvement projects. It will also show how such projects need to be tightly aligned to support one or more specific SIGs.

Chapter 7

Demand Quantifiable Results

Driving shareholder value is what executives get rewarded for.

— Popular Six Sigma saying

You need to make sure you quantify your 6 Sigma benefits, but also trace those benefits to the bottom line. That's because while cost, growth, quality, and reliability improvements from 6 Sigma can all flow to the bottom line, there are leaks in any company's operations that, if unaccounted for, will adversely affect the numbers you claim from 6 Sigma projects. They will give people the impression that the results you claim from 6 Sigma are soft and not real. This can badly damage the credibility of a 6 Sigma deployment.

— Denny Huber, Corporate 6 Sigma Metrics Manager
Caterpillar

As part of choosing and prioritizing Strategic Six Sigma initiatives, it's important that leaders choose DMAIC and DFSS projects whose successful completion will effectively impact the company's strategic improvement goals (SIGs). These SIGs represent optimal points of leverage in an organization where, if effort is effectively applied, tremendous improvements in customer satisfaction, core processes, or successful support of business strategy can be realized. It is through concerted activity and action directed at SIGs that organizations can ultimately realize quantum leaps in business perform-ance—be it in profitability, customer satisfaction, innovation, improved quality, or in any of many other indicators, as noted on a company's family of measures.

As Figure 7.1 reveals, SIGs lie at the nexus of customer requirements, core processes, and business strategies. It is an organization's SIGs that help drive the prioritization of potential Six Sigma projects, from which a final set of active projects is ultimately selected.

■ HOW TO PRIORITIZE SIX SIGMA DMAIC AND DFSS PROJECTS

How does a company go about prioritizing potential Strate-gic Six Sigma projects? There are a number of guidelines that leaders should use in evaluating the value and potential payback of Six Sigma projects.

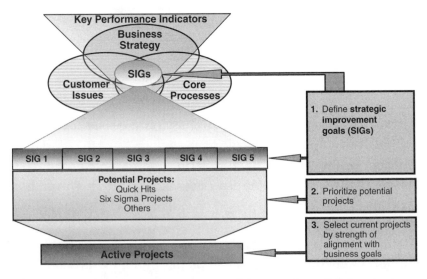

Figure 7.1 Creating alignment to achieve goals and drive strategy.

First, a company's leaders should put a premium on identifying projects with optimal, short-term benefits. The reasons are clear: If a company can secure some quick gains (wins) from initial Six Sigma project implementation, it helps build momentum for further projects down the line, in part by proving to people that Six Sigma approaches work, and by registering great benefits (cost reductions, cycle time reductions, improved efficiency, etc.) in a short period of time. In turn this helps overcome organizational resistance to change and drives cultural transformation (e.g., new ways of working, greater focus on accountability, the application of performance metrics to business processes, greater consensus about the efficacy of Six Sigma principles).

Second, projects should be chosen, based on a clear understanding of their potential financial impact to the organization. How much is a given Strategic Six Sigma project likely to generate in terms of cost savings, increased sales, reduced cycle times for new product development, or improved levels of customer service and satisfaction? While projects will vary, depending on their size, scope, and industry, some early projects, especially in industries such as chemicals and petroleum, have yielded $1 million to $2 million. A single project at a well-known entertainment company yielded over $10 million in benefits. It is not unusual for individual Six Sigma projects to generate $250,000 to $450,000 in pretax savings or increased sales/sales opportunities. Some companies, such as Dow Chemical, have achieved significantly greater results.

Third, understand where the organization is most likely to generate savings or improvements from specific Six Sigma projects. What is a Six Sigma benefit? Six Sigma benefits can accrue to an organization as the result of revenue increases, cost reductions, or productivity gains. *Level 1* benefits refer to benefits that directly impact on the company's overall profit margin (e.g., projects that have a clear, hard dollar impact on the profitability of the business). Here, we are talking about projects that decrease costs, increase revenue, or that lead to increased levels of customer satisfaction that thereby increase customer repurchases. *Level 2* projects are those that bring about the redeployment of resources where there is a budgeted need, thereby increasing operational efficiency or productivity. Here, we are speaking of projects that impact back-office operations of a company (e.g., that bring about greater efficiency in subprocesses that in turn support a company's core business processes or operations). *Level 3* projects are those that directly impact operations by avoiding expenditures or that increase the likelihood of increased revenues in the future.

To pass muster at one leading automaker, Six Sigma projects must meet three specific criteria according to the company's vice president of quality: (1) They must focus on customer satisfaction; (2) project results must cut defects by at least 70 percent; and (3) each individual project should average $250,000 in cost savings. Other companies, such as Dow Chemical, use a variety of yardsticks, both financial and nonfinancial to choose and judge the success of their Six Sigma projects. (See the sidebar, "How Dow Chemical Picks Six Sigma Projects and Shapes Results.")

Still other companies, such as ServiceMaster, are refining their voice-of-the-customer (VOC) and voice-of-the-marketplace (VOM) processes to the point that they establish actionable attributes for projects by individual branch office, based on localized VOC profiles. "Going forward, we'll be able to select and implement projects that precisely meet the needs of customers," says Patricia Asp, senior vice president. "In other cases, understanding critical *employee satisfaction*

HOW DOW CHEMICAL PICKS SIX SIGMA PROJECTS
AND SHAPES RESULTS

Does every Six Sigma project a company selects have to generate concrete results? Not necessarily. Dow Chemical, for example, uses at least three different criteria to choose Six Sigma projects. "They should do one of several things," says Kathleen Bader, Business Group President for Styrenics and Engineered Products, and the company's enterprise-wide Corporate Vice President for Quality and Business Excellence.*

In the best case, a project will "support the business strategy—be driven absolutely from the critical three- to five-year breakthrough objectives of the business, or from the annual objectives for the [individual Dow] business," says Bader. Such projects typically are selected because of their likely positive impact on the company's bottom line, or for what they are likely to contribute to Dow accomplishing a critical three- to five-year business objective.

Dow also selects projects to reduce what Bader describes as the company's "environmental footprint"—in other words, to impact company operations from a health, safety, and ecological standpoint. "We have a specific objective throughout our Environmental Health and Safety organization to do exactly that," says Bader, adding that Six Sigma's methodology and toolkit offer unique approaches to helping Dow reduce this footprint.

Finally, says Bader, many Dow Six Sigma projects are designed to help Dow gain a better understanding of its customers, and to help it develop customer relationship management best practices that will differentiate it from competitors. "Across all our marketing groups we have a clear understanding that we will [sometimes select] projects that fail to create any EBIT for Dow's results, if these projects are driven from certain determinants of customer loyalty," she says.* "You can't afford to support [such projects] forever, if you can't prove that to be the case. But we fundamentally believe that to be the case, and are willing to absorb some cost to create projects that drive customer loyalty without necessarily impacting Dow's bottom line."† — *The Authors*

*EBIT, earnings before interest and taxes.
†Kathleen Bader, interview with Richard Koonce, PricewaterhouseCoopers, Midland, MI, 14 December 2001.

attributes will help us choose projects that improve employee loyalty, resulting in reduced turnover. In either case, the projects we select will help make service levels consistent and predictable from customer to customer and branch to branch, thus enhancing customer loyalty, and improving customer and employee retention."[1]

Ideally, a company will choose DMAIC and DFSS projects (and judge project results) using a variety of metrics. Dave Burritt, Corporate 6 Sigma Champion at Caterpillar says that as Caterpillar began its 6 Sigma deployment, it focused on rewarding mostly level 1 and level 2 results "because we wanted to prove to the stock market, to our shareholders, to employees, and to our customers that we could make money at 6 Sigma," he says. But going forward, Caterpillar will begin to strive for (and reward) level 3 benefits as well, he says. The reason? "In some cases level 3 benefits will drive more enduring benefits but will take a little longer."[2]

Fourth, projects should be assessed in terms of their overall fit with the organization's strategic goals and vision. A project may in fact be doable, but does it necessarily mean it is appropriate or will add value to the goals? For example, will the project get management commitment? Can it be leveraged to other parts of the organization, and/or easily replicated to create multiplier effects in terms of process improvements, cost savings, and so on? Can the company's operating systems, information technology (IT) infrastructure, and management performance and appraisal systems easily support the project or not? And how long will the project take? Desmond Bell, VP of Six Sigma at Bombardier Transportation, says that in the early days of Six Sigma deployment in his company, "we didn't have a very good way to develop a project pipeline that was clearly linked with the strategic plan. There wasn't exactly a shot gun approach to project selection, but we were picking projects in different parts of the business based on local issues," not on the potential of project benefits to be leveraged enterprise-wide.[3]

Fifth, potential projects must always be prioritized against a company's key performance indicators, otherwise known as its family of metrics. Let's say that a company's key performance indicators include: "innovation," "profitable sales growth," improvement of customer satisfaction," "improvement of employee satisfaction," and "improvement of process/product quality and reliability." Specific SIGs (e.g., "To bring products A and B online by _____." "To increase service revenues to 30 percent of total by _____," and "To reduce manufacturing cycle times of product C by _____") need to be evaluated against these key performance indicators (KPIs), each of which is weighted in its importance by senior management. After SIGs are weighted in importance against KPIs, the top four or five SIGs are selected as the focus of improvement. Projects are then identified and prioritized against the SIGs.

As one can see, the alignment of projects to support business goals and strategy is a multitiered process of driving line-of-sight relevance and accountability at each level of decision making and action taking. It is through the rigorous analysis of projects in terms of how they support SIGs and, in turn, how they support the corporate strategies of the organization that a company can ultimately align Six Sigma projects to have maximum impact.

■ SIX SIGMA PROJECT FILTERS

Given the intense focus and organizational resources required to implement Strategic Six Sigma in an organization, however, there are still factors that CEOs and their leadership teams must consider as they plan Strategic Six Sigma deployments and the rollouts of individual DMAIC and DFSS projects. Think of these as filters for whether pursuing a particular Six Sigma project makes sense or not.

➤ *Is the solution to a particular defect or problem known?* If it is known, the solution should be implemented. If not, the problem is a suitable candidate for a Six Sigma project, because it will require structured data collection, analysis, and exploration of possible solutions.

➤ *Are sufficient data available to quantify the problem?* If the answer is no, implement a simple data collection plan to further qualify and quantify the nature of the problem before proceeding further. If the answer is yes, consider undertaking a Six Sigma project to measure and analyze it, and either explore designs for fixing it, or how improvement of current processes can eliminate it.

➤ *Is the root cause of the problem known and supported by facts?* If yes, go ahead and fix the problem. If no, consider implementing a Six Sigma project to probe the root cause of the problem, and to set steps in motion to analyze how best to address it—be it through process improvement or process development and design.

➤ *Is the problem being addressed elsewhere?* If the answer is yes, pursuit of a solution to the problem in that venue should be allowed to play itself out, before being considered as a Six Sigma project. If the answer is no, it is a ripe candidate for a Six Sigma project.

➤ *Does the potential project address a SIG?* If the answer is no, it is not worthy of consideration for Six Sigma implementation, at least not initially. If the answer is yes, application of Six Sigma principles to an analysis and measurement of the problem could well result in exponential increases in productivity, efficiency, and cost reduction—especially if the solution leads to the replication of solutions across the business.

➤ *Do the total savings to be potentially realized from a project meet financial targets?* If no, the project is not worth pursuing. If the answer is yes, the project is a good potential Six Sigma project. Many companies set a minimum financial benefit, such as $200,000 to $250,000, as the filter here.

➤ *Does the problem to be addressed involve a new product, process, service, or plant?* If the answer is yes, use DFSS methods to address it. If the answer is no, use DMAIC approaches to address the problem instead. Business success with Strategic Six Sigma is best achieved through multiple focused projects, aimed at identifying multiple root causes of individual defects in products, services, and processes. This enables deployment of Six Sigma to proceed at a speed and scale sufficient to overcome organizational inertia and build momentum for the long-term.

■ SCORING QUICK WINS

Some processes have been neglected for so long that a simple value mapping exercise may illuminate many easy and obvious improvement opportunities. Conducting this common-sense assessment of process steps may help to identify such opportunities, referred to as *quick wins,* or *low-hanging fruit.* Strategic Six Sigma project teams should always be prepared to identify and pursue quick-win opportunities because the return on investment (ROI) of time, people, skills, and resources can be very high. Moreover, their successful (and rapid) completion can create excitement and build momentum

---

QUICK WINS FROM SIX SIGMA
TAKE DIFFERENT FORMS

Quick-win opportunities from Six Sigma can take many forms. At ServiceMaster, for example, the introduction of Six Sigma practices into the company's branch and service center operations in Spring 2002 quickly generated significant cost savings. For example, "We identified $200,000 that could be saved enterprise-wide just by cutting back on long distance calls and use of Directory Assistance in our branches," notes Pat Asp, senior vice president who serves as one of the executive Six Sigma sponsors for ServiceMaster. "The monthly cost for Directory Assistance might be only $20 a month per branch, and might not even register on anyone's radar screen, but when you begin to replicate savings across hundreds or thousands of branch offices and across different brands in the ServiceMaster family," the savings can really add up.*

Other quick wins that ServiceMaster has identified include cutting uniform costs by $100,000 a year, improving call capture rates in the company's service centers, slashing office supply costs through consistent ordering practices, and even making tire pressures on corporate vehicles consistent across the entire fleet of all ServiceMaster brands, thus reducing vehicle maintenance costs. "Our goal is to identify savings and then to leverage those savings or other improvements both from branch to branch and from brand to brand wherever we can," says Asp. — *The Authors*

*Patricia Asp, telephone interview with Richard Koonce, Pricewater- houseCoopers, Arlington, VA, 21 March 2002.

---

for pursuing longer-term improvement opportunities. (See the sidebar, "Quick Wins from Six Sigma Take Different Forms.")

What are the criteria for defining an improvement opportunity as a quick win? First, it should be easy to implement. Making the change or improvement should not require a great deal of coordination and planning. Second, implementing changes should have immediate impact, and require very little time to actually get online. Third, quick wins should be cheap to implement, requiring little in terms of capital, people, time, equipment or technology. Fourth, quick wins should be within a project team's direct control. The team and its leaders should be able to readily gain the support of those needed to make the changes in the organization. Finally, quick wins should result in increased momentum for Six Sigma deployments, by generating enthusiasm for and belief in the power of Six Sigma principles to transform how a company operates.

■ ASSESSING SUCCESS WITH INDIVIDUAL PROJECTS

Launching (and subsequently assessing) how well individual Six Sigma projects are doing at achieving their desired ends, requires that leaders assess and measure success at regular intervals, be it every 30 to 60 days, once a quarter, twice a year, or on some other timetable. Key questions that need to be asked before project launch and at regular intervals thereafter include the following:

➤ Does the project have top-level leadership commitment?

➤ Is the project's stated goal in alignment with corporate strategy?

➤ Does the project have a strong customer/market focus?

➤ Is a supporting infrastructure (systems, metrics, performance appraisal mechanisms, performance feedback loops, and other tools) in place to support regular analysis and measurement and success of the project on a going-forward basis?

➤ Has the organization fielded a sufficiently robust team of Black Belts to drive project direction/completion?

➤ Are the organization's IT capabilities sufficiently robust to provide project support to measure, analyze, and assess the progress of Six Sigma projects going forward?

➤ Using process management techniques, can the benefits of this project be successfully leveraged across the organization?

➤ Does the project team itself consist of members from across all levels and functions in the organization? (This is key to getting broad-based organizational support for project goals.)

➤ Are the emerging (or final) business results what the organization envisioned? What needs to be done to improve results going forward?

■ GET FINANCE AND ACCOUNTING PEOPLE INVOLVED AS SIX SIGMA PROJECT TEAM MEMBERS

Holding leaders at *all* levels of a company responsible for Six Sigma results is critical to success with project deployments. But what should leaders do to ensure that momentum doesn't dissipate and projects don't stall, due to organizational resistance or insufficient championship of initiatives at every organizational level? Consultant Bob Norris recalls the story of one organization that was implementing Six Sigma, but which didn't build a sufficiently strong coalition of leaders at all levels to support the effort. "Black Belts and project teams were well-trained in [Six Sigma] methodology, and were successfully applying the tools and techniques," he writes (with Debbie Neuscheler-Fritsch) in the May 2001 issue of *Quality Progress*. "There was also high esprit de corps among teams, and significant operating improvements had been identified as well."[4]

Unfortunately, however, when the benefits were presented to top management, company executives, though appreciative of the teams' work, were underwhelmed and disenchanted with team results. They asked teams, "What is the impact on the bottom line? Why should we implement the improvements you've identified, if we can't determine their financial impact?"[4]

In conducting postmortems of Six Sigma projects that have failed to achieve results, we have learned that one reason project teams are sometimes perceived as less than successful is that the CFO and his or her staff are never engaged by teams in blessing the final results. Without this blessing, the improvements are then discounted by senior executives in the organization, dismissed with comments such as, "These improvements will not play on Wall Street," and "What do operating personnel know about translating results to the bottom line?"

As we've emphasized, Strategic Six Sigma organizations follow robust process improvement methodologies (either DMAIC or DFSS), managing by fact with data and measurement tools, techniques, and systems. While this description of Six Sigma is correct from a textbook perspective, there is a larger truth that must be spoken of here as well.

■ DELIVERING VALUE TO SHAREHOLDERS

First and foremost, Six Sigma is about delivering value to shareholders. It is all about driving results: creating, preserving, and realizing value. It is in this way that Six Sigma links a company, its processes, products, and services to customers and shareholders.

Unfortunately, what sometimes gets lost in the excitement of deploying Six Sigma methodology in an organization "is the discipline required in tying Six Sigma projects to clearly defined and auditable financial results," note Norris and Neuscheler-Fritsch.[4]

Norris and Neuscheler-Fritsch say there are five key principles to abide by when implementing Six Sigma projects inside business organizations today. Keeping these guideposts in mind will help Six Sigma organizations effectively translate operating results into meaningful financial results that will resonate with customers, employees, shareholders, and Wall Street analysts.[4]

■ THE KEYS TO ENSURING SIX SIGMA PROJECT TEAM SUCCESS

➤ Item 1: Adopt an Accountant

Why is it so important to involve the finance/accounting function in a company's Six Sigma efforts? To answer this question, it's important to understand that one of the primary roles the finance/accounting function plays in an organization is that of scorekeeper.

By using systems that capture key operating and financial data, the finance organization of a company manages and reports on key business metrics, such as revenue dollars, labor rates, fixed and variable unit costs, gross margin rates, operating margin rates, inventory costs, general and administrative expenses, and cash flow.

All these measures become critical in helping teams translate process improvements into the bottom-line impact that creates shareholder value—ultimately determining the success of process improvement teams.

The composition of Six Sigma improvement teams is always a hot topic of debate. Certainly, those closest to the processes being studied need to be directly involved in applying Six Sigma tools to the analysis and measurement of problems and to developing solutions. In our experience, one of the most effective things organizations can do to accelerate the work of Six Sigma project teams and to create strong internal buy-in for projects is to add finance/accounting subject matter experts (SMEs) to improvement teams.

By 1997, while conducting Black Belt training at GE Capital, we began to notice a new job classification appearing there—Quality Analyst. This was the result of Jack Welch's directive at that time to have a finance person in every business unit track each project's benefit to the company's profit and loss (P&L) statement. At Bombardier Transportation, finance people are likewise involved both during and after Six Sigma projects, to validate first the anticipated (then actual) business results. "Bombardier is a very conservative organization when it comes to calculating savings from Six Sigma projects," says Desmond Bell, Bombardier Transportation's VP for Six Sigma:

First, the finance people will validate the potential business benefits during a project so that we have an idea of what the potential impacts will be. Then, at the end of the project, there's a formal validation before the project is considered complete. [Finally] we have a rolling audit process that takes place 6 to 12 months after completion of the project. At that time, the [Black Belt] or project owner and the finance person go back and do a formal review of the actual benefits that have been achieved as

*a result of completing the project. If we have any doubts
about the reality of the savings from a project or workshop, we won't claim any savings. In our tracking data-
bases, the savings value will appear as a "0."*[3]

The role of finance/accounting SMEs is to help translate
what the team will discover into dollars and cents. The discoveries that teams make can include examples of process
ineffectiveness, inefficiencies, poor quality, and ways to
increase capacity of output and eliminate non-value-added
steps. With finance/accounting SMEs on board, the full dollar value and impact of these defects can be determined.

Our experience suggests that the earlier a project team
involves a team member from the finance/accounting area,
the sooner that SME will:

> ➤ Become intimate with the process being studied and
> be able to translate process steps into unit costs and
> calculate the costs of poor quality.
> ➤ Be able to develop cost-benefit scenarios to help sell
> the improvement recommendations to upper man-
> agement. [This involves tracking the potential dollar
> impact from project(s) to the company's profit and
> loss statement.]
> ➤ Minimize the potential adversarial relationships that
> typically develop between a specific operating unit
> within a company and the finance/accounting func-
> tion.

As a project team moves from the *define* to the *control* stage
of the DMAIC process, for example, the finance/accounting
SME plays an influential role, as shown in Table 7.1.

Another key success factor in any Six Sigma implementation effort is to link improvement efforts with incentives.

Table 7.1 Finance and Accounting Contribution
to the Six Sigma Methodology

Six Sigma Improvement Methodology	Finance/Accounting SME Roles and Responsibilities
Define	➤ (Team charter): Develop financial benefits that team will realize when the project is complete. ➤ (Team charter): Assist team to determine the cost of the pain the organization is experiencing, and thus what the financial opportunity is for the improvement effort.
Measure	➤ As an expert in measurement, assist the team in developing key and realistic output, process, and input measures. ➤ As the process is mapped in the define stage, establish specific unit cost measures for each critical process step.
Analyze	➤ As the team is discovering root causes and non-value-added process steps, translate the root causes of defects into the cost of poor quality using the unit cost analysis established in the measure stage.
Improve	➤ As the team is developing process improvement scenarios, assist in running process simulations to determine unit costs to be saved by redesigning the process. ➤ Prepare cost-benefit analysis using key financial tools [e.g., net present value (NPV), internal rate of return (IRR), payback period] to help select the improvement idea with the largest net benefit impact to the organization.
Control	➤ Assist in developing the monitoring system (i.e., dashboards, scorecards) management requires to sustain the gains of the improvement implemented and to control the process by the process owners.

Note: It has been shown that one critical success factor in any Six Sigma implementation effort is to link improvement efforts with incentives. (See Chapter 8.) The finance/accounting SME, playing the role of the scorekeeper, can interface with the company's human resources department and management on behalf of the team helping the company.

The finance/accounting SME, playing the role of the scorekeeper, can interface with human resources (HR) and upper management on the team's behalf, to help the company determine the right incentives for the team. (We'll have more to say about incentives in Chapter 8.)

When finance/accounting SMEs play critical roles on Strategic Six Sigma project teams, it helps bolster the confidence of upper management that team results have been reviewed by the appropriate numbers experts, have their blessing, and are not loosy-goosy numbers incapable of being documented. Ultimately, management will believe the benefits are auditable and can be broadly communicated to the organization, customers, and shareholders. The team's efforts, in other words, "will now play in the capital markets."

➤ Item 2: Document and Reinforce Financial Guidelines for Quantifying Project Benefits

When a company's top leadership team documents and reinforces financial guidelines to guide the work of Strategic Six Sigma project teams from the moment Six Sigma is deployed, it helps everyone in the organization develop a sense for what will or will not constitute a good Six Sigma project. Many organizations set a dollar threshold as they begin the project prioritization process, so from the outset, projects provide returns that will pay for up-front investments in Six Sigma training and full-time Black Belt team leaders. Clearly defining what types of savings are considered hard or soft is also critical. It will focus team energies and drive team behaviors to seek out and identify quick-win opportunities first, before tackling other possibilities.

In many organizations, soft or indirect benefits fall into categories such as cost avoidance related to regulatory or legal compliance or benefits related to improving employee morale or efficiency. Such benefits can't be directly tied to operating margins or incremental revenues through a specific measurement.

➤ Item 3: Use Project Reviews (Tollgates) to Align Six Sigma with the Finance Organization

From the moment a Strategic Six Sigma team creates its project charter, it is critical that the Six Sigma Black Belt (team leader), the project sponsor (champion), and the finance organization all agree on the assumptions that will drive initial estimates of the potential value of a given project to the business.

Once an operational definition of the defect has been agreed on and data from the existing process is captured, a preliminary analysis of possible benefits and their sources (revenue, cost reduction, etc.) can be developed.

Throughout each phase of the Six Sigma process, a representative from the finance team should be present at each tollgate to ensure key assumptions have not changed. In many organizations, the analyze phase is the point at which the finance team is charged with revalidating and documenting the expected benefits. Obviously, this analyze exercise is repeated once the team has identified and selected the necessary improvements (improve phase) so the costs of implementing improvements can be factored into the final numbers.

Use a self-assessment, such as the one displayed in Figure 7.2, to evaluate whether the financial benefits process is in control.

➤ Item 4: Consistently Communicate the Financial Benefits to Your Organization and Recognize Those Individuals Who Have Helped Achieve Them

By creating highly visible dashboards or scorecards—and referencing them often in employee meetings, staff meetings, and in other settings—a company's top leaders can foster employee enthusiasm for Six Sigma, and also spark healthy internal competition among Six Sigma project teams. It also drives home the point that Six Sigma is about delivering results and is a message that Six Sigma leaders, at *all* levels,

Rating Scale
1—Never or 0%
2—Seldom or <25%
3—About half the time or 50%
4—Frequently or 75%
5—Always or 100%

Rating

1. Revenue and cost reduction benefit guidelines are documented and are being applied.
2. Master Black Belts, Black Belts, and Green Belts understand and follow the quality revenue and cost reduction benefit guidelines.
3. Financial representatives are present at tollgates.

4. Initial opportunity estimate calculations and assumptions are validated by Finance.
5. Business leaders use financial opportunity estimates as criteria for project approval.
6. Process owner and Master Black Belt validate and approve final impact calculations prior to claiming benefits.
7. Postcontrol reviews of project results are conducted to ensure benefits are continuing to be realized.
8. Finance reviews and approves quarterly submission of actual and estimated quality benefits.
9. Operating plans and budgets are updated based on realization of quality project benefits.
10. Six Sigma database is updated with timely and accurate results.

Figure 7.2   Six Sigma financial discipline self-assessment.

need to consistently and frequently repeat within the organization to keep everybody's eyes on the objectives at hand.

Depending on the nature of the workforce and the business, a company's Six Sigma leaders, champions, and Black Belts can use visuals such as horse races, football fields, and thermometers to clearly create energy around specific financial targets. Companies such as GE make extensive use of scorecards and dashboards to communicate the status of specific projects, and to galvanize group energy around team problem solving and project completion. (See the sample of an executive dashboard that we showed you in Figure 6.8.)

➤ Item 5: Integrate Business Risk Management into Process Improvement

As more and more companies use Six Sigma to improve and design core processes, the concept of *business risk management* (BRM) is becoming central to companies fully realizing the financial benefits from their improvement/design efforts, and to avoiding collateral damage that can occur if redesign efforts are undertaken without full and adequate planning.

Company processes, for example, can be severely damaged or disrupted as teams eliminate process steps. In some cases, this can have significant downstream impacts on a business. When doing value-added analysis, teams often consider controls (for example, inspection and legal review) on process steps as non-value-added tasks, and therefore may not consider the inherent risks associated with eliminating these control steps.

Following are examples of what can happen when controls are eliminated without a project team fully assessing the risk of their elimination:

➤ A company eliminates a key report. As a result, cash balances aren't swept (consolidated into one master account) on a nightly basis. Thus, the company leaves excess cash in a number of bank accounts, costing it $200,000 per year in unnecessary fees.

➤ A change in a company's tax reporting process results in the company submitting incorrect tax returns, exposing it to tax penalties of $3.5 million.

To help companies determine the impact of business risk on their financial results, it is essential to factor business risk into process improvement and design work. See Figure 7.3 for a snapshot of the different kinds of business risk that Six Sigma teams need to consider.

Figure 7.3 Layers of business risk.

Strategic Risks—What should we do? Which path should we take?	Organization Design/Structure, Mergers and Acquisitions, Capital Structure	Business Vision, Resource Allocation/Alignment, Leadership	New Technology, New Markets/Products, E-commerce	
Organizational/Cultural Risks—Soft, hard to measure, impossible to quantify.	Integrity and Ethical Values, Accountability, Empowerment	Responsibility, Authority, Intellectual Property	Communication, Reputation, Brand Image	
Business Operational Risks—Doing the right things, but are we doing them wrong (efficiency and effectiveness)?	Outsourcing, Taxation, Contract Commitment, Product/Software Development	Product Liability, Product Recall, Product Tampering	Customer Relations/Satisfaction, Cycle Time, Performance Gap	Product Marketing, Product Distribution, Business Continuity
Process Risks—Universal risks inherent in any process, at any organization (basic blocking and tackling)	Warranty, Purchasing, Procurement, IT Security, Inventory	Revenue, Shipping, Receiving, Accounting, Cash	Business Measurements Management, Capital Assets, Copyright/Patent, Sales Discounts	Foreign Exchange, Cash Flow, Pricing, Suppliers, Vendors, and Contractors, Accounts Payable, Benefits, Payroll, Employment Practices, Incentives
Compliance Risks—Policies, procedures, regulations, etc.	Human Resources, EPA, OSHA	Purchasing Practices, Policy Letters, SEC Regulations	Regulatory Reporting, Accounting Principles	

194

As a company deploys Six Sigma, use BRM as a filter to evaluate proposed process redesigns and to determine the costs/benefits of recommendations that teams present to top management. Melding BRM and Six Sigma together for this purpose can be accomplished by embedding BRM concepts into a company's Six Sigma methodology and training, and by reviewing toolsets for both Six Sigma and BRM and incorporating their use on projects wherever possible. For example, a project team Black Belt might consider adapting a key quality Six Sigma tool, failure mode effects analysis (FMEA), to measure and assess how key business risk elements potentially impact the financial health of an organization.

If a company wants to successfully create and preserve value—and realize that value for its customers and shareholders—it should give serious consideration to incorporating BRM elements into its deployment of Six Sigma throughout its organization.

■ INTEGRATING SIX SIGMA WITH OTHER IMPROVEMENT METHODOLOGIES

By bringing up BRM, we are obviously suggesting one way that Six Sigma methodology, robust as it is, can nonetheless be integrated with other process improvement disciplines, adapted to suit the needs of a particular organization, or to deal with unique industry-specific concerns that may be impacting profitability, productivity, or process efficiency. In this vein, Six Sigma deployments can also be integrated with other improvement methodologies, such as Kaizen projects and Lean Manufacturing approaches. *Kaizen* is a process improvement activity that involves the use of chartered process improvement teams to identify waste in different processes, and to implement immediate, sustainable solutions to sustain waste elimination or reduction. *Lean Manufacturing* is a process that entails improving cycle time while eliminating waste. It involves a multistep process of defining value, mapping value streams, optimizing workflows, enabling customers to pull work through an organization, and embracing continuous improvement.

■ CHAPTER CONCLUSIONS

This chapter has focused on the importance of developing quantifiable metrics with which to prioritize the selection of Six Sigma projects, and gauge the success of such projects over time. As financial results from projects begin to be generated, it can quickly strengthen leadership resolve and commitment to Strategic Six Sigma principles and practices as key to a company's financial health, to improved business performance, and to enhanced levels of customer satisfaction and marketplace responsiveness. Thus, we recommend that as successes from completion of initial Six Sigma projects emerge, CEOs and their top leadership teams move quickly to leverage both project learnings and Six Sigma thinking into their companies' strategy and growth processes.

Notwithstanding this, executives and managers charged with Six Sigma initiatives must understand that introducing true accountability—and a measurement mentality—into their companies today often represents a huge culture change in how business traditionally has been conducted. Thus, they are likely to face pushback from employees (at least initially) in the earliest stages of Six Sigma deployments. "The reality is that people resist measurement," says Dr. David Wilkerson, a managing director with PricewaterhouseCoopers who has been involved in numerous Six Sigma client engagements. "There are a number of reasons for this," he says:

> *First, people have more flexibility when they aren't held accountable to specific goals. You take a manager of a specific function for example. He has a lot of wiggle room if you don't hold him directly accountable for resources, for example. He may have 500 people assigned to him and he can use them however he likes if there isn't a measurement system being applied to how people do their jobs. But when it gets down to businesses being competitive today, and producing products at the lowest cost possible, companies don't have the luxury of allowing managers a lot of wiggle room anymore. To be successful, companies have to measure what they do, and be certain they are meeting the needs of their customers. For this reason, metrics must be consistently applied to tracking data and information, and to determining expenditures for people, raw materials and other resources.*[5]

➤ Best Practices for Developing Quantifiable Measures for Projects

In the wake of the accounting debacles associated with the failures of companies such as Enron and Global Crossing, financial accountability has become more vital to the accurate operation of businesses than ever before, and to public and market perceptions and confidence that companies are being run in legal, ethical, and professional ways. One of the key benefits of employing Strategic Six Sigma in an organization is that it can rapidly generate concrete financial benefits including reduced costs, increased revenues, and enhanced productivity.

Nevertheless, a company's leaders must still agree on the specific measures that will be used to assess results from Six Sigma projects. And, they must be certain that process improvements can be readily translated into bottom-line benefits for the business that, in turn, will increase shareholder value. To optimize success in achieving these things, a company's leaders must:

1. **Choose Six Sigma projects based on a clear understanding of their potential financial impact to the organization, and their overall fit with the organization's strategic goals and values.** Companies should choose some projects to have immediate, short-term benefits, while others can be chosen to yield medium- and long-term benefits.

2. **Prioritize projects against a company's KPIs, otherwise known as the company's family of metrics.** Not all projects must generate immediate financial paybacks. However, if other goals are stipulated, such as increased understanding of how to foster customer loyalty/retention, executives must agree on when hard financial impacts need to result from given projects.

3. **Involve finance/accounting. Build in-house support and momentum for Strategic Six Sigma initiatives through engaging the company's CFO and the accounting staff as allies.** Accounting professionals can play critical roles in tracking the potential dollar impact from individual Six Sigma projects to the company's bottom line. They can also help reassure business leaders and outside stakeholders (stockholders, analysts, etc.) that a company's business performance (including business improvement) is being accurately tracked and reported.

4. **Document and reinforce financial guidelines for quantifying project benefits.** When a company's top leadership team documents and reinforces financial guidelines to guide the work of Six Sigma project teams, it brings added consistency and discipline to the process of Six Sigma project selection. It also helps everyone in the organization develop an understanding of what constitutes a good Six Sigma project.

5. **Use project reviews to continuously align Six Sigma projects with strategic goals, and be certain that finance agrees with the assumptions that will drive estimates of the value of projects.** Ensuring the alignment of projects with top leadership goals and financial reporting procedures is key to ensuring that results from Six Sigma projects are accurately measured and viewed with credibility by all of a company's stakeholders, including shareholders, analysts, capital markets, and others.

Let's turn now to Chapter 8, where we discuss how to shape people's work behaviors by providing them with the right inducements and incentives to embrace Strategic Six Sigma principles and practices in an enthusiastic way.

Chapter

Develop Incentives and Create Accountability

What motivates people? Sure, Maslow's hierarchy does—you've got to take care of some basic things for people. But [beyond that] people want to be part of a winning organization. They want to do what their company and especially customers think is important, and they want to have a chance to share in that success with other people and feel good about it. There's no mystery here. We're all wired the same!

—Dan Burnham,
Chairman and CEO
Raytheon Corporation

In Chapter 7, we dealt with how to derive quantifiable, tangible results from people when planning and completing Strategic Six Sigma projects. While both making new performance expectations clear to people and giving them Six Sigma methods to do their jobs in new ways are big parts of achieving success with Six Sigma deployments, these aren't enough. To achieve long-term success, a company must truly transform how it does business. In essence, to use Jack Welch's term, it must change its organizational "DNA".

This requires that companies do more than drive simple compliance to Six Sigma standards and work requirements. They must also build leadership and employee *commitment* to new ways of working. To do this, a company must create a strong culture of accountability, redesign people's jobs, and develop appropriate incentive plans to shape new behaviors and reinforce new work approaches. Dealing with these and related human resources (HR) issues constitutes the softer side of managing Strategic Six Sigma implementations. It doesn't get a lot of emphasis in technical discussions of Six Sigma deployments. Yet, in our experience, it is absolutely critical to success. As a matter of fact, it's part of the critical operating system that must exist in an organization, if Strategic Six Sigma initiatives are to endure over time.

■ PROVIDING APPROPRIATE INCENTIVES AT DIFFERENT ORGANIZATIONAL LEVELS

So, how does a company create a culture of accountability and provide incentives to those individuals—Six Sigma project and corporate champions, Black Belts, Green Belts, project sponsors, process owners, and Six Sigma project team members—who play vital roles in Strategic Six Sigma initiatives? Because companies "get what they reward," they must pay close attention to developing incentive and recognition systems that foster accountability and drive results—at *every* level.

For example, a CEO, members of his or her leadership team, and the specific deployment champions that emerge from this leadership group must be strongly motivated to drive the initial deployment and large-scale rollout of Six Sigma within an organization. Typically, this entails making a large part of the variable-pay packages of top executives (stock options, bonuses, etc.) weighted toward completion of specific Six Sigma project benchmarks throughout the initial years of Strategic Six Sigma initiatives. All of these performance goals should be outlined on the performance scorecards of these executives.

■ REWARDS AND COMPENSATION FOR THE CEO, TOP LEADERSHIP TEAM, AND STRATEGIC SIX SIGMA PROJECT CHAMPIONS

Writing in *Jack: Straight from the Gut,* former General Electric (GE) CEO Jack Welch writes that tweaking GE's stock options plan had a tremendous effect in helping to jumpstart a number of key business initiatives at GE. One of these was the 1990 launch of the emphasis on boundaryless behavior by GE employees to boost corporate profitability and enhance customer satisfaction. Playing with the company's stock options "drove idea sharing" inside the company, reports Welch. Indeed, "[S]tock ownership changes behavior. In 1981, the value of exercised options for everyone at GE was only $6 million. Four years later, that number increased to $52 million. In 1997, 10,000 GE people cashed in options worth $1 billion. In 1999, about 15,000 employees got $2.1 billion from them."[1] These options, along with others, says Welch, not only ensured that year after year, an increasing proportion of GE executives, managers, and employees had "skin in the game" of corporate change, but also found themselves in a position to be better able to take care of elderly parents, send kids to college, or to buy a vacation home.[1]

Likewise, when Caterpillar launched its Six Sigma efforts in January 2001, top executives were incented to drive 6 Sigma goals and objectives to successful completion. "One of the things that [Caterpillar CEO] Glen Barton did early on was to decide that 20 [percent] of the incentive pay of the company's executive leaders, the top 33 people in the company, would be tied directly to the success of 6 Sigma," says Dave Burritt, Caterpillar's Corporate 6 Sigma Champion.

"Now, to take it to the next level, all eligible employees (an even larger group) will have at least 20 [percent] of their incentive pay based on the success of 6 Sigma as we move into 2002."[2]

When Caterpillar went through a reorganization in the 1990s, I was one of those people who didn't buy into the notion of incentive pay. I used to think, "Just tell me what the goal is, I'll do my best, I can't work any harder or any smarter. This is as good as it gets." But what I've come to understand is that incentives provide greater focus to people. When you pay people more for doing certain things, it helps people realize what they need to concentrate on. So, as we've rolled out 6 Sigma we've said, "There are going to be rewards for Black Belts, there are going to be rewards for Project Sponsors and Deployment Champions and for team members." So, we've found that rewards are very important to the success of 6 Sigma. . . .

Dave Burritt
Corporate 6 Sigma Champion—Caterpillar

Because variable compensation is a huge motivator for top executives, we believe companies should establish incentive plans that award stock options and similar benefits to top-level executives who complete critical milestones in Strategic Six Sigma deployments. In the first year of a Six Sigma implementation, for example, variable pay and bonuses should be awarded to top execs for:

➤ Introducing Six Sigma effectively to the top leadership team
➤ Identifying how Six Sigma will be used to deploy other business strategies

➤ Communicating the business case for Six Sigma to the entire organization, along with financial targets for Six Sigma projects

➤ Setting up the infrastructure (e.g., systems, metrics, project deployment schedules, initial Six Sigma leadership training) to support subsequent project planning and rollout

➤ Achieving specific targets for numbers of Black Belts and Green Belts trained

Beginning in year two, rewards and incentives for the CEO and top executive team need to be awarded to top leaders for:

➤ Taking an active and visible role in overseeing the successful enterprise-wide completion of Design, Measure, Analyze, Improve, and Control (DMAIC) and Design for Six Sigma (DFSS) projects, and rolling up the improvements (dollars) realized from these projects into their corporate profit and loss (P/L) statements

➤ Continuing to articulate the business case and priorities behind introducing Six Sigma in the organization

➤ Continuing to link successful completion of Six Sigma projects to the organization's mission, strategies, and financial objectives

➤ Cascading Six Sigma leadership involvement and training to all levels of the organization

➤ Building a culture of accountability to sustain Six Sigma for the long term by using process management

There are several ways that successful completion of Black Belt projects can be described and used as a basis to assess top leadership performance. Top leaders may be evaluated based on realized financial benefits from projects (audited by financial or accounting representatives). Success can also be evaluated based on such criteria as:

➤ Number of Black Belts deployed in an organization
➤ Dollars saved or accrued per Black Belt
➤ Ratio of DMAIC to DFSS projects
➤ Revenue increases
➤ Increases in customer satisfaction

➤ Incentives for Business Unit and Division-Level Executives

At the business unit/divisional level of the organization, executives should be evaluated and rewarded based on the degree to which they:

➤ Become directly involved in identifying strategic improvement goals (SIGs), which are clear, concrete, measurable, and time-bounded
➤ Select and develop successfully champions, Black Belts, and Green Belts to lead individual Six Sigma projects
➤ Prioritize and select DMAIC and DFSS projects within the organization
➤ Establish a robust, repeatable process management system through which future Six Sigma projects will be selected, launched, and aligned to meet business priorities

The ability of executives at this level to explicitly state SIGs and choose Strategic Six Sigma projects based on their alignment with corporate goals is crucial to optimizing the benefits that Six Sigma approaches can bring to the organization.

➤ Incentives for Master Black Belts and Black Belts

As with the senior levels of leadership, an organization may well decide that its Master Black Belts and Black Belts should have significant portions of their variable compensation, including stock options and cash bonuses, tied to achievement of specific Six Sigma project results. It certainly sends the message that Six Sigma is about achieving specific financial gains and process improvement.

Because Black Belts are responsible for driving successful completion of Black Belt projects, and because such projects are critical to achieving specific financial targets (or deploying certain aspects of strategy), Black Belts need to be specifically compensated for the degree to which they drive cost reductions, defect reductions, and process improvements. Thus, incentives and variable compensation for Black Belts should be tied directly to the following:

- ➤ Successful delivery of chartered financial results to the business units and the entire enterprise.
- ➤ Success in addressing SIGs (achieving hard dollars in savings, reduced number of product, service or product defects, etc.)
- ➤ Leadership ability in guiding the activities of cross-functional process improvement teams.
- ➤ Ability to coach/mentor process improvement team members.

➤ Ability to build sustainability into Six Sigma projects/results.

➤ Ability to advise middle management on the formulation and implementation of breakthrough improvement projects.

➤ Mastery and application of specific Six Sigma tools/techniques to achieve results. This should include hard skills in statistical Six Sigma tools, as well as soft skills in coaching, conflict resolution, communications, group facilitation, and process management.

➤ Rewards for Others Involved in Strategic Six Sigma Deployments

A company might well decide that all those who have a hand in Six Sigma initiatives—including Green Belts (part-time participants on Black Belt projects), Yellow Belts (occasional participants on Six Sigma projects), and even all employees of the organization—should share in the success a company has in achieving Six Sigma results. One organization we worked with, for example, arranged for both the team leader and team members of its Six Sigma projects to get takes of the total savings realized as a result of their team completing a successful project that was sustainable.

If incentives are put in place at the team level, however, team members need to be evaluated based on the following:

➤ Success in contributing to the team's overall financial success (either revenue or cost savings)

➤ Success in demonstrating team member behaviors and skills that are critical to team success (e.g., group problem solving; ability to brainstorm, analyze, measure, and diagnose problems; ability to continuously learn and apply new learning to problem-solving activities; ability to cooperate/collaborate with other team members)

➤ Successful completion of project milestones (e.g., adherence to project deployment schedules, completion of team and subteam assignments)

■ LEADERSHIP TIME REQUIREMENTS FOR STRATEGIC SIX SIGMA DEPLOYMENTS

To be successful with Strategic Six Sigma, the time requirements of CEOs and top executives will be enormous. In most cases, they'll be far greater than leaders expect. (That's why we argue that having a full-time cadre of Six Sigma leaders is critical to success with Strategic Six Sigma in most cases. See Chapter 9.)

Unlike traditional leadership approaches, which emphasize delegation and handoffs, Six Sigma leadership cannot be delegated, only cascaded. And while leadership teams generally get the intellectual content of Six Sigma rather quickly, embracing it as something they must personally drive the acceptance of in their organizations—using their personal time, talent, and charm to do so—takes much longer. This is one reason why the very top executive in a Strategic Six Sigma organization needs to be strongly and personally committed to the importance of Six Sigma to his or her company. It's why Jack Welch described it as the most important business initiative GE has ever undertaken, and why other executives—such as Caterpillar CEO Glen Barton and 3M Chief Jim McNerney—both give it tremendous emphasis in their communications with employees, customers, and stakeholders. (See the sidebar, "How Caterpillar Created a

Rapid and Unstoppable Six Sigma Deployment Force Using High-Energy Deployment Champion Summits.")

We normally coach executives of all levels that when they become involved with Six Sigma, they will have to exercise shirtsleeve leadership to a degree that has never been required of them before. The examples of Jack Welch, Larry Bossidy, Glen Barton, Mike Parker, Dan Burnham and others whom we've profiled in this book are testimony to that fact.

■ RECOGNITION: THE OTHER HALF OF THE COMMITMENT EQUATION

As important as accountability is to driving Strategic Six Sigma results, giving people recognition for work well done, and for achieving difficult financial or process improvement targets is also important. This is key to driving long-term acceptance of Strategic Six Sigma—not as a flavor-of-the-month leadership initiative, but as a long-term systemic approach to business change and organizational transformation.

Typically, organizations speak of reward and recognition systems in the same breath, while in fact, the two things are quite different. Incentive and reward systems are linked directly to specific performance benchmarks, personnel policies, or HR practices governing compensation and other remuneration for levels of work completed or accomplishments achieved. Recognition systems, on the other hand, typically are activated *after* performance criteria for meeting rewards have been met, job evaluations are complete, and work has been privately acknowledged. They come into play when a more public acknowledgment of an individual or a team's success is appropriate to reinforce new ways of working, to acknowledge new levels of performance realized,

HOW CATERPILLAR CREATED A RAPID AND UNSTOPPABLE 6 SIGMA DEPLOYMENT FORCE USING HIGH-ENERGY DEPLOYMENT CHAMPION SUMMITS

Reward/recognition systems are key ways to *incentivize* a company's top executives to drive Strategic Six Sigma initiatives forward, and are useful in motivating leaders at *other* levels to champion Six Sigma projects and remove roadblocks to their successful completion. However, other motivational tools must be employed as well—especially in the earliest stages of Strategic Six Sigma implementation—to make sure that efforts do not stall or get seriously derailed.

For example, to sustain deployment of Six Sigma at Caterpillar, Corporate 6 Sigma Project Champion Dave Burritt convened a series of deployment champion summits at strategic points throughout 2001. These three-day events at Caterpillar's Peoria, Illinois, headquarters were designed as part training and networking opportunity, and part motivational seminar. They brought together 45 deployment champions from Caterpillar's 27 business divisions around the globe for intense periods of learning, bonding, sharing of best practices and war stories, teambuilding, celebration of early successes, and fun as deployment efforts progressed. "These sessions were designed to meet a number of needs," says Caterpillar's Communications Director for 6 Sigma, Julie Hammond. "We wanted people to get to know and trust one another, identify resources they could call on, and to shamelessly steal ideas from one another that they could use as part of the deployment activities they were engaged in back in their home regions."*

To that end, the summits involved high-level talks by senior Caterpillar executives, like CEO Glen Barton, and energizing team-building activities designed to emphasize to deployment champions the importance of following specific 6 Sigma deployment guidelines—"the deployment recipe," as Hammond puts it—back in their regions. One exercise, designed to reinforce the importance of collaborative teamwork and the ability to follow specific directions, had small teams of deployment champions brew their own beer, design beer bottle labels, bottle their stock (using the facilities of Peoria microbreweries to do so), and of course, taste-test the final product.

(Continued)

(Continued)

STAGING 6 SIGMA COMMITMENT CEREMONIES

Other activities involved staging commitment ceremonies at which deployment champions were asked to commit themselves to getting 6 Sigma tattoos. Caterpillar's CEO Glen Barton even got into the act, displaying his own 6 Sigma tattoo in several 6 Sigma gatherings. The tattoos were temporary, notes Hammond (although not all participants realized this at first, and sometimes balked at the idea of being tattooed).

Hammond is emphatic that staging such activities as these was critical to helping Caterpillar achieve its aggressive first-year 6 Sigma deployment goals. "People sometimes complain about training and group events that focus on soft stuff—things like communications, teambuilding, and collaborative decision making," she says. "People call them 'crap.' But I disagree. We designed our summits to help deployment champions bond as a team, and be able to actualize their power and role as change agents back in their divisions."*

FOCUSING ON THE SOFT STUFF IS CRITICAL

Indeed, Hammond says that each time deployment champions came together for both informational downloads and group bonding activities, it helped strengthen their ability as deployment champions, giving them a venue in which they could talk about issues, share concerns, and even whine about problems, when necessary. That way, she says, "they wouldn't do it back in their divisions where there was too much work to do."*

Besides ongoing deployment champion summits, Caterpillar is devising still other ways to sustain the rapid deployment of 6 Sigma projects and teams within Caterpillar. To help support Caterpillar's worldwide community of 6 Sigma practitioners, for example, the company has developed what it calls a Knowledge Network, a corporate intranet that links all of the company's different 6 Sigma communities together in a single site. Here, Master Black Belts and Black Belts can swap ideas with one another, and share best practices they've developed in completing specific projects. Here also deployment champions can keep abreast of specific 6 Sigma projects, both DMAIC and DMEDI efforts.[†] Meanwhile, Green Belts can come to be schooled in the various steps involved in the DMAIC process by reviewing a project storyboard that focuses on improving the quality of a fictional company's chocolate chip cookies. Finally, any Caterpillar employee worldwide can come to learn about the work of specific 6 Sigma teams, or to take virtual gallery walks and hear 6 Sigma Black Belts describe their teams' success stories.[*]

— The Authors

[*]Julie Hammond, interview with Richard Koonce, Pricewaterhouse-Coopers, Peoria, IL, 4 December 2001.
[†]Caterpillar's DFSS methodology, *DMEDI* stands for *Define, Measure, Explore, Develop, and Implement.*

or to celebrate the success of an organization and key individuals meeting or exceeding financial targets.

➤ Recognition Systems Can Have a Powerful Psychological Impact on Employees

It's important for a company's leaders to understand the full psychological impact that having the right recognition programs in place can have in supporting Strategic Six Sigma initiatives going forward. Recognition programs have always been important to organizational and corporate success, most notably in sales organizations, customer service operations, and elsewhere in cases where fostering strong team spirit and individual accomplishment has been critical to the bottom line. In recent years, however, their importance in virtually every realm of organizational operations has become increasingly important, especially in launching

➤ Reengineering initiatives
➤ Information technology (IT) implementations
➤ Culture change programs
➤ Mergers and acquisitions
➤ Changes in strategic vision/mission
➤ Process design/redesign and improvement efforts.

This has occurred because such initiatives typically require large amounts of employee commitment and participation, as well as project or team-driven work. Such initiatives cannot be achieved by a single individual—even a CEO—working alone or with only a small top leadership team.

Recognition programs are important not only because they publicly reinforce new ways of working, but also because they motivate masses of people to work differently—to *change behavior*. They play an incredibly important psychological role in building employee morale, solidifying team cohesion, and fostering better working relationships among people—especially in times of transition. Their very existence also serves as an acknowledgment by an organization to the tough work, long hours, stress, and changes that individuals and work teams often go through as part of taking on new job roles, functions, responsibilities, and reporting relationships. Individuals involved in Six Sigma initiatives, for example, typically experience

➤ Changes in their job roles, titles, functions, reporting relationships, and even professional status
➤ New performance expectations/metrics that increasingly reward team-based work more than individual contribution
➤ Changes in work schedules, work locations, and job requirements

➤ Changes in skill requirements
➤ Potential concerns and stress about job competence or job security

➤ Monetary or Nonmonetary Recognition for a Job Well Done?

So, what kinds of recognition programs might an organization put in place, both to acknowledge people's contributions to Strategic Six Sigma projects, and to reinforce new ways of working? Contrary to what one might think, recognition approaches need not always be monetary—a fact that Tom Peters and Nancy Austin recognized years ago in their best-selling book, *A Passion for Excellence*. ["P]eople will work eighteen hours a day for months for a T-shirt, if the context is meaningful and the presenter is sincere," they write. "[B]ig cash awards [on the other hand] can be horribly disruptive, leading to 'hide the idea,' 'Screw the other guy,' and 'Don't help them' behavior."[3]

Sometimes offering people symbolic awards works just as well, if not better than monetary recognition piled on top of other bonuses. Some years ago the McLean, Virginia, sales offices of a leading telecommunications company experimented with different recognition approaches. To recognize sales reps for superlative sales performance in closing large telecommunications sales over the phone, it awarded expensive big-ticket awards such as microwaves, toaster ovens, and TVs to people who met or exceeded sales quotas. In one case, however, it ran out of awards before it had run out of award recipients. So, during a subsequent sales team competition, the company changed tactics. It awarded Big Hitter recognition awards—baseball bats ascribed with winners' names. The company found that people competed just as hard to win the baseball bats (retail purchase price about $15.00) as they had for the expensive consumer items. And the budget for sales recognition went way down!

Strategic Six Sigma companies today use a variety of recognition approaches to acknowledge the hard work of Six Sigma project teams. Virtually all use team recognition events such as dinners, lunches, pins, and small personal awards to recognize team members for their contributions. Another popular recognition award is the opportunity for select individuals to get special training. Offering Black Belt and Green Belt training to selected employees sends a strong message about who is considered a valued team player and high-potential future leader in their organization. After all, training is considered one of the highest, most valued forms of recognition. As such, it can be a powerful way to unify people behind achievement of specific goals, especially when it holds the promise of ensuring future advancement opportunities and greater leadership responsibility. Bombardier, for example, uses training as a key behavioral change tool. At Bombardier, roughly 40 to 50 percent of Black Belts are viewed as high-potential employees, on the fast track to senior-level leadership job opportunities. Thus, being accepted into this elite cadre is seen as prestigious and is consequently something employees keenly seek.

► Other Approaches to Six Sigma Recognition

Still another recognition approach some companies use is to stage internal competitions among Strategic Six Sigma project teams. One insurance company we've worked with holds what they refer to as a Six Sigma Skills Olympics, pitting the Six Sigma skills of one project team against others to solve key business problems or to eliminate process defects. Another holds regular awards competitions that pit company employees from different parts of the organization against one another to solve critical process and service problems.

Dow Chemical takes a still different approach. All Dow employees share financially in the success of Six Sigma projects that are brought to full completion. The company also provides Black Belts with high-visibility opportunities to meet and mingle with Dow's CEO Mike Parker and members of Dow's board of directors, a group that includes luminaries such as former Missouri Senator John Danforth and Willie Davis, an NFL Hall of Fame Lineman for the Green Bay Packers. Recently, for example, the company invited 31 of its Black Belts with their best projects to come in and make presentations about their projects to the board of directors and Dow employees. This so-called Gallery Walk event attracted some 1,700 Dow employees from Dow's Midland, Michigan, headquarters in a 90-minute period, and enabled Dow Black Belts to showcase their projects, and be recognized by their peers and superiors for superlative business performance.

Individual Dow business units also hold high-end certification events for Black Belts, including the awarding of special pins for completing Black Belt training, and gold pins with diamonds in them for being certified as Black Belts. "These gestures are symbolic, and very meaningful to those people who have earned certification," notes Jeff Schatzer, Dow's Communications Leader for Six Sigma. The company also holds recognition events to honor Six Sigma project team members who do yeoman work in delivering Six Sigma results.[4]

■ EMBEDDING SIX SIGMA SKILLS TRAINING IN CORPORATE LEADERSHIP DEVELOPMENT PROGRAMS

While reward and recognition systems are obviously effective ways to develop and mold leaders to drive Strategic Six Sigma initiatives, there are other, longer-term things companies can do to ensure that Six Sigma mind-sets and skill sets are implanted in current and emerging leaders. We've already noted the use of training to encourage people to develop Six Sigma skills. (Read more about this in Chapter 10.) Taking a longer view, we feel it's critical that as companies embark on Six Sigma deployments they put formal, institutional plans in place to embed Six Sigma skill requirements in all their leadership development and training programs. Six Sigma competencies should also be integrated into the competency profile templates used by companies to assess and preselect individuals for long-term promotional potential as part of succession planning activities. We recommend to organizational clients, for example, that individuals who are identified as having Black Belt potential be seriously considered for senior-level leadership positions after a period of at least two years in active Black Belt roles. Over the course of five to six years, this approach can ensure that strong and substantive Six Sigma skills exist in an organization at *all* leadership levels, and that mid- and senior-level leadership pools will be constantly refreshed with new injections of managers with Six Sigma skills and hands-on Six Sigma project experience.

■ CHAPTER SUMMARY

This chapter has explored how companies can create a culture of accountability and put effective reward and recognition systems in place to drive new ways of working as part of Strategic Six Sigma initiatives. Putting such structures in place is critical because they address the all-important human factors associated with getting people to work differently and assume greater accountability and responsibility as part of Strategic Six Sigma deployments.

➤ Best Practices in Developing Incentives and Creating Accountability

1. **Incentive and reward/recognition systems are critical to success with Strategic Six Sigma initiatives.** For that reason, take time to tailor incentives to the specific levels at which key individuals work, bearing in mind the specific tasks and responsibilities they shoulder.

2. **Stock options and variable compensation are powerful ways to create accountability and induce changes in people's behavior—especially at the executive level.** They are especially critical to have in place at the beginning of Strategic Six Sigma initiatives.

3. **When it comes to rewards and recognition however, nonmonetary approaches work just as well—if not better than monetary approaches.** This is because being recognized for one's contribution to a team is sometimes a stronger motivator of people's behavior, than the possibility of winning an expensive prize for one's efforts (or even a cash award.)

4. **If your company wants to give monetary recognition awards to key individuals, be cautious.** They sometimes create undesirable competition among people, when in fact, Strategic Six Sigma initiatives require unprecedented amounts of group work and effective collaboration among people to succeed.

5. **One of the very best recognition awards to give people is training.** Therefore, look for ways to use it as a reward and recognition tool with your company's most valuable Six Sigma executives and leaders.

Let's go on now to Chapter 9, which deals with the importance of companies committing themselves to having full-time Six Sigma team leaders in place to drive Strategic Six Sigma initiatives forward on a sustained basis.

Chapter

Success with Strategic Six Sigma Projects Requires Full-Time, Well-Trained Six Sigma Leaders

Our implementation of Six Sigma is taking place across Dow—in every business and function. We have full-time individuals in place in each of the businesses, and our goal is to have 3 percent of our employee population be full-time Black Belts.

—Tom Gurd, Vice President
Quality and Business Excellence
Dow Chemical Company

We emphasized in Chapter 3 that the single biggest factor in launching and managing successful Six Sigma business initiatives is having a committed team of leaders, at *all* levels of the organization, in place to help drive initiatives forward. So, it stands to reason that *sustaining* success with Six Sigma over the long-term requires that an organization make a full-time commitment to it, and have the people in place, in various critical Six Sigma roles, to ensure project and team success.

Launching and sustaining Strategic Six Sigma initiatives requires continuous and rigorous cooperation and coordination among Six Sigma team leaders at various levels in an

221

organization. This leadership necessarily originates at the top of the organization, with senior executives and business unit leaders. It then must cascade down through all levels of the organization, by being embraced and implemented by Six Sigma deployment champions, project sponsors, project team members, process owners, and of course, by Black Belts, Green Belts, and Yellow Belts.

We have touched on these individuals' roles briefly elsewhere in this book, but in this chapter we focus in more detail on the critical roles each person plays as part of a successful Six Sigma deployment. In so doing, we will again emphasize that Strategic Six Sigma leadership is as much about managing successful change as it is about dealing with the technical aspects of Six Sigma implementations. It is as much about successfully managing and motivating people to work in new ways, as it is about embracing a data-driven approach to customer relationship management, corporate goal setting, and strategy execution.

■ AN ENTERPRISE-WIDE APPROACH TO PROCESS MANAGEMENT

Most quality initiatives [e.g., total quality management (TQM) and business process reengineering (BPR)] are deployed at an *operational* level in organizations where they are designed to bring about incremental results. They are intended to cut costs and/or improve operations. Strategic Six Sigma, on the other hand, is intended to work at a *transformational* level, enterprise-wide in organizations. Not only does it change how work gets done at the everyday level in the organization. It is also capable of generating quantum leaps in business performance, customer satisfaction, innovation, supply chain efficiency, and so on. This results from the exponential benefits to process improvement that occur when there is a process management structure in place, enabling improvements to be leveraged across an entire organization.

But building this business process framework—and creating the climate of organizational alignment to sustain it—takes work. And people power. No wonder then that organizations such as Dow Chemical, which are deeply committed to Six Sigma, concentrate so intently on applying the people power needed for Six Sigma to succeed.

"We've got a steering team of Six Sigma business champions in place in each of our businesses and functions throughout the company. The job of the steering team is to drive change throughout Dow" by determining how projects can best be managed across all Dow businesses and functions, says Tom Gurd, Dow's Vice President of Quality and Business Excellence.[1] Each of Dow's business units vice presidents also has a business champion in place to help them implement Six Sigma, according to Gurd. This is in addition to more than 1,500 Black Belts and Master Black Belts that are leading projects forward throughout the organization.

Talk to other companies that are Six Sigma leaders—Du Pont, Caterpillar, Bombardier, Raytheon—and one finds a similar commitment of people to the successful planning and sustaining of Six Sigma initiatives over time. Moreover, they realize that commitment needs to be full-time—and enterprise-wide.

■ THE CHIEF PLAYERS IN STRATEGIC SIX SIGMA INITIATIVES

Let's talk now about the key roles and responsibilities of Strategic Six Sigma leaders at all levels of an organization.

➤ Executives and Business Unit Leaders

As we have already outlined, the top executives of an organization have the most critical roles to play in successfully driving the implementation of Six Sigma programs and projects inside their organizations. Here are some of the most critical things they must do, to ensure the success of Strategic Six Sigma initiatives.

They must do the necessary legwork ahead of Six Sigma implementation to determine how the methodology can best be deployed in the organization, and what compelling business drivers are necessitating its use. This prework, which may consist of external environmental scans, benchmarking, and internal organizational assessments, can help leaders determine the precise pitch that their introduction of Six Sigma into the organization must take. Will Strategic Six Sigma be used to drive supply chain redesign? To accelerate globalization or e-business initiatives? To transform the company's culture? To facilitate the introduction/rollout of a new product line? To expedite a merger/acquisition? To develop a national brand? In each instance, how will the initiative benefit customers? And in what ways will it be employed not only to ensure customer satisfaction (tactical-level customer relationship management), but also to build strategic, long-term customer loyalty?

Senior leaders must then articulate and own a vision of how Six Sigma will help the organization, and provide the organizational resources to systematically set up the infrastructure to support projects and drive new ways of working. In Chapters 7 and 8, we described many of the elements required in setting up the infrastructure (metrics, roles, responsibilities, incentives, and rewards) necessary to propel

Strategic Six Sigma initiatives forward. As part of doing this, leaders must articulate the compelling reasons why the organization must embrace Six Sigma principles, and then communicate this with clarity, consistency, and commitment on a going-forward basis. "Walking the talk," if you will, is absolutely essential here. As we've said elsewhere in this book, Six Sigma leadership cannot be delegated to others. It will take large amounts of leaders' personal time, at *all* levels, to drive acceptance of and commitment to Six Sigma principles and practices going-forward. The time commitment will be especially high in the initial two years of implementation as leaders

➤ Create strong organizational focus around Six Sigma goals, approaches, and benefits

➤ Drive fundamental culture change in their organizations (risk taking, data-driven decision making, a customer focus)

➤ Deal with initial employee ignorance or lack of awareness about Six Sigma and with organizational inertia to changing how work gets done

➤ Handle periodic project setbacks that inevitably occur as the organization deals with scattered pockets of resistance to Six Sigma methods

➤ Generate sufficient speed and scale with new project launches to drive momentum for sustained organizational change

➤ Hold their organizations and themselves accountable for the success of Six Sigma—with what gets measured and what gets done—at *all* levels

➤ Identify the greatest areas of opportunity (for process, product, and service improvements) at both the enterprise-wide and business unit levels

When embarking on Strategic Six Sigma deployments, "CEO passion is clearly critical," notes Dan Burnham, CEO of Raytheon. Tim Jubach, an independent consultant who has worked closely with Burnham and Ratheon over the years, as the company has pursued Six Sigma, agrees. He says Burnham, who got much of his early leadership training under the tutelage of Honeywell CEO Larry Bossidy, is "among the best when it comes to displaying leadership passion for Six Sigma, and conveying that passion to others in his organization, including executives, managers, and [rank-and-file] employees." Moreover, Jubach says, Burnham brings other dimensions to his Six Sigma leadership. "Not only is he passionate about Six Sigma, he also thoroughly understands the methodology," he says. "Consequently, he's not only able to lead his organization forward to achieve Six Sigma financial targets. He also plays an active role in the teaching of Six Sigma principles to *other* leaders at Raytheon. Even among today's top Six Sigma leaders, that's rare!"[2]

➤ The Senior Six Sigma Champion

The senior Six Sigma champion is responsible to the CEO for the projected benefits to be generated by Six Sigma within a company's different business units. He or she ensures that the activities and goals of all Six Sigma projects are aligned with business priorities, and provides for the funding necessary to support Six Sigma within the enterprise (or sometimes) the enabling business unit. The senior Six Sigma champion

> ➤ Serves as a role model of Six Sigma leadership best practices, continually emphasizing the importance of customer focus, process/quality improvement, and data-driven decision making to others

➤ Provides coaching and support for executives, champions, and Master Black Belts

➤ Coordinates organizational support for Six Sigma projects at high levels, championing the importance of Six Sigma to others in the organization

➤ Removes roadblocks when and if they are encountered

➤ Drives the development of the human resources (HR) and financial infrastructure needed to support Strategic Six Sigma over the long term

➤ Is involved in selecting Black Belts and Master Black Belts for project assignments

➤ Is involved in developing a Six Sigma training curriculum

➤ Six Sigma Deployment Champions

Six Sigma champions are responsible for developing and implementing Six Sigma deployment plans within their respective business units. They are also responsible for the effectiveness and efficiency of a company's Six Sigma infrastructure, and for communications efforts across the organization and among business units. Champions

➤ Assist business unit leaders with resource allocation and the prioritization of projects

➤ Coordinate project selection and training with project sponsors and corporate champions

➤ Work closely with the senior champion to select Black Belts and to nominate Master Black Belts within the business units

➤ Serve as role models of Six Sigma leadership practices, emphasizing the importance of customer focus, and applying data-driven statistical

techniques to drive process improvement and design efforts
➤ Report business unit results
➤ Leverage or replicate lessons learned across other business units

➤ Project Sponsors (Process Owners)

Project sponsors/process owners are line managers who are responsible for identifying and executing Six Sigma Black Belt projects. They work closely with champions to select and prioritize projects, and oversee the details associated with deployment plans and implementation schedules. Project sponsors

➤ Are personally accountable for the performance of given processes and assigned projects, and control the resources associated with a given process. (Put another way: Project sponsors/process owners own the jobs where "the rubber meets the road" in terms of project implementation and results!)
➤ Are personally responsible for the largest number of people working within a critical process or project area.
➤ Have an end-to-end understanding of given processes, and how their process interacts with other departments and internal (other business units) or external (customer/supplier) organizations.
➤ Possess a strong granular grasp of how business priorities and strategic objectives get translated into operational terms for given processes.
➤ Exert a great deal of influence and authority, even outside their immediate process area to remove barriers.

➤ Master Black Belts

Master Black Belts are full-time Six Sigma specialists who are responsible for the long-range technical vision of Six Sigma. Master Black Belts

- ➤ Develop the technology roadmaps to support Six Sigma process improvement and process design/redesign efforts
- ➤ Oversee the technical process work associated with implementing Six Sigma projects across different functional areas and businesses
- ➤ Are responsible for training and coaching Black Belts and Green Belts
- ➤ Possess strong leadership abilities and technical skills, and have a proven track record of ensuring rapid implementation of Six Sigma projects
- ➤ Report results to project sponsors, deployment champions, and business leaders

■ BLACK BELTS

Black Belts, who typically represent between 1 and 3 percent of the total workforce in Strategic Six Sigma companies, are full-time, dedicated Six Sigma specialists that are responsible for delivering promised financial results to business units and the overall business enterprise. Black belts

- ➤ Are full-time Six Sigma team leaders
- ➤ Lead functional or cross-functional process improvement teams and are responsible for training and coaching Green Belts and other team members as well

➤ Work with, mentor, and advise middle management on formulating and implementing breakaway improvement plans
➤ Use and disseminate Six Sigma tools and methods, and network/collaborate with other Black Belts around the world to benefit their businesses, and to benchmark and exchange Black Belt best practices
➤ Are accountable to sponsors/deployment champions for project results

---

The Black Belt role is like [that of] a sculptor, trying to create art pieces of consistent standard using different methods. That's a real challenge. Some pieces take longer than others, and some turn out to be less than perfect. [Black Belts] use the same tools but the quality of the art pieces is very much reliant on many other factors, including the skills of the [Black Belt], and the commitment and beliefs of all employees who collectively determine the culture of the organization.

Caterpillar Black Belt
Singapore

The selection of Black Belts is particularly critical to the success of Strategic Six Sigma initiatives. They need to possess a strong set of both hard (analytical/statistical) and soft (leadership/people) skills in order to be Black Belts. Typically, Black Belt candidates possess

➤ A clear understanding of business objectives
➤ A strong process orientation
➤ A firm grounding in analytical techniques and methods
➤ Strong facilitation and teaching skills

➤ Strong communications skills
➤ Change management experience
➤ Effective team-building skills
➤ Cross-functional business and organizational work experience

In many cases, Black Belts are viewed by their company's top leadership as high-potential future leaders of their organizations. Thus, a great deal of time and care needs to be taken in selecting them for Six Sigma projects. The form shown in Figure 9.1 is typical of that used by Strategic Six Sigma organizations as part of the Black Belt's selection and vetting process.

➤ Green Belts

Green Belts work part-time on specific Six Sigma projects, under the guidance and direction of Black Belts. They also integrate use of Six Sigma tools and methodology into performance of their daily jobs, and seek the advice and counsel of Black Belts, when necessary, to address productivity and process improvement issues.

■ CERTIFICATION OF KEY SIX SIGMA LEADERS

The selection of a company's Green Belts, Black Belts, and Master Black Belts is critical to the overall success of Six Sigma efforts, primarily because these individuals represent the bulk of the ground forces that an organization applies to Six Sigma projects and priorities. For that reason, individuals not only receive robust Six Sigma training but are also certified in their roles. (This is one of the key differences between Six Sigma and earlier quality improvement approaches, such as TQM and BPR, where certification was not required.)

Identify Best Black Belt Candidates (Rate 1–10)

Black Belt Candidate	Selection Criteria	Leadership	Analytical Skills	Process Orientation	Teaching Skills	Interpersonal Skills	Change Management Experience	Team Building Skills	Collaboration
	Total								

Figure 9.1 Black Belt selection matrix.

Green Belts, for example, typically complete a minimum of 5 to 10 days' training in either Define, Measure, Analyze, Improve, and Control (DMAIC) or Design for Six Sigma (DFSS) methods, after which they must pass an online or written exam. To be certified, they must also participate on one team that successfully delivers financial results of $150,000 to $250,000 in annualized benefits.

Black Belts complete extended classroom training as well, from a minimum of three weeks to up to five weeks if they will be working in a manufacturing environment. They, too, must pass an online or written exam. In addition, they must lead at least two project teams, which deliver combined annualized benefits of at least $300,000.

A typical curriculum for Black Belts includes four to five weeks of training, delivered just in time as a team begins its first project. Because they are dedicated Six Sigma experts, Black Belts will often manage or take part in numerous projects at once. A typical General Electric (GE) Black Belt, for example, leads three to five improvement teams, and a Master Black Belt will advise 10 to 15.

Because Six Sigma is such an intense approach to quality improvement, it requires the disciplined training and commitment of dedicated Six Sigma practitioners. GE's Black Belts, who currently number more than 5,000, receive rigorous training in quality tools, root-cause analysis, and statistical methods. The result is a cadre of change management leaders who can map, measure, and analyze any process and who are highly sought after to help run GE's diverse businesses.

Master Black Belts complete an additional 10 to 15 days of training beyond standard Black Belt training, and must pass an online or written exam. In addition, they generally must teach three sessions of Black Belt training, and coach Black Belts on at least 10 projects with combined annualized benefits of $1.5 million, although this last requirement varies by organization.

■ INDUSTRY-WIDE CERTIFICATION OF SIX SIGMA PRACTITIONERS

Currently, the training and certification of Master Black Belts, Black Belts, and Green Belts varies by industry and organization. But efforts are underway to create industry-wide certification standards for Six Sigma practitioners, according to Roxanne O'Brasky, President of the International Society of Six Sigma Professionals (ISSSP), a group that is championing this endeavor. ISSSP (pronounced I–triple S–P) is a Scottsdale, Arizona–based professional society whose members include thousands of Six Sigma practitioners—Master Black Belts, Black Belts, and Green Belts—as well as companies and Six Sigma service providers. The society "is dedicated to promoting the advancement of the Six Sigma methodology and enhancing the growth of individuals associated with Six Sigma," says O'Brasky. "It's also dedicated to serving as an information source about Six Sigma practices, and as a champion for the adoption of Six Sigma throughout all of industry." O'Brasky says the formal certification of Six Sigma professionals "will help ensure that practitioners have a consistent knowledge base that they bring to their project work, and that companies reap the maximum results from Six Sigma deployments."[3] She expects certification standards to be fully in place by 2003.

As we've noted, companies considering Six Sigma should give careful thought to selection and deployment of improvement team members and leaders. The number of teams established should be weighed against the number of improvement projects the company plans to run simultaneously and the amount of change the organization can absorb. By requiring all its business leaders and emerging business leaders to complete Green Belt or the equivalent of Black Belt training before they are qualified for promotion, GE, for example, has produced a cadre of more than 70,000 part-time improvement team leaders. Efforts such as GE's and those of other companies to develop strong populations of Six Sigma leaders sends a powerful message that Six Sigma is critical to the business, not just for the short term, but for the long term.

■ CHAPTER SUMMARY AND BEST PRACTICES

This chapter has outlined the importance of having full-time Six Sigma practitioners involved in both launching and sustaining Six Sigma initiatives over time. There are three reasons for this: (1) Implementing Six Sigma successfully requires rigorous and continuous leadership sponsorship and support from the top of the organization. (2) It requires a strong infrastructure of systems, performance metrics, teams, and goals with which to ensure that process improvements are identified, initiated, and sustained. (3) It needs the heartfelt involvement of a dedicated cadre of Six Sigma leaders both to champion Six Sigma improvement targets and to break down organizational resistance and roadblocks to their achievement.

Here, then, are some best practices to keep in mind as part of developing a full-time cadre of Six Sigma practitioners to drive Strategic Six Sigma improvements in your organization:

1. **Identify high-potential individuals in your organization as candidates to be Master Black Belts, Black Belts, and Green Belts. Then, give them high-quality/**

high-impact Six Sigma training. Doing so will help you launch Strategic Six Sigma initiatives with sufficient scale and velocity for efforts to ramp up quickly, and to rapidly begin generating concrete, measurable returns.

2. **Benchmark other companies to determine what percentage of managers should ultimately be designated as Master Black Belts, Black Belts, and Green Belts in your organization.** Coming up with a specific percentage here will give you concrete targets to aim for in developing a critical mass of Six Sigma leaders with the expertise to drive and sustain Six Sigma initiatives over time. As noted, Dow Chemical is committed to having 3 percent of its employee population designated full-time Black Belts and Master Black Belts. What percentage of managers or employees do you think is appropriate to have designated as full-time Six Sigma practitioners in *your* organization?

3. **Make Six Sigma leadership and skills training an integral part of your company's leadership development programs and succession planning efforts.** To develop and continuously nurture a population of leaders with Six Sigma expertise, Six Sigma leadership and technical training needs to be embedded in leadership development and training programs, recruitment activities, and succession planning efforts. (See Chapter 10.) This is the best way to build a robust talent pool and pipeline of both existing and emerging Six Sigma leaders.

4. **Create attractive career paths for your company's best and brightest Six Sigma Leaders (Champions, Sponsors, Master Black Belts, Black Belts, and Green Belts.)** This sends a strong message to employees

about what the company's goals and priorities are, what skills and competencies the company values, and what it is willing to do to reward those who make significant contributions to the company's Six Sigma initiatives.

5. **As part of creating career paths for your company's Six Sigma leaders, require that Master Black Belts, Black Belts, and Green Belts be certified Six Sigma practitioners.** This lends prestige to their positions, acknowledges their specialized expertise, and conveys to the employee population at large that Six Sigma skills are critical to the company's future business success.

Chapter 10

Why Training Is Critical to Making Strategic Six Sigma Initiatives Work

The change challenges in adopting Six Sigma are in many ways similar to adopting any other initiative you might have, but in some ways substantially different. They're similar in the sense that if you can't put in front of people the fundamental reasons for change, then you're not going to get people to change. And if you can't show people what's in it for them personally—and what's in it for the business that hopefully they already care a lot about—you won't get there. However, with Six Sigma there is an additional step. It's the adoption of a different way of thinking: looking at inputs versus outputs, adopting an intolerance for variation, developing a focus on data, and having an absolute belief in the need for sustainability of results. Some of these things mean that people really need to change how they do their daily work in significant ways, and that creates an additional barrier to change...

— Kathleen Bader, Group President
Polystyrene and Engineering Plastics Unit
Dow Chemical

Throughout this book, we've repeatedly emphasized that *committed leadership* is the single most important ingredient in ensuring that Strategic Six Sigma initiatives are effectively planned and launched within a company. We've talked as well about how important it is to

➤ Integrate deployment of Strategic Six Sigma approaches with a company's other business strategies

➤ Develop a disciplined and consistent process to stay in touch with customers and the marketplace

➤ Think of one's company as a family of processes that must be designed and aligned to address both customer and marketplace requirements

➤ Develop quantifiable measures with which to assess success in meeting critical customer requirements (CCRs) and with which to monitor and measure project team and individual work performance

➤ Develop appropriate incentives and create accountability for specific Strategic Six Sigma projects

➤ Make a full-time commitment to Strategic Six Sigma planning and implementation of projects

■ THE NATURE OF STRATEGIC SIX SIGMA CHAMPIONS TRAINING

Achieving Strategic Six Sigma leadership goals in each of the areas we've talked about in this book requires rigorous training, not just in Six Sigma statistical and analytical principles, but in the equally important tasks of articulating a vision, driving change, and leading people. Moreover, change acceleration studies show that providing people with the right training can dramatically accelerate organizational change efforts. For both these reasons, we typically introduce a company's CEO and top leadership team to Strategic Six Sigma leadership principles in a three-to-five day Six Sigma champions workshop. (See Figure 10.1.) This workshop has eight main goals. It is designed to:

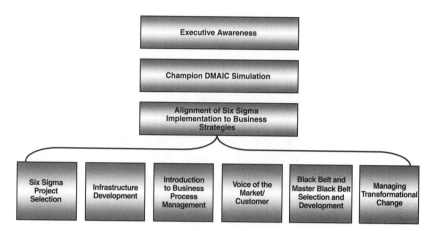

Figure 10.1 Typical format of a Strategic Six Sigma champions workshop.

1. Build top leadership awareness of Six Sigma methods and tools, and how best to apply them in a transformational way on an enterprise-wide basis
2. Foster top leadership understanding of the three elements of Strategic Six Sigma: Define, Measure, Analyze, Improve, and Control (DMAIC), Design for Six Sigma (DFSS), and process management
3. Help top leaders understand the individual roles they must play as leaders, in cascading awareness and knowledge of Six Sigma principles and practices throughout the organization
4. Build top leadership consensus about the goals and strategies of the organization, and to quantify strategies and business objectives as clearly as possible
5. Identify strategic improvement goals (SIGs), and specific Six Sigma projects that can be undertaken to meet strategic improvement needs

6. Help leaders build the infrastructure of systems, people, skills, processes, and metrics necessary to effectively identify, launch, and successfully complete Six Sigma (DMAIC and DFSS) projects
7. Help leaders select other leaders to spearhead the work of individual Six Sigma project teams and projects
8. Craft compelling communications messages that will be used to build leadership and employee commitment to Six Sigma principles at all levels.

Let's now look at each of these workshop stages in more detail.

➤ Module 1: Building Executive Awareness

The first part of Strategic Six Sigma champion training includes outlining and emphasizing to a company's CEO and top leadership team the critical roles that a company's top leaders play in effective deployment of Strategic Six Sigma inside an organization. We typically focus a good deal of time in this module, not only on the tasks involved with successful Six Sigma deployments, but also on the importance of top executives playing vigorous and visible hands-on roles as Six Sigma champions. Because Strategic Six Sigma is fundamentally a team effort, we also sometimes deal with top leadership team process issues that need to be resolved, if team members are to work effectively together. Everyone in the room, for example, needs to understand that while they retain key functional roles in the organization, they must now also begin to work more closely in concert with one another, giving up rivalries and turf issues for the sake of adopting a robust common approach to strategy deployment, and the building of a business process framework. Finding consensus about all these issues is not always easy (see the sidebar in Chapter 4, "Why Is It So Tough to Form Top Leadership Teams?"), but the rewards are well worth the time spent on creating it. Not only does it forge strong top-team focus around key business issues, strategies, and priorities, it also serves to catalyze group energies toward pursuit of common goals, using a commonly agreed-to set of metrics to get there.

As top teams begin to recognize their own teaming issues, they are then ready to roll up their sleeves and focus on deployment issues. We thus help top executives

➤ Define their company's business goals and strategies
➤ Quantify those strategies to the extent possible (i.e., attaching specific metrics, timelines, percentages, and/or numbers to business goals)
➤ Identify required areas of business improvement
➤ Develop detailed (and quantifiable) SIGs and group consensus for moving toward achieving them

Amazingly, what we often find in working with CEOs and their top leadership teams is that a company has never effectively quantified its business goals or its operating strategies. Individual top leaders may know (or presume they know) what they contribute to the company's bottom line. But in many cases, they do not understand their roles and contributions vis-à-vis their colleagues. Nor, are systems and mechanisms in place to help different components of the company operate within a common framework of key performance indicators.

Thus, much of the work we do with executives in module 1 focuses on helping them specify a family of measures by which they will gauge their own job performance. We help them identify key performance indicators, both for themselves, their business units/divisions, and for the organization as a whole. We help them articulate (or in some cases develop from scratch) specific business strategies (clear, measurable, and bounded by time). And finally, we help them come to consensus about how all these things need to be put in place within a common framework of how the business will be run.

Typical of the questions we ask of executives in module 1 are the following:

> How do you define success in your business (organization/business unit?)
> What will you tell your people they need to achieve for the business (and for them) to be judged successful?
> What are the metrics by which performance (business/team/individual) is judged?
> Are these metrics quantifiable? (Are they specific, measurable, and bounded by time?)
> What is the state of customer satisfaction in your organization? (By customer size, revenue, etc.)
> How does your company assess customer satisfaction? Is it based on your perceptions of customer requirements, on anecdotal data, or on systematic and disciplined collection, analysis, and synthesis of customer data on a regular basis?
> What are the specific performance metrics you employ to link completion of work and customer satisfaction levels back to corporate strategy or to key business goals?

Question sets that we use in Strategic Six Sigma champion's workshops are always customized to the needs of individual companies and industries. In any case, however, questions such as those just outlined are designed to elicit intense leadership discussion of a company's business strategies, and where key performance issues exist that need to be addressed to improve performance or boost customer satisfaction. The end result of doing this is that a company's CEO and top executives are forced to quantify their business model. Once they've done that, they can then see where performance gaps exist, the extent to which customers are being satisfied (or not), and what SIGs may need to be put in place to reduce production errors, improve product delivery times, reduce research and development (R&D) cycles, or to achieve any of hundreds of possible improvement objectives.

What we're doing with executives, even in this early stage of a champions workshop, is helping them to become conscious about the links between their job performance, work activities, and measurement systems on the one hand, and the overall organizational performance and financial health of their company on the other. Where are the linkages? Where are the disconnects? Executives need to quantify how and where they spend their time. This is critical so they can begin to focus on those activities and tasks that will improve business performance, efficiency, and productivity, or that will improve customer satisfaction, corporate innovation, marketplace responsiveness, and so forth. This is a key step to undertake, prior to embarking on specific performance improvement initiatives (Six Sigma projects) to improve business performance. It's also key to creating consistent leader behaviors across levels, aligning resources to support Strategic Six Sigma projects, and to creating the organizational focus that will be necessary to successfully derive benefits from Six Sigma projects.

➤ Module 2: Champion DMAIC Simulation

Module 2 of champion training steps participants through a DMAIC project exercise to help them understand the various steps that are involved in planning and managing successful DMAIC projects. Top leaders need to be intimately acquainted with what's involved in the DMAIC project process, because ultimately they will select and prioritize Six Sigma projects for completion, and be charging their subordinates with effectively managing these projects to specific performance targets. Consequently, executives are introduced to process management and DMAIC concepts and tools, including project chartering, process mapping, VOC methods, sampling, statistical thinking, and root-cause analysis. Other subjects covered include how process improvement ideas are generated, how project pilots are designed and implemented, and how process management is used to effectively derive benefits from DMAIC (and also DFSS) projects. As part of module 2, we facilitate a discussion of the "Good Questions for Champions to Ask" of their project teams as they identify the best Six Sigma projects to undertake, and implement those projects. As we do this, we challenge Six Sigma leader champions to challenge their teams about the business case for undertaking specific projects. The idea here is to identify those projects that hold the best potential for generating concrete and measurable results—in terms of reduced costs; reduced defects; improved revenues; improved product, service, or process quality; and so forth.

Different companies will be concerned with different projects. Some companies we've worked with, for example, identify cost reduction projects as being the most important to undertake, at least in the early stages of Strategic Six Sigma project implementation. With results from these in hand, they then feel positioned to make a broader business case about how Six Sigma can be applied to other areas of their business. Other executive groups focus almost immediately on revenue generation, through the use of DFSS tools.

➤ Module 3: Aligning Six Sigma Projects to Business Strategies

As part of the group storming-and-forming process in module 1, and the subsequent brainstorming and prioritization of business goals/strategies that then follows, it becomes possible in module 3 for executives to begin identifying and aligning projects to meet specifically identified business strategies. The scope of workshop discussion narrows, and begins to focus specifically on choosing projects to address key business goals.

In Figure 10.2, for example, a large aerospace manufacturer has determined that a business opportunity exists in

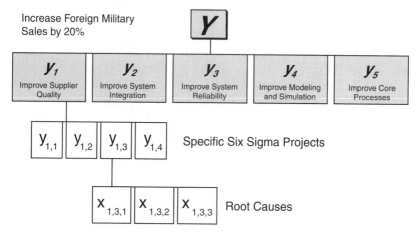

Figure 10.2 Business success is achieved through multiple focused projects.

the global marketplace for military aircraft with enhanced avionics. As part of defining this opportunity, business executives have also identified a strategic business goal of increasing foreign military sales by 20 percent. To achieve this goal, a group of business executives from the company has identified five SIGs to help the company realize its financial targets. These goals include: (1) improving supplier quality; (2) improving system integration efforts; (3) improving systems reliability; (4) improving modeling and simulation efforts as part of R&D efforts; and (5) improving core manufacturing processes. In this example, four specific Six Sigma projects were then identified and prioritized as being of help to the company in impacting its SIGs.

As Figure 10.2 shows, the ultimate selection of Six Sigma projects is rigorously determined by an executive team based on the potential of those projects to impact SIGs and, in turn, financial goals and business strategy. The exercise of mapping the connections that link projects *to* SIGs *to* strategy is a powerful group experience for executives, who begin clearly to understand Six Sigma's horsepower in driving strategy, once they connect these dots. Module 3, in fact, is often a breakthrough experience for executives that in some cases have resisted Six Sigma up to this point. All of a sudden, they get it and recognize its power and potential to dramatically impact business performance. This module is a perfect setup then for the tasks that await the team in module 4.

➤ Module 4: Infrastructure Development

In module 4 of champions training, we focus on helping a company's leaders determine the resources, tools, and people they will need to actually implement strategic Six Sigma projects. For example:

➤ What kinds of organizational resources will be required?

➤ In what ways will leaders at different levels need to be enlisted to help sponsor the ongoing work of project teams, and to remove organizational roadblocks when and if they are encountered?

➤ Who in the organization needs to be enlisted as part of Six Sigma project teams? Specifically, how will finance people be brought into the effort, and what will be the company policy on tracing project benefits through to the bottom line? (Care is given to organizing teams that have broad, cross-functional representation on them, so that teams can work easily across all functions of the organization in brainstorming solutions to specific organizational problems.)

➤ What kinds of rewards and recognition systems need to be put in place to reward performance and build commitment to new ways of working?

➤ What kinds of communications channels need to be used to communicate key messages to the organization, as Six Sigma deployment proceeds across the company?

➤ Module 5: Introduction to Business Process Management

As noted earlier, business process management is the approach by which Strategic Six Sigma improvement efforts (both DMAIC and DFSS projects) can be strategically leveraged across an entire organization. Thus, this module focuses on how leaders can best drive and align Six Sigma efforts strategically to get maximum leverage from Six Sigma projects.

Considerable time is spent in this module helping executives to identify and clarify the core processes in their organization, whose improvement will yield the most dramatic changes (and benefits) both for customers and the organization.

The definition of *core processes* that we use with clients is "those processes that are closely linked to customers and the organization's key competencies, and which are at the heart of the company's identity with its customers and markets." Thus, a core process for one company (e.g., Intel) might be its famed manufacturing processes. A core process for another company (e.g., 3M) might be its reputation for innovation. A core process for still another company (e.g., Dell Computer) might be its approach to sales and customer service that makes it a marketplace standout.

We also identify core processes as those "whose overall improvement, redesign (or development) holds the most potential to help a company achieve its strategic objectives, and which are essential to satisfying shareholders' expectations of excellent financial returns." Typical core processes within most organizations include:

➤ Marketing
➤ Sales
➤ New product development
➤ Product manufacturing
➤ Customer service

Once we've helped executives define their business core processes, we assist them in developing comprehensive plans to achieve their priorities. Issues discussed include:

➤ How to align improvement initiatives to the business-based priorities of the organization

➤ How to focus the organization first on short-term priorities (linked to long-term objectives)

➤ How to build a foundation of best practices and organizational experience that enables the company to leverage Six Sigma learning faster and more efficiently with successful completion of each additional (and similar) Six Sigma project

➤ Module 6: Leveraging VOC and VOM Data

As a follow-on to module 5, module 6 focuses on how to effectively use VOC and VOM data to drive Six Sigma efforts. We take care to ensure that as part of setting improvement targets for Six Sigma projects, executives pay close attention not just to meeting or exceeding critical customer requirements (CCRs) for individual customers, but also to benchmarking the performance of their competitors, and to assessing future performance requirements that the marketplace may make of the company in the near- or medium-term future. We assess and discuss the effectiveness of current VOC/VOM processes, and steps to make them more effective.

➤ Module 7: Black Belt and Master Black Belt Selection and Development

This module covers the critical process of selecting appropriate Black Belts and Master Black Belts to spearhead specific Six Sigma projects, a process we have already discussed in other chapters. Once selected for their roles, Master Black Belts will work as expert consultants, advising both the senior leadership team and business unit leaders on Six Sigma project selection and targets. Black Belts will work at the level of project improvement teams, driving all stages of DMAIC and DFSS projects.

A constant thread running throughout all aspects of champions training is the importance of an organization's top leaders being aware of and attuned to the change management dynamics associated with effective Strategic Six Sigma deployment. We argue that leaders simply can't afford to stop communicating the urgency of change, even when they tire of doing so. For if they do, they run the risk that their organization will fail to fully embrace the change principles and practices that are critical to successfully deploying and sustaining Strategic Six Sigma initiatives over the long term. (See the sidebar, "The Hidden Challenges in Communicating the Urgency of Six Sigma to an Organization.")

A significant side benefit of introducing Six Sigma training into organizations is that it frequently leads to the identification and nurturing of a broader and more diverse leadership team. So says Desmond Bell, Vice President of Six Sigma at Bombardier Transportation. Bell says that as Six Sigma methods and practices have been introduced at Bombardier, it has helped advance the professional and executive careers of many women who have taken on roles as Master Agents (Master Black Belts) and Agents (Black Belts), garnering them attention and recognition they may have not received in other job assignments. This is a good thing, says Bell. "Our female Master Agents and Agents are as capable as their male colleagues in generating results from Six Sigma projects, and as such are recognized and rewarded for their efforts," he says. "This is a meritocracy, and Six Sigma is about rewarding and recognizing those who generate results."[1]

STAYING THE COURSE: THE HIDDEN CHALLENGES IN COMMUNICATING THE URGENCY OF SIX SIGMA TO AN ORGANIZATION OVER THE LONG TERM

What's the biggest challenge a company faces when it comes to communicating the details and vision of Six Sigma to employees? Ask Tom Gurd, Vice President of Quality and Business Excellence at Dow Chemical Company, and he'll likely say it's making sure a company's top leaders stay the course when it comes to repeating critical messages about Six Sigma to employees—again, again, and again.

"At Dow, we're very focused on creating constancy of purpose around Six Sigma. Consequently, our leaders have maintained a focused, high-energy approach to communicating the urgency of Six Sigma to the company's employees around the world."*

Indeed, Dow's top leaders *have* done a very effective job at getting employees on board the Six Sigma bandwagon. When Six Sigma first rolled out at Dow two years ago, Kathleen Bader, the Dow business group president leading Dow's Six Sigma drive, did 36 Six Sigma road shows around the world, meeting with employees at the grassroots, and building commitment to the importance of Six Sigma as a key business priority. At one presentation in Milan, Italy, she even took time to deliver the first few minutes of her talk in Italian. Nowadays, Dow CEO Mike Parker and other senior executives routinely take part in Six Sigma road shows and training sessions. And Parker personally keeps Six Sigma on the front burner of business concerns as part of Dow's monthly meetings of its corporate operating board. Such hands-on efforts by a company's top leaders are key to building strong commitment to change initiatives of any kind. They also put a human face on leaders, and on the changes they're asking employees of their organizations to make.

*Tom Gurd, interview with Richard Koonce, PricewaterhouseCoopers, Midland, MI, 20 November 2001.

(Continued)

(Continued)

Notwithstanding such efforts, Jeff Schatzer, Dow's Communications Leader for Six Sigma, warns that there's always a danger that a company's top leaders will become complacent about the importance of acting as change agents, when introducing large-gauge change initiatives such as Six Sigma into an organization.

There's always "a lag time between when leaders start delivering significant change messages to employees, and when an organization's employees begin to absorb, understand, embrace and act on those messages," says Schatzer. This is especially true of large, multinational corporations with layered communications channels. "In other companies I've seen corporate leaders sometimes tire of delivering critical messages of change to people, before their organization has fully digested the essence of what they're trying to communicate."[†]

If a leader stops communicating the importance of change just as people are beginning *to* change, it can create dissonance or disconnects in the organization. This can lead to increased resistance to change in the future. "If a change initiative is given great emphasis one month but gets pushed to the back burner of business concerns the next, it sends the wrong impression to employees. People become cynical and that's when employees begin to complain about every new business initiative simply being another flavor-of-the month leadership priority," says Schatzer.[†]

To avoid this problem, a company's leaders must never let up communicating Six Sigma priorities to the organization. They must consistently display visible and vigorous leadership of Six Sigma initiatives, so that people have no doubt of where the organization is headed. At the same time, a company's communications plans must consistently reinforce key executive messages to employees through high-energy, multichannel communications efforts that penetrate to all levels, functions, and organizational units of the enterprise.

— The Authors

[†]Jeff Schatzer, telephone interview with Richard Koonce, Pricewater-houseCoopers, Arlington, VA, 8 November 2001.

Bell says that the emergence of women in Six Sigma roles has been good for the company in several ways. Besides giving greater visibility to women's leadership talents, it has "established a healthy balance of both women and men in Six Sigma roles." Second, it has created a pull effect, generating interest on the part of still other women to work their way up Bombardier's career ladder, says Bell. "This is good for us because it not only engages more people in Six Sigma projects, but over time will enrich the pool of prospective leaders from which we can draw people to fill senior level jobs."[1]

■ CHAPTER CONCLUSIONS

As one can see from this chapter, champions (executives) training consists of a robust mix of change leadership training and specific technical training on Six Sigma tools and methodologies. The primary goals of Strategic Six Sigma champion workshops are to equip top leaders of organizations with the tools to oversee both the hard (technical) and soft (people and processes) aspects of Strategic Six Sigma deployment, and to build consensus and commitment to the tasks ahead. In essence, we want Strategic Six Sigma leaders to have at their fingertips both the tools and mindsets they will need to effectively execute Strategic Six Sigma plans and initiatives, and to sustain them over time in their organization.

While the training we've described here is primarily for an organization's CEO and top leadership team, versions of this same training must also be cascaded down to successively lower leadership levels in the organization— first to business unit/divisional-level leaders, and then to middle-level executives, process owners, and Six Sigma project managers. (See Figure 10.3.) The core aim throughout is to build a robust and highly competent population of Six Sigma leaders within an organization that can implement Six Sigma projects with sufficient speed and scale to drive massive transformation in the company, while achieving concrete and measurable results from individual Six Sigma projects in the process.

The importance of doing this cannot be overstated. It is critical not just to training Six Sigma leaders at *all* levels in one's organization. It's also essential if one hopes to ultimately embed Six Sigma principles in the makeup of the organization and in the approaches people take to doing their jobs on an everyday basis.

The training of Six Sigma leaders, in other words, is vital not only to create consistent leadership behaviors, and drive alignment of people, processes, and projects to support Strategic Six Sigma goals. It's also key to ensuring continuous organizational learning, which is the prerequisite to ensure *ongoing* process, product, and service improvement. Put another way, Six Sigma champion training helps to ensure that Strategic Six Sigma organizations not only learn how to apply Strategic Six Sigma methods and best practices to the here and now, but over time learn how to leverage their growing knowledge of process improvement in increasingly efficient and rapid ways.

► Best Practices

As this chapter has shown, training is essential to the effective preparation of Six Sigma leaders and to the effective launch and sustaining of Strategic Six Sigma initiatives. To

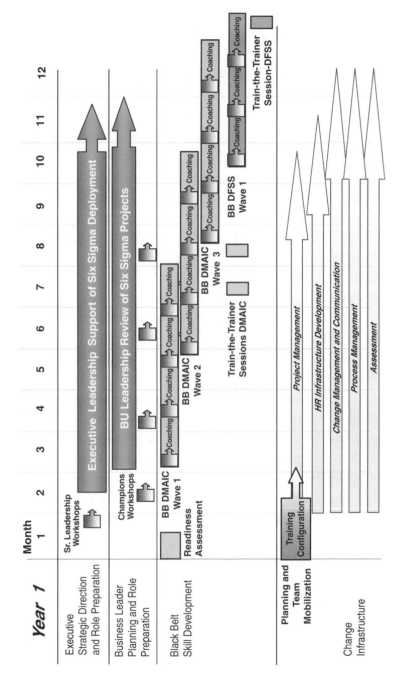

Figure 10.3 Typical Six Sigma deployment timeline.

prepare executives and managers for their Six Sigma roles, it
is critical to do the following:

1. **Train leaders at *all* levels of the organization both in
   the leadership and technical skills needed to launch
   and successfully manage Six Sigma initiatives.** All
   training programs need to incorporate action learning approaches, whereby individuals learn by doing,
   and by working on real-life business projects and
   problems.
2. **In companies that are true Six Sigma leaders, top
   executives spend time developing Six Sigma leaders
   at *other* levels in the organization.** This is clearly
   evident in companies like Caterpillar, Dow, Bombardier, Raytheon, and GE, where CEOs and members
   of their top leadership teams become personally
   involved in teaching Six Sigma leadership and technical skills to others.
3. **Training programs need to be continuously updated
   and refreshed, to remain relevant and aligned to the
   business.** They must also be cascaded to all levels of
   leadership in an organization, although the format
   and specific content of training programs will vary by
   leadership group.
4. **Finally, companies that are Strategic Six Sigma leaders create a strong learning ethic in their organizations. This encourages continuous knowledge
   sharing, exchange of business best practices, and the
   constant integration of VOC and VOM data into the
   redesign of the company's business model.** Corporate web sites, intranets, web casts, and e-learning programs can all play powerful roles in this regard,
   supplementing classroom-based training, champions

workshops, and other face-to-face learning encounters. As noted in Chapter 8, Caterpillar uses a proprietary web site both to share Six Sigma best practices among its Six Sigma practitioner community, and as a venue in which people can share Six Sigma success stories, project updates, and other relevant information.

Chapter

Sustaining Gains with Strategic Six Sigma over Time

There's a difference between saying you want to do Six Sigma and that you want to be a Six Sigma company. If you want to do Six Sigma, you can complete projects, you can take costs out of the business, and you can be very successful. But the strategy at Bombardier is that we want to become a Six Sigma company. That means we have to change how people work. That's where the challenge of change comes in. It's where the soft side of change becomes very important. You've got to work on the culture of the organization. You've got to have an aligned set of values that reinforce what you're trying to do. Your recruitment policies and training and development strategies have to underpin it. Your communications strategies have to support it. There's a lot of work in there that typically organizations aren't aware of when they first embark on the Six Sigma journey. . . .

> —Desmond Bell, Vice President, Six Sigma
> *Bombardier Transportation*

Throughout *Strategic Six Sigma: Best Practices from the Executive Suite,* we have talked about the importance of taking a planned and systematic approach to Strategic Six Sigma implementation. We've discussed the seven critical success factors involved in rolling out Strategic Six Sigma initiatives, and stressed time and time again the importance of seeing Strategic Six Sigma deployment not just from a *technical implementation* perspective, but also from a *people* and *change management* perspective. And that's where we want to conclude this book—with some additional thoughts about that.

It should be obvious by now that it takes enormous leadership will and organizational energy to make Strategic Six Sigma initiatives successful. Nonetheless, the benefits of successfully introducing Strategic Six Sigma into an organization are enormous. Once implemented, they are likely to transform the operations and cultures of companies forever afterward. As noted in Chapter 4, Dow Chemical CEO Mike Parker sees the potential of Six Sigma to spur *value creation* at Dow to be almost limitless, and likely to generate benefits "forever." And as we observed in Chapter 2, Honeywell CEO Larry Bossidy sees Six Sigma as key to his company sustaining productivity improvements—again, "forever."

The examples of what's taking place today at companies like Dow, General Electric (GE), Du Pont, Caterpillar, Lockheed Martin, and others testify to the fact that the strategic implementation of Six Sigma principles and practices can lead not just to large, order-of-magnitude improvements in business processes, products, and services, but also to exponential business growth. We believe its future is very bright, especially in the commercial and business environment of post-September 11.

Notwithstanding that, the implementation of Strategic Six Sigma is still in its infancy in many companies today. Consequently, firms need to be sure that they don't embark on Strategic Six Sigma initiatives in a piecemeal way. To do so is to risk a Strategic Six Sigma deployment being seen by employees as little more than just another leadership fad, or as the latest flavor-of-the-month management project. As Dow's Kathleen Bader points out in Chapter 3, "A half-hearted implementation of Six Sigma is worse than no implementation at all!"

To achieve long-term success and sustainability with Strategic Six Sigma deployments, a company must therefore do several things:

1. It must tailor its efforts to suit its unique goals and business strategy: top-line growth, e-business design and implementation, innovation, global brand building, supply chain improvement, new product development and introduction, facilitation of mergers and acquisitions, acceleration of information technology/enterprise resource planning (IT/ERP) initiatives, and so forth.

2. It must create a robust process management system by automating performance scorecards and customer dashboards—by putting them on the web, for example, and dynamically coupling business performance with customer expectations on a continuous basis. This will ensure the building of a finely honed *operating system* to drive continuous process improvement and strategy execution. When fully actualized, this operating system serves as the organizational backbone necessary to sustain the long-term curve A Six Sigma initiatives we described in Chapter 2.

3. Its deployments must take into account key environmental drivers that, in many cases, are specific to a company's particular industry (e.g., deregulation and the utility industry) as well as other factors—such as organizational culture, leadership, and management legacy issues—that can affect deployments for either good or ill.

■ GOING BEYOND COMPLIANCE TO BUILD COMMITMENT TO STRATEGIC SIX SIGMA

Finally, and most important, achieving maximum returns from Strategic Six Sigma initiatives means doing more than just forcing employee compliance to Six Sigma work standards, performance expectations and business goals. A company's top leaders (the CEO and his or her top leadership team) must in fact build strong organizational *commitment* to Six Sigma principles, and do so in leaders at *all* organizational levels. This commitment to a Six Sigma way of working must then be cascaded down into the organization. It must permeate the company's operating system, and begin to impact how rank-and-file employees do their jobs on an everyday basis. (See Figure 11.1.)

There's no way we can overstate the importance of leaders building strong employee commitment to Strategic Six Sigma at *every* level. As we said earlier in this book, the end result

Compliance
"I have to do it this new way."

Commitment
"I want to do this the new way."

Reaction
"I will react to this change – if I must."

Action
"I will act to achieve this change."

Testing
"I must absorb this change."

Testing
"I will put myself at stake for this change."

Negative perception
"I feel threatened by this change."

Positive perception
"I see the opportunity in this change."

Engagement
"I see the implications for me/us."

Understanding
"I know why and what will change."

Awareness
"I am being told about something."

Figure 11.1 Change—compliance versus commitment.

and *ultimate goal* of implementing Strategic Six Sigma inside an organization is to unleash enormous amounts of focused organizational energy—energy that can be used to drive strategy, improve efficiency and productivity, and ensure breakaway levels of business performance and profitability. To initially create and channel this energy requires enormous top-level leadership commitment. To *sustain* it entails getting permanently past initial thresholds of resistance, inertia, and indifference, and successfully building a leadership and employee community that has internalized Six Sigma principles and work practices as an integral part of the design—the construct of everyday work.

If a company's CEO can build true commitment to Six Sigma principles and practices—by generating awareness, creating understanding of Six Sigma tools and approaches, and engaging employees in meaningful Six Sigma projects—it creates positive perceptions and experiences in employees of how Six Sigma can be used enterprise-wide to impact all areas of the business. (See Figure 11.1.) At the same time, it fosters a strong action orientation on people's parts, encourages job ownership, and personal commitment to Six Sigma principles and work practices. Indeed, we've seen employees who were initially hesitant to adopt Six Sigma methods embrace them with a passion, once they get it, and begin to see how Six Sigma principles and approaches provide not only the necessary structure for people to do their jobs, but also greater clarity and focus as individuals go about their daily work. In such cases, employee morale rises, team unity tightens, and greater individual and group performance become possible. It is at *this* point that Strategic Six Sigma becomes the powerful engine of continuous improvement, ongoing change, and ultimately profound business transformation that we first outlined in this book's introduction.

■ CREATING TRUE BELIEVERS

Companies such as Dow, GE, Du Pont, Caterpillar, Raytheon, 3M, and others all recognize that creating impassioned true believers in Six Sigma is far preferable to simply shoving Six Sigma principles and work practices down employees' throats, coercing people to do their jobs differently.

While taking the compliance path may be necessary in some organizations at the very beginning of a Six Sigma effort (as it was at GE), it isn't a recipe for long-term business success. So says Mike Joyce, Vice President of LM-21, Lockheed Martin's corporate-wide continuous improvement initiative that incorporates use of Six Sigma, Lean Enterprise, and Kaizen improvement techniques. Indeed, pursuing a compliance approach can potentially be disastrous if a firm's leaders don't take into account the specific character traits of an organization—its culture, customers, product sets, employee work attitudes, habits, and so forth, he says.[1]

■ LEVERAGING EXISTING CULTURAL STRENGTHS TO DRIVE CHANGE

For example, at Lockheed Martin, there was already a strong customer-centric culture in place when the company embarked on Six Sigma as part of LM-21 back in 1998. Thus, to have simply forced compliance with Six Sigma tools and metrics, without getting input from employees, or incorporating existing customer and quality assurance processes and best practices into the initiative, might well have backfired, says Joyce. "We have a very rich database of things that work well. Moreover, within the Lockheed Martin culture we are very programmatic and customer-focused and the customer value [was already] down there at the program level." We wanted to "be careful not to spoil that." The introduction of LM-21, therefore, was positioned in such a way that it leveraged already existing values that focused on customers, product quality, innovation, and the application of new technologies to solving business problems.[1]

We wanted to have elements of the following in our Six Sigma approach: First, we wanted to have the precepts of Lean Manufacturing. Second, we wanted to have a strong component of Design for Six Sigma. (P.S: The people who taught the world about DFSS were at Texas Instruments Defense, which we owned, so we had the benefit of having people who really understood this.) We also wanted to include Motorola precepts—the disciplined application of statistical tools, statistical analysis, design of experiments, and so forth. So, we had a lot of technical content that we wanted to include.

Next, we brought in a lot of content around change leadership. We said to our Black Belts, "Your job isn't simply to be experts with respect to the tools. All the tools in the world aren't going to get us anywhere unless you become change drivers." So we gave them training in change leadership. And that's a heavy portion of our training.

Finally, we knew none of this would work unless we had an active pull from management. So early on, we trained our senior middle management on what Six Sigma was going to do for them. Not to make them highly knowledgeable about the tools, but to get them avaricious in their demand for it to help them make their numbers.

Dan Burnham
Chairman and Chief Executive Officer / Raytheon

■ EMPLOYEES MUST PROVIDE THE ARMS AND LEGS FOR THE EFFORT

At the same time, Joyce says a company must factor the characteristics of its employee population into the planning and design of Six Sigma deployments. A company's leaders have to embark on Six Sigma based on "what is right for their business culture," he says. "You have to spend some time saying, 'What's our culture? What will make this work?' " Joyce says that for Lockheed Martin, this discussion resulted in the realization that "we have 50,000 scientists and engineers in our company. The culture of scientists and engineers is that they do not respond to threat. They do [however] respond to challenge." Thus, Joyce and his company's top leadership team rolled out LM-21 using incentives and goal-setting techniques that capitalized on the existing work attitudes and achievement orientation of Lockheed-Martin employees.[1]

At Caterpillar, a similar respect by top leadership for organizational character traits—in Caterpillar's case, a legacy of operating units that historically had operated autonomously—heavily influenced how Strategic Six Sigma was deployed. Caterpillar's Corporate 6 Sigma Champion Dave Burritt notes that as his company rolled out 6 Sigma in 2001, the company took care to ensure that there was as much self-determination of 6 Sigma improvement goals at a business unit level as possible, and 2002 will see more of that:

> We can't pretend to say that we're a fact-based, data-driven company just yet. So, 2001 was definitely about compliance. We had top-level commitment to 6 Sigma, but sometimes we had to push things through to remove obstacles. We said to people, "Find something you like about 6 Sigma and just do it [because] you will follow

the recipe. You will use red light and green light charts, you're [either] on the train or off the train. You will do it this way." But we know that compliance is not something that's sustainable. You have to move from compliance to commitment. You have to release the reins and allow people to make more autonomous decisions relating to 6 Sigma.[2]

At Caterpillar, Burritt says this will occur going forward, as the company doubles the number of Black Belts from 700 in 2001 to 1,400 in 2002:

We're increasing the density of Black Belts, increasing the complexity and interdependencies among different areas. Consequently, we'll have a lot of bright people really questioning the methodology and the way we do things. Plus, we'll also be moving to the Extended Enterprise concept, bringing suppliers and dealers into our 6 Sigma efforts as well. We'll want them all to follow the recipe. But what's key here is self-determination. They will pick the projects and they will get the benefits. . . .[2]

■ USING BLACK BELT TRAINING TO BUILD MOMENTUM FOR INITIATIVES

Like Lockheed Martin and Caterpillar, Dow Chemical also believes in the importance of building strong commitment to Six Sigma goals and work approaches, not just compliance *to* them. This is a key goal of the Black Belt training that Dow undertakes, says Tom Gurd, Dow's Vice President of Quality and Business Excellence, who gets personally involved in virtually every wave of Black Belt training that Dow undertakes at its Atlanta, Georgia, Six Sigma training facility.

"When you look for Black Belts, you look for people that are technically competent, and who can also drive change," he says.[3] Gurd acknowledges, however, that some of those recruited to be Black Belts display the same initial resistance and skepticism to Six Sigma that Dow employees occasionally do. "Some people come in and are very excited to be here for training. They've waited a long time to become Black Belts and their attitude is 'Let's go.' Others come in either apprehensive about what's expected of them, or, sit in the back of the room in training classes with their arms crossed, saying, 'You know what, I don't know if I want to do this. I don't know if this is a good thing.' "[3]

How does Dow overcome this resistance? Surprisingly, Gurd says that those who are initially resistant to Six Sigma methodology and training often turn out to be "your biggest advocates" as training proceeds. This occurs because Black Belt training provides a powerful bonding experience for everybody who attends it. That bonding begins when people come together from all over the organization, mingle, network with others, get over their fears, and are exposed to learning "both the nuts and bolts of Six Sigma statistical tools, as well as critical soft skills necessary to lead people effectively," according to Gurd. In many cases, he says, people help one another learn Black Belt skills (like statistical analysis or project management) that they never thought they'd fully master:

Some folks come to [Black Belt] training and already have experience with statistics and project management. They're very comfortable with those things. But you also get commercial folks who are very experienced with cus-

tomers and customer interactions that don't feel that comfortable working with statistics. As time goes by, you see people teaching each other things. People team up to help one another learn new skills, or more fully grasp concepts and ideas they can use back in their organization. A person with project management experience might say to somebody else, "Hey, I've got the project management skills and the statistical background. You've got the direct experience and know-how with the customer. Let's learn from each other. . . ."[3]

Gurd says this buddying up in training classes helps people move from initial skepticism and apprehension with Six Sigma to eventual enthusiasm and commitment *to* it. He says it happens every time Dow stages a Black Belt training class, and as Black Belts begin to tackle individual Six Sigma projects. "When you put 200 Black Belts into a [Black Belt] training class you see this happen every day. People start exchanging war stories, helping each other, and exchanging best practices and skill sets across the organization in different areas," he says. "It's powerful and over time it helps to create culture change."[3]

Energized by their training, Black Belts then return to their business units to move forward with their own Strategic Six Sigma projects, says Gurd. But they're not totally alone. The camaraderie and learning community that Black Belts establish with one another while in training together often helps them out later on, when occasionally they must call on class colleagues for ideas, help, feedback, or guidance after formal Black Belt training has been completed.[3]

Clearly, as the aforementioned discussion suggests, there are many ways that companies can effectively turn initial employee compliance with Six Sigma methods and approaches into heartfelt commitment to Six Sigma principles. In summary:

➤ By tailoring initiatives to accommodate the culture traits and history of an organization
➤ By capitalizing on already embedded values and business approaches to accelerate deployment
➤ By engaging employees and key players in Six Sigma initiatives with empowering training programs
➤ By ensuring that a company's top leaders stay clearly out in front at all times, consistently communicating with people, and championing the importance of Strategic Six Sigma to company goals and business strategies

■ A RECIPE—NOT A PRESCRIPTION FOR BUSINESS SUCCESS

While implementing Strategic Six Sigma initiatives inside a company does in fact involve a critical recipe of steps and actions, as we've noted elsewhere in this book, one can't simply take a one-size-fits-all approach to implementations and hope everything turns out all right.

"Different companies will approach Six Sigma implementation in different ways," says principal PwC consultant George Byrne. "When Du Pont implemented Six Sigma they did it business unit by business unit. In each unit you saw them following the exact same series of steps. When Caterpillar did it they did a global deployment, introducing it everywhere at once. So there are different approaches companies can take," he says. "Implementing Strategic Six Sigma is a little bit like baking a chocolate layer cake. Two people might both make a chocolate layer cake but they might well do it in two different ways with slightly different ingredients. In the end, though, it's still a chocolate layer cake."[4]

■ THE FUTURE OF SIX SIGMA: SOME PREDICTIONS

Throughout this book, we have focused extensive time on showcasing some of the leading examples of Strategic Six Sigma initiatives in the corporate world today—in companies such as GE, Dow, Du Pont, Caterpillar, and others. We've shared not only lessons learned, best practices developed, and key executive insights acquired from successful Six Sigma deployments. We've also stressed the importance of corporate leaders taking firm control of Strategic Six Sigma deployments, if such efforts are to succeed.

So, how will Strategic Six Sigma principles and concepts be used by companies going forward? Here are some predictions.

First, as organizations everywhere are forced to do more with less, to trim costs while growing profits, and to move quickly in new business directions, Strategic Six Sigma thinking and best practices will play a growing role in business strategy deployment in companies worldwide. This will happen because Strategic Six Sigma's emphasis on data-driven decision making provides a powerful lever to create strong organizational focus, and to forge strong alignment of a company's leaders and employees around a commonly understood language of metrics and business goals.

Today, the community of companies subscribing to Strategic Six Sigma principles and practices is growing. In this book, we've talked extensively about efforts underway at companies such as Dow, GE, Du Pont, Caterpillar, 3M, Lockheed Martin, and Bombardier. But today enthusiasm for the use of Strategic Six Sigma principles as part of the strategy deployment process is beginning to be seen elsewhere: in companies such as Bank of America, ServiceMaster, and JP Morgan Chase, among others. These companies and others have begun to discover both the efficiencies and enormous value creation that can result, when Strategic Six Sigma principles are applied in a purposeful way to a company's business planning processes.

Second, companies will increasingly use Strategic Six Sigma principles and methods to make their customer relationship management processes as robust, responsive, interactive, and customer-friendly as possible. They will use Strategic Six Sigma principles, tools, and practices to identify, target, capture, acquire, and segment new customers, and to increase customer satisfaction, loyalty, and retention levels with key accounts. They will create detailed and dynamic value models by clearly linking customer needs and expectations with specific business processes to address those needs and expectations. The inability of companies to make this clear and compelling linkage is one of the most common weak points in many Six Sigma initiatives. Yet, nowadays, more and more companies are experimenting with approaches to doing this.

Dow's effort to create The Perfect Order is just one example of what more and more companies will do in the future: monitor their business performance against hundreds of customer attributes, spread across different product sets and business units, designing their business processes not only in response to customer requirements, but also in a collaborative way *with* customers.

Other companies that are doing pioneering work in creating dynamic value models include AT&T and Johnson Controls. Johnson Controls, for example, has developed a highly nuanced customer satisfaction index—a detailed value model—that measures customer satisfaction across a range of criteria (e.g., image, product attributes, ordering, and billing) on a monthly basis. The information is then used to create targets and goals for monitoring and managing customer satisfaction improvement across the company's customer base on a continuous basis.[5]

Some of the hottest emerging CRM applications for Strategic Six Sigma (as we noted in Chapter 1) are in the e-business arena, as companies continue to evolve their e-business models, roll out increasingly complex web applications, and migrate more and more customers (both commercial and retail) to the web for all types of interactions. The reasons to do this are both obvious and compelling, says Peter Amico, a principal consultant with PricewaterhouseCoopers and a leading practitioner in applying Strategic Six Sigma methodology to web-based business applications:

A lot of the early dot.coms didn't have a good business case. They didn't define who their customers were, and when they did define their customers they didn't do the appropriate segmentation, because the requirements are different by segment. Even when they did do the segmentation, they didn't prioritize things in an appropriate way. They tried to give everybody everything too soon, and that's not cost-effective.[6]

For this reason, Amico says, "anybody that's doing web applications today really needs to be thinking about measurement, and getting [behaviorally based] customer requirements by segment. Six Sigma can be a powerful tool to do that."[6]

Third, Strategic Six Sigma principles and approaches will also be applied to support a wide variety of other strategic priorities from globalization and mergers and acquisitions, to sustainable growth, national/global branding, innovation, outsourcing, and new product introductions. As more and more companies strive to operate globally, Strategic Six Sigma tools and techniques will be applied to bring cost-effective scale to global business operations, to align and streamline supply and value chains, to solidify relationships among companies, customers, and suppliers, and to support increasingly cross-culture/cross-boundary business alliances and partnerships.

Fourth, we submit that Strategic Six Sigma tools and approaches will become increasingly critical to the accelerated design, planning, and deployment of IT projects, ERP initiatives, just-in-time (JIT) accounting strategies, and other large-gauge technology and systems implementations. How? As such initiatives are undertaken, the principles of Six Sigma will be applied enterprise-wide to help companies capture the detailed and highly complex critical customer requirements (CCRs) of both internal and external customers; design processes that exactly meet the needs of these customers; and identify strategic improvement goals (SIGs) and potential Six Sigma projects to address problems, eliminate defects, and improve processes.

At the same time, Six Sigma metrics and analytical tools will be of continuing use to companies after ERP/IT implementations have been completed. They will be incorporated into the design and operation of robust performance monitoring systems. These systems will have the power to identify, diagnose, and resolve problems on an enterprise-wide basis, thus helping companies avoid unforeseen systems failures, downtime, and unacceptable levels of business or operating risk.

■ USING STRATEGIC SIX SIGMA AS A LEADERSHIP ALIGNMENT TOOL

Fifth, and finally, given the reality that Strategic Six Sigma tools and practices are increasingly being used in all areas of business today, we believe it will be vital for companies to incorporate Strategic Six Sigma principles and thinking into the design of leadership development and training programs. Why? Because driving Strategic Six Sigma initiatives inside organizations today requires more than a vision and more than the commitment of a company's top leadership team. As we have said many times in this book, it requires that leaders *at all levels* of an organization work together and perform their jobs in new ways. In essence, it requires that a company's outfield team (its midlevel executives, process owners, managers, and subject matter experts) be clearly aligned with its infield (its top leadership team).

At Bombardier Transportation, for example, the company has already begun to embed the teaching of Six Sigma leadership and technical skills in its leadership development, training, and succession plans, says Desmond Bell, Vice President for Six Sigma. "Today customers expect more from our products and people than they did in the past. They expect us to deliver more, to get it to them faster, and to provide them with a [high-quality] product that will serve them well and generate revenue for them over a [twenty-year-plus] product life cycle," he says. "To do all that, we need to have people in this company with robust Six Sigma skills and customer experience. We need people with statistical knowledge, of course, but we need people who can exercise strong leadership as well—in leading teams, determining customers' requirements, and in coordinating specific projects with customers and suppliers."[7]

By embedding Six Sigma skills training in leadership development and training programs, a company can effectively align everyone's job performance and professional development for the same clear purposes. It can ensure that all members of its leadership team possess a common baseline of skills; a common understanding of business priorities and goals; and a common approach to organizing, prioritizing, managing, and measuring work. We can think of no more powerful way to build organizational vitality and resilience, and to prepare a company to realize breakaway business success in today's brutally competitive business environment.

■ PARTING THOUGHTS

Clearly, the potential power of Strategic Six Sigma thinking and concepts—to transform organizations and forever change how people do their jobs—is tremendous. So, where do you, a senior business leader, go from here?

If there is any one theme we want to leave you with as we end this book, it's this: While Six Sigma tools and approaches can be powerful when used as part of individual improvement projects, the organizational leverage or power a company's leaders can achieve by framing their use within a *strategic* context—to support and drive strategy deployment—is *enormous*. Not only does Strategic Six Sigma provide an engine—to drive top-line growth, process improvement, and culture change, it will boost human performance and organizational profitability at the same time. In doing these things, Strategic Six Sigma will help companies increase their operating agility, their market resilience, and their organizational vitality.

Jack Welch is fond of saying that a company's business strategy must be both dynamic and anticipatory. We agree with that, and submit that Strategic Six Sigma provides both the *mind-set* and *toolset* to make it so. Regardless of your company—its history, its goals, its strategy—Strategic Six Sigma is a vehicle to help you achieve your business destiny. It will forever transform your company, your customers, your people, and your processes. It will change how people do their jobs and, in so doing, alter the DNA of your organization. We wish you the best of luck as you embark upon that transformation journey, and we know that it will be an exciting one.

Dick and Jerry

Afterword: Some Parting Thoughts

Throughout this book, we've discussed the myriad ways that companies today are using Six Sigma principles and practices in a strategic manner to deploy business strategies and to foster robust, top-line growth. We've explored how Six Sigma can serve as a catalyst for sustained business transformation, leadership development, and organizational renewal. And, we have outlined many of the emerging ways that Six Sigma principles and practices are being applied to drive globalization efforts, mergers and acquisitions (M&A) activities, customer loyalty, national and international brand building, enterprise resource planning (ERP) projects, e-business initiatives, and other business priorities.

In light of recent news events, however, there is still another area where application of Strategic Six Sigma principles is likely to make its mark in coming years. That's in the area of corporate governance and business integrity. In the wake of the Enron meltdown, the recent bankruptcies of companies from Global Crossing to Kmart, and the high-impact dot-com train wreck of 2001, the need for companies to apply greater financial discipline to their accounting practices, and to how they report corporate performance to stakeholders and Wall Street has never been more in the spotlight.

Perhaps no corporate executive has spoken more eloquently about the need to apply Strategic Six Sigma principles to the assurance of business integrity than Dan Burnham, Chairman and Chief Executive of Raytheon.

Raytheon, one of the world's leading defense and aerospace systems suppliers, today uses its own brand of Six Sigma, called Raytheon Six Sigma to drive operational excellence in all areas of its business, from Missile Defense, Intelligence, Surveillance and Reconnaissance, to Precision Strike technologies and Homeland defense. While Raytheon uses Six Sigma principles and practices enterprise-wide to drive customer satisfaction, growth, and productivity, Burnham sees an equally important opportunity for Six Sigma rigor and discipline to be applied to the assurance of business integrity and stakeholder confidence.

"How do you define a company's integrity? Very often such discussions start and end with mindless aphorisms, and then go to the internal mechanisms that support 'integrity,' " says Burnham. He adds that while many companies, including Raytheon, have evolved highly effective ethical processes, hotlines, and ombudsmen, to assure ethical practices are adhered to, recent revelations about corporate accounting practices are driving companies beyond aphorisms and integrity programs to think about *corporate governance as a set of processes* in its own right, to which the rules of precision, perfection, and measurement must be applied as they would be anywhere else in an organization.[1]

In that vein, Burnham says companies are well advised to apply a Six Sigma level of rigor and vigor today to corporate governance and integrity assurance. They need to ask themselves questions like, "What *is* the role of the audit committee?

What is the role of the Board?" says Burnham. "Let's define those roles and define how we're going to measure success in those roles. At Raytheon we have tried to be particularly thoughtful on these issues in the last few months. We now use data, board questionnaires for example [that] measure [performance] in the areas of corporate governance. So, I think the whole issue of defining what's important, establishing your 'end state,' and measuring progress, applies as much to governance mechanisms and processes as it does to anything else."[1]

Clearly, Strategic Six Sigma has a powerful role to play today, not only in ensuring the efficiency of business processes, and the successful deployment of business strategies, but also in guaranteeing business integrity and ethical corporate governance. As you read and use this book in your daily work as a business leader, we're confident you will develop still other strategic applications of Six Sigma in your business, the practice of which will drive the optimal alignment of people and processes to support corporate growth and increasing shareholder value.

Notes

Introduction

1. Foundation for the Malcolm Baldrige National Quality Award, "The Nation's CEOs Look to the Future," 1998, New York, Study 818407.

Chapter 1

1. Barton, Glen. Caterpillar 2000 Annual Report.
2. Joyce, Mike. Interview with Richard Koonce. Bethesda, MD: PricewaterhouseCoopers, 11 October 2001.
3. Dauphinais, G. W., G. Means, and C. Price. *Wisdom of the CEO*. New York: John Wiley & Sons, 2000, p. 19.
4. Parker, Mike. Interview with Richard Koonce. Midland, MI: PricewaterhouseCoopers, 19 November 2001.
5. Schatzer, Jeff. Telephone interview with Richard Koonce. Arlington, VA: PricewaterhouseCoopers, 8 November 2001.
6. Bell, Desmond. Interview with Richard Koonce. Arlington, VA: PricewaterhouseCoopers, 18 February 2002.
7. Whittaker, Sheelagh. "Making the Web Work: 'I' Before 'E'—No Exceptions." *The Industry Standard*, 21 August 2001, p. 1.
8. McCartney, Don. "E-Business and the Lessons of the Titanic." PwC web site article by Don McCartney, p. 1.
9. Carnegie Mellon University and PricewaterhouseCoopers. *Emm@, New E-Business Maturity Model*, 6 January 2000: p. 1.
10. Maler, Kevin. "New 3M Chairman Meets Wall Street." *Knight-Ridder Tribune Business News: Saint Paul Pioneer Press*, 31 May 2001.

11. Merrick, Amy. "Spreading the GE Gospel: As 3M Chief, McNerney Wastes No Time Starting Systems Favored by Ex-Boss Welch." *Wall Street Journal,* 5 June 2001.
12. Zyman, Sergio. *The End of Marketing as We Know It.* HarperBusiness, 2000, p. 233.
13. Asp, Pat. Telephone interview with Richard Koonce. Arlington, VA: PricewaterhouseCoopers, 21 March 2002.
14. Welch, Jack. *JACK: Straight from the Gut.* New York: Warner Books, 2001, pp. 334–335.
15. Deutsch, Claudia H. "Managers Seek Corporate Nirvana Through Quality Control." *New York Times,* 7 December 1998.
16. Holliday, Chad. "Sustainable Growth, the DuPont Way." *Harvard Business Review,* September 2001, pp. 129–134.
17. Chang, Kenneth. "IBM Creates a Tiny Circuit Out of Carbon." *New York Times,* 27 August 2001.
18. Sherman, Erik. "Global Warning: Protecting Data and Systems in a Global Marketplace Brings a Whole New Meaning to Finding the Weakest Link." *Catalyst,* Summer 2001, p. 40.

Chapter 2

1. Welch, Jack. *JACK: Straight from the Gut.* New York: Warner Books, 2001, p. 331.
2. Ibid., p. 333.
3. Ibid., p. 335.
4. Ibid., p. 333.
5. Ibid., p. 337.
6. AlliedSignal 1998 Annual Report.
7. Harry, Mikel, and Richard Schroeder. *Six Sigma.* New York: Doubleday, 2000, p. 216.
8. Honeywell web site. *Six Sigma Plus Methodologies.* www.honeywell.com/sixsigma/page1_1.html.
9. Welch, Jack. *JACK: Straight from the Gut.* New York: Warner Books, 2001, p. 332.
10. Harry, Mikel, and Richard Schroeder. *Six Sigma.* New York: Doubleday, 2000, p. 217.

11. Bell, Desmond. Interview with Richard Koonce. Arlington, VA: PricewaterhouseCoopers, 18 February 2002.
12. Pasternack, Bruce, and Albert Viscio. *The Centerless Corporation.* New York: Fireside Books, 1999.
13. PwC Survey, "Organizations Accelerating Change." Fairfax, VA: PricewaterhouseCoopers, 2001.

Chapter 3

1. Kotter, John. *Leading Change.* Boston: Harvard Business School, 1996, p. 21.
2. Maler, Kevin. "3M Adopts Quality Control Program to Boost Performance." *Saint Paul Pioneer Press,* 4 April 2001.
3. Bader, Kathleen. "Six Sigma at Dow: A Cultural Transformation." Presentation at The Conference Board's 2001 Annual Quality and Performance Excellence Conference, New York, 27–28 February 2001.
4. Schmitt, Bill. "Moving Ahead with Six Sigma." *Chemical Week,* 26 April 2001.
5. Bader, Kathleen. "Six Sigma at Dow: A Cultural Transformation." Presentation at The Conference Board's 2001 Annual Quality and Performance Excellence Conference, New York, 27–28 February 2001.
6. Schmitt, Bill. "Expanding Six Sigma: Have You Signed up Yet?" *Chemical Week,* 21 February 2001.
7. Byrne, George, and Robert Norris. "Six Sigma: A Practitioner's Perspective." Presentation at The Conference Board, New York, 14 July 2000.
8. Statement by Caterpillar CEO Glen Barton.
9. Byrne, George. Interview with Richard Koonce. Fairfax, VA: PricewaterhouseCoopers, 15 September 2001.
10. Welch, Jack. *Jack: Straight from the Gut.* New York: Warner Books, 2001, p. 337.
11. Yearout, Steve, Gerry Miles, with Richard Koonce. *Growing Leaders.* Alexandria, VA: American Society for Training and Development, 2001, pp. 152–156.

12. Byrne, George, and Robert Norris. "Six Sigma: A Practitioner's Perspective." Presentation at The Conference Board, New York, 14 July 2000.
13. PricewaterhouseCoopers. Six Sigma Performance Improvement Presentation Packet. Arlington, VA: PricewaterhouseCoopers, p. 11.
14. Schmitt, Bill. "Expanding Six Sigma: Have You Signed up Yet?" *Chemical Week*, 21 February 2001.
15. Bader, Kathleen. "Six Sigma at Dow: A Cultural Transformation." Presentation at The Conference Board's 2001 Annual Quality and Performance Excellence Conference, New York, 27–28 February 2001.

Chapter 4

1. "What is Six Sigma? The Roadmap to Customer Impact." General Electric. www.ge.com/sixsigma/.
2. Bader, Kathleen. "Six Sigma at Dow: A Cultural Transformation." Presentation at The Conference Board's 2001 Annual Quality and Performance Excellence Conference, New York, 27–28 February 2001.
3. "Du Pont Intensifies Market Orientation as a Key Factor Driving Sustainable Growth." *Du Pont News Release*, 1 June 2001.
4. Lortie, Pierre. Interview with Richard Koonce. Montreal, PQ, Canada: PricewaterhouseCoopers, 7 March 2002.
5. Burritt, David. Interview with Richard Koonce. Peoria, IL: PricewaterhouseCoopers, 4 December 2001.
6. Unnamed Executive. Client interview with Richard Koonce. Washington, DC: PricewaterhouseCoopers, 27 March 2001.
7. Unnamed Executive. Client interview with Richard Koonce. Washington, DC: PricewaterhouseCoopers, 27 March 2001.

Chapter 5

1. Niemes, Jim. Phone interview with Richard Koonce. Arlington, VA: PricewaterhouseCoopers, 14 December 2001.

2. Brown, Stanley. *Strategic Customer Care: An Evolutionary Approach to Increasing Customer Value and Profitability.* New York: Wiley, 1999.

Chapter 6

1. Burritt, David. Interview with Richard Koonce. Peoria, IL: PricewaterhouseCoopers, 4 December 2001.
2. Bell, Desmond. Interview with Richard Koonce. Arlington, VA: PricewaterhouseCoopers, 18 February 2002.

Chapter 7

1. Asp, Patricia. Telephone interview with Richard Koonce. Arlington, VA: PricewaterhouseCoopers, 21 March 2002.
2. Burritt, David. Interview with Richard Koonce. Peoria, IL: PricewaterhouseCoopers, 4 December 2001.
3. Bell, Desmond. Interview with Richard Koonce. Arlington, VA: PricewaterhouseCoopers, 18 February 2002.
4. Neuscheler-Fritsch, Debbie, and Robert Norris. "Capturing Financial Benefits from Six Sigma." *Quality Progress,* May 2001, pp. 39–44.
5. Wilkerson, David. Telephone interview with Richard Koonce. Arlington, VA: PricewaterhouseCoopers, 27 February 2002.

Chapter 8

1. Welch, Jack. *Jack: Straight from the Gut.* New York: WarnerBooks, 2001, p. 192.
2. Burritt, David. Interview with Richard Koonce. Peoria, IL: PricewaterhouseCoopers, 4 December 2001.
3. Peters, Tom, and Nancy Austin. *A Passion for Excellence.* New York: WarnerBooks, 1986, p. 306.
4. Schatzer, J. Phone interview with Richard Koonce. Midland, MI: PricewaterhouseCoopers, 8 November 2001.

Chapter 9

1. Gurd, Thomas. Interview with Richard Koonce. Midland, MI: PricewaterhouseCoopers, 20 November 2001.
2. Jubach, Tim. Telephone interview with Richard Koonce. Boston: PricewaterhouseCoopers, 13 April 2002.
3. O'Brasky, Roxanne. Telephone interview with Richard Koonce. Arlington, VA: PricewaterhouseCoopers, 20 February 2002.

Chapter 10

1. Bell, Desmond. Interview with Richard Koonce. Montreal, PQ, Canada: PricewaterhouseCoopers, 7 March 2002.

Chapter 11

1. Joyce, Mike. Interview with Richard Koonce. Bethesda, MD: PricewaterhouseCoopers, 11 October 2001.
2. Burritt, D. Interview with Richard Koonce. Peoria, IL: PricewaterhouseCoopers, 4 December 2001.
3. Gurd, T. Interview with Richard Koonce: Midland, MI: PricewaterhouseCoopers, 20 November 2001.
4. Byrne, G. Interview with Richard Koonce: Fairfax, VA: PricewaterhouseCoopers, 15 September 2001.
5. Nauman, Earl, and Steven H. Hoisington. *Customer Centered Six Sigma: Linking Customers, Process Improvement and Financial Results.* Milwaukee, WI: ASQ Quality Press, 2001, p. 197.
6. Amico, Peter. Telephone interview with Richard Koonce. Arlington, VA, 14 December 2001.
7. Bell, Desmond. Interview with Richard Koonce. Montreal, PQ, Canada: PricewaterhouseCoopers, 7 March 2002.

Afterword

1. Burnham, Dan. Interview with Richard Koonce. Lexington, MA: PricewaterhouseCoopers, 12 April 2002.

Credits

Introduction

p. xviii: All of the documents published by the Baldrige National Quality Program are considered to be in the public domain.

Chapter 1

p. 1: Reprinted from the May 2000 issue of *Fast Company* magazine. All rights reserved. To subscribe, please call 800-542-6029, or visit www.fastcompany.com.

p. 11: Permission received on 11 October 2001 to reproduce excerpts from interview with Michael Joyce, VPLM21, at Lockheed-Martin.

p. 14: *Wisdom of the CEO* by G. W. Dauphinais, G. Means, and C. Price. Copyright © 2000, John Wiley & Sons, Inc. Reprinted by permission of John Wiley & Sons, Inc.

p. 14: Permission received on 20 November 2001 from Thomas J. Gurd, VP Quality & Business Excellence, Dow Chemical, to reproduce excerpts from an interview with Mike Parker.

p. 16: Permission received on 4 March 2002 from Desmond Bell at Bombardier Transportation to reproduce excerpts from an interview with Desmond Bell.

p. 17: "Making the Web Work: I before E—No Exceptions" by Sheelagh Whitaker, CEO, EDS Canada, *The Industry Standard* (advertorial). Article published 21 August 2001.

p. 24: Reprinted by permission of the *Wall Street Journal,* Copyright © 2001 Dow Jones & Company, Inc. All Rights Reserved Worldwide. License number 446031250229.

p. 27: Permission received on 2 April 2002 from Pat Asp at ServiceMaster to reproduce excerpts from an interview with Pat Asp.

pp. 29, 30: From *JACK: Straight from the Gut* by Jack Welch. Copyright © 2001 by John F. Welch, Jr. Foundation. By permission of Warner Books, Inc.

p. 30: "Managers Seek Corporate Nirvana through Quality Control" by Claudia H. Deutsch, *New York Times.* Article published 7 December 1998. Copyright © 1998 by The New York Times Co. Reprinted by permission.

pp. 31, 32: "Sustainable Growth, the DuPont Way" by Chad Holliday, *Harvard Business Review.* Article published September 2001. Quoted material allowed under fair use. No permission required.

p. 36: "Global Warning: Protecting Data and Systems in a Global Marketplace Brings a Whole New Meaning to Finding the Weakest Link" by Erik Sherman, as published in the summer 2001 issue of *Catalyst,* Reprinted with permission, American Management Systems, Inc.

Chapter 2

pp. 39, 50–52, 54: From *JACK: Straight from the Gut* by Jack Welch. Copyright © 2001 by John F. Welch, Jr. Foundation. By permission of Warner Books, Inc.

p. 44: Permission received on 16 April 2002 from Dan Burnham, CEO Raytheon Company, to reproduce excerpts from an interview with Dan Burnham.

p. 47: Permission received on 4 December 2001 from D. B. Burritt, Six Sigma Corporate Champion at Caterpillar, to use quoted material by Glen Barton, CEO, Caterpillar, in a January 2001 message to all 75,000 Caterpillar employees.

p. 54: Permission received on 19 March 2002 from Edward Romanoff at Honeywell to reproduce excerpts from the Honeywell corporate web site, *Six Sigma Plus Methodologies.*

Chapter 3

Chapter 4

Chapter 5

Chapter 6

p. 149: Reprinted from "Process Management and the Future of Six Sigma" by Michael Hammer, as printed in *MIT Sloan Management Review*, Winter 2001 issue, by permission of publisher. Copyright © 2001 by Massachusetts Institute of Technology. All rights reserved.

p. 168 (Figure 6.9): Reprinted by permission of Air Products and Chemicals.

Chapter 7

p. 185: From "Capturing Financial Benefits from Six Sigma" by Debbie Neuschler-Fritsch and Robert Norris, as printed in the May 2001 issue of *Quality Progress*, pp. 39–44.

Chapter 8

p. 203: From *JACK: Straight from the Gut* by Jack Welch. Copyright © 2001 by John F. Welch, Jr. Foundation. By permission of Warner Books, Inc.

p. 215: From *A Passion for Excellence* by Tom Peters and Nancy Austin, p. 306. published by WarnerBooks, New York, 1986. Quoted material allowed under fair use. No permission required.

Chapter 9

p. 226: Permission received on 17 May 2002 from Tim Jubach, Independent Consultant, to reproduce excerpts from an interview with Tim Jubach.

p. 234: Permission received on 26 February 2002 from Roxanne O'Brasky, President of the International Society of Six Sigma Professionals (ISSSP), to reproduce excerpts from an interview with Roxanne O'Brasky.

Bibliography and Recommended Reading

AlliedSignal. *Annual Report,* 1998.

Amico, Peter. Interview by Richard Koonce. Arlington, VA: 14 December 2001.

Asp, Patricia. Telephone interview with Richard Koonce. Arlington, VA: PricewaterhouseCoopers, 21 March 2002.

Bader, Kathleen. "Six Sigma at Dow: A Cultural Transformation." Presentation at The Conference Board's 2001 Annual Quality and Performance Excellence Conference, New York, 27–28 February 2001.

Bader, Kathleen. Interview by Richard Koonce. Midland, MI: PricewaterhouseCoopers, 14 December 2001.

Bell, Desmond. Interview by Richard Koonce. Arlington, VA: PricewaterhouseCoopers, 18 February 2002.

Bell, Desmond. Interview by Richard Koonce. Montreal, PQ, Canada: PricewaterhouseCoopers, 7 March 2002.

Blakeslee, Jerry. "Six Sigma Performance Improvement." Fairfax, VA: PricewaterhouseCoopers. Slide deck, Fall 2001, Slide 11.

Blakeslee, Jerry. (1999, July). "Implementing the Six Sigma Solution." *Quality Progress,* July 1999, pp. 77–84.

Brown, Stanley. *Strategic Customer Care: An Evolutionary Approach to Increasing Customer Value and Profitability.* New York: John Wiley & Sons, 1999.

Brue, Greg, and Morningstar Communications Group. *6 Sigma for Team Members: Applying the 6 Sigma Seven Principles of Problem-Solving Technology^sm*. Pagosa Springs, CO: Morningstar Communications Group, 2001.

Burke, Warner, Bill Trahant, with Richard Koonce. *Business Climate Shifts: Profiles of Change Makers.* Woburn, MA: Butterworth-Heinemann, 1999, pp. 18–20.

Burnham, Dan. Interview with Richard Koonce and Dick Smith. Lexington, MA: PricewaterhouseCoopers, 12 April 2002.

Burritt, David. Interview by Richard Koonce. Peoria, IL: PricewaterhouseCoopers, 4 December 2001.

Byrne, George. Interview by Richard Koonce. Fairfax, VA: PricewaterhouseCoopers, 15 September 2001.

Byrne, George, and Robert Norris. "Six Sigma: A Practitioner's Perspective." Presentation at The Conference Board, New York, 14 July 2000, slide 13.

Carnegie Mellon University and PricewaterhouseCoopers University. *Emm@, New E-Business Maturity Model,* 6 January 2000, p. 1.

Chang, Kenneth. "IBM Creates a Tiny Circuit Out of Carbon." *New York Times,* 27 August 2001.

Dauphinais, G. W., G. Means, and C. Price. *Wisdom of the CEO.* New York: John Wiley & Sons, 2000, p. 19.

Deutsch, Claudia H. "Managers Seek Corporate Nirvana Through Quality Control." *New York Times,* 7 December 1998.

"Dupont Intensifies Market Orientation as a Key Factor Driving Sustainable Growth." *Dupont News Release,* 1 June 2001.

Foundation for the Malcolm Baldrige National Quality Award, "The Nation's CEOs Look to the Future," 1998, New York, NY, Study 818407.

General Electric web site: www.ge.com/sixsigma/.

Gurd, Thomas. Interview by Richard Koonce. Midland, MI: PricewaterhouseCoopers, 20 November 2001.

Hammond, Julie. Interview by Richard Koonce. Peoria, IL: PricewaterhouseCoopers, 4 December 2001.

Harry, Mikel, and Richard Schroeder. *Six Sigma.* New York: Doubleday, 2000, pp. 216–217.

Holliday, Chad. "Sustainable Growth, the DuPont Way." *Harvard Business Review,* September 2001, pp. 129–134.

Honeywell. *Six Sigma Plus Methodologies.* www.honeywell.com/sixsigma/page1_1.html.

Joyce, Michael. Interview by Richard Koonce. Bethesda, MD: PricewaterhouseCoopers, 11 October 2001.

Jubach, Tim. Interview with Richard Koonce. Boston: PricewaterhouseCoopers, 13 April 2002.

Kotter, John. *Leading Change.* Boston: Harvard Business School Press, 1996, p. 21.

Lortie, Pierre. Interview by Richard Koonce. Montreal, PQ, Canada: PricewaterhouseCoopers, 7 March 2002.

Maler, Kevin. "New 3M Chairman Meets Wall Street." *Knight-Ridder Tribune Business News: Saint Paul Pioneer Press,* 31 May 2001.

Maler, Kevin. "3M Adopts Quality Control Program to Boost Performance." *Knight-Ridder Tribune Business News: Saint Paul Pioneer Press,* 4 April 2001.

McCartney, Don. "E-Business and the Lessons of the Titanic." www.pwcglobal.com.

Merrick, Amy. "Spreading the GE Gospel: As 3M Chief, McNerney Wastes no Time Starting Systems Favored by Ex-Boss Welch." *Wall Street Journal,* 5 June 2001.

Miles, Gerry, Steve Yearout with Richard Koonce. *Growing Leaders.* Alexandria, VA: American Society for Training and Development, 2001, pp. 145, 152–156.

Mittal, Banwari, and Jagdish Sheth. *ValueSpace: Winning the Battle for Market Leadership.* New York: McGraw-Hill, 2001, pp. 31, 225.

Niemes, Jim. Telephone interview by Richard Koonce. PricewaterhouseCoopers, 14 December 2001.

Neuscheler-Fritsch, Debbie, and Robert Norris. "Capturing Financial Benefits from Six Sigma." *Quality Progress,* May 2001, pp. 39–44.

Norris, Robert. Interview by Richard Koonce. Fairfax, VA: PricewaterhouseCoopers, 28 August 2001.

O'Toole, James. *Leadership A–Z.* New York: Jossey-Bass, 1999, p. 38.

Parker, Michael. Interview by Richard Koonce and Jerry Blakeslee. Midland, MI: PricewaterhouseCoopers, 19 November 2001.

Peters, Tom, and Nancy Austin. *A Passion for Excellence.* New York: Warner Books, 1986, p. 306.

Potter, Frank. "Event to Knowledge: A New Metric for Finance Department Efficiency." *Strategic Finance Magazine,* July 2001.

PricewaterhouseCoopers LLP, Survey, "Organizations Accelerating Change." Fairfax, VA: PricewaterhouseCoopers, 2001.

Schatzer, Jeffrey. Telephone interview by Richard Koonce. PricewaterhouseCoopers, 8 November 2001.

Schmitt, Bill. "Expanding Six Sigma: Have You Signed up Yet?" *Chemical Week,* 21 February 2001.

——. "Moving Ahead with Six Sigma." *Chemical Week,* 26 April 2001.

Sherman, Erik. "Global Warning: Protecting Data and Systems in a Global Marketplace Brings a Whole New Meaning to Finding the Weakest Link." *Catalyst,* Summer 2001, p. 40.

Viscio, Albert, and Bruce Pasternack. *The Centerless Corporation.* New York: Fireside Books, 1999.

Welch, Jack. *Jack: Straight from the Gut.* New York: Warner Books, 2001, pp. 192, 331–335, 337.

Whittaker, Sheelagh. "Making the Web Work: 'I' Before 'E'—No Exceptions." *The Industry Standard,* 21 August 2001, p. 1.

Zyman, Sergio. *The End of Marketing as We Know It.* New York: Harper Business, 2000, p. 233.

About the Authors

■ DICK C. SMITH, PARTNER

Dick Smith is a Partner in PwC's Strategic Change Practice and the Partner-in-Charge of the Center of Excellence for Six Sigma Process Improvement located in the Washington Consulting Practice. He has over 12 years of strategy, change management, and process consulting experience. Combined with over 20 years of corporate background in sales and marketing, operational experience and quality management, he brings a wide range of expertise to his clients. Dick's background with PwC includes consulting and training to firms on strategy, customer satisfaction, quality deployment, change management, business process reengineering, and Baldrige assessments. In the Six Sigma practice area, he focuses his efforts on assisting executives in both government and commercial accounts on aligning business strategy with the deployment of Six Sigma process improvement initiatives to drive overall business results.

Over the past five years, Dick has led the expansion of PwC's Six Sigma consulting group in the United States and supported the establishment of PwC's Six Sigma practices in Europe and Asia. Currently, the Center of Excellence for Six Sigma has global brand recognition and several global clients, including Caterpillar, Dow Chemical, and Shell Oil.

His client projects in recent years include: GE Capital, J.P. Morgan, Dow Chemical, LG Group (Korea), Air Products, Dana Corporation, Honeywell (AlliedSignal), AIG Insurance, Caterpillar, Du Pont, Bank of America, GMAC, and Wellmark (Blue Cross of Iowa).

Mr. Smith is a frequent speaker on the topics of strategy deployment, organizational change, process reengineering and Six Sigma deployment at conferences, such as the Conference Board, the American Society for Quality (ASQ), and the International Quality and Productivity Council (IQPC). He has published several articles on change management and reengineering.

Mr. Smith is a member of the American Society for Quality, the International Society for Six Sigma Professionals, the American Society for Training & Development, and Quality New Jersey (QNJ). He is a State Examiner for QNJ Quality Award (Baldrige).

■ JERRY BLAKESLEE

Jerry Blakeslee is a Global Partner at PwC Consulting's Center of Excellence for Six Sigma Services based in Fairfax, Virginia. Jerry leads a core team of professionals providing Six Sigma business improvement and corporate transformation services to a wide variety of organizations. These services include leadership development, strategy development, process management, and change management.

Jerry is extensively involved in providing executive consulting and Six Sigma business improvement services to numerous global organizations. He was one of the primary architects of the PwC Six Sigma approach and is responsible for developing global support capability for PwC clients. He is currently the project partner for Six Sigma implementations at Royal Dutch Shell, Dow Chemical, Dow Corning, Formosa Plastics, ServiceMaster, and in Korea, POSCO Steel and Samsung Financial. In 1999, he was the project director for the PwC Six Sigma implementation at LG Group in Seoul, Korea, that includes LG Chemicals, LG Telecom, and nine other LG Companies. He spent two years developing and delivering Black Belt and Master Black Belt training for GE Capital, primarily in Europe, where he was responsible for developing PwC's capability to deliver the GE material in seven different languages. He is author of the article, "Achieving Quantum Leaps in Quality and Competitiveness— Implementing the Six Sigma Solution," in the July 1999 issue of *Quality Progress Magazine.*

Prior to joining PwC, Jerry spent 26 years in responsible leadership positions with PPL Corporation, where he held a variety of leadership positions in nuclear plant operations and engineering, corporate planning, and continuous improvement.

Jerry holds a B.S. in mechanical engineering from Lafayette College, and an M.S. in nuclear engineering from the Pennsylvania State University. Jerry and his wife, Bonnie, live in Pennsylvania's Lehigh Valley near Bethlehem.

■ RICHARD KOONCE

Richard Koonce is an accomplished interviewer, radio commentator, author, and business consultant who is the author or coauthor of three previous books: *Growing Leaders* (ASTD, 2001), with Steve Yearout and Gerry Miles; *Business Climate Shifts: Profiles of Change Makers* (Butterworth-Heinemann, 2000), with Bill Trahant and Warner Burke; and *Career Power!* (Amacom, 1994). A former broadcast journalist and contributing commentator to Public Radio's *Marketplace* program, Richard has interviewed numerous business and public figures over the years, ranging from CEOs and celebrities to authors and U.S. presidents. Besides his work as a writer and interviewer, Rick is also a senior contract consultant to PwC and a nationally known expert on job and workplace trends. He has been interviewed on job and workplace issues by the *Wall Street Journal*, the *New York Times*, *Money* magazine, *U.S. News & World Report*, *USA Today*, ABCNEWS radio, the *Washington Post*, and *Working Woman*, among others. Rick is a member of The National Press Club, *Leadership Washington*, Washington Independent Writers, and The American Society for Training & Development.

Index